Pure Beauty

Pure Beauty

Judging Race in Japanese American
Beauty Pageants

REBECCA CHIYOKO KING-O'RIAIN

 University of Minnesota Press
Minneapolis
London

Chapter 3 originally appeared as "Miss Tomodachi Meets Mainstream America: Japanese American Beauty Pageants as Cultural and Symbolic Productions," in *East Main Street: Asian American Popular Culture,* edited by Shilpa Dave, Tasha Oren, and Leilani Nishime (New York: New York University Press, 2005); reprinted with permission of New York University Press. Portions of chapter 4 originally appeared as "Multiraciality Reigns Supreme? Mixed Race Japanese Americans and the Cherry Blossom Queen Pageant," *Amerasia Journal* 23, no. 1 (1997): 113–28; reprinted with permission from the UCLA Asian American Studies Center Press.

Published by the University of Minnesota Press
111 Third Avenue South, Suite 290
Minneapolis, MN 55401-2520
http://www.upress.umn.edu

Library of Congress Cataloging-in-Publication Data
King-O'Riain, Rebecca Chiyoko.
  Pure beauty : judging race in Japanese American beauty pageants / Rebecca Chiyoko King-O'Riain.
    p.   cm.
  Includes bibliographical references and index.
  ISBN-13: 978-0-8166-4789-7 (hc : alk. paper)
  ISBN-10: 0-8166-4789-5 (hc : alk. paper)
  ISBN-13: 978-0-8166-4790-3 (pb : alk. paper)
  ISBN-10: 0-8166-4790-9 (pb : alk. paper)
  1. Beauty contests—United States. 2. Japanese Americans. 3. Japanese American women. 4. Race awareness—United States. I. Title.
  HQ1220.U5K56 2006
  791.6'2—dc22
                                                              2006019972

Printed in the United States of America on acid-free paper

The University of Minnesota is an equal-opportunity educator and employer.

12 11 10 09 08 07 06   10 9 8 7 6 5 4 3 2 1

Contents

vii   Preface

1   Introduction: Negotiating Racial Hybridity in Community Beauty Pageants

21   1. Race Work and the Effort of Racial Claims

37   2. The Japanese American Community in Transition

59   3. Japanese American Beauty Pageants in Historical Perspective

74   4. Cultural Impostors and Eggs: Race without Culture and Culture without Race

116   5. Patrolling Bodies: The Social Control of Race through Gender

148   6. The "Ambassadress" Queen: Moving Authentically between Racial Communities in the United States and Japan

186   7. Percentages, Parts, and Power: Racial Eligibility Rules and Local Versions of Japanese Americanness in Context

227   Conclusion: Japanese Americanness, Beauty Pageants, and Race Work

235   Notes

239   Bibliography

255   Index

Preface

WHEN MY GREAT-GRANDMOTHER, Toku Yoshimura, immigrated to the United States as a picture bride in the early 1900s, she was not the typical picture bride and yet her destiny may not have worked out as she had wished. She left Mifune village in Kumamoto prefecture to join a husband she had never met, except in photographs. Rumors of her strong will and advancing age (she was nineteen at the time) eventually made their way across the ocean but not before she had opted not for the man she was married to through photographs, but instead his younger, better-looking cousin. As an accomplished seamstress, she made her way into the sewing industry in Gardena, California, and had a family of four children; the eldest, Chieko, died in late childhood and left my grandmother, Toshi, to take on the mantle of eldest daughter.

Toshi, also a rebel of sorts, married Yoshio Kobata of Kobata Brothers Nursery in Gardena, and theirs was the wedding of the year. Their first child, my mother, was so adorable that she won the Nisei Week Beautiful Baby Contest—and my fate as a researcher of Nisei Week was cast.

When the family was relocated during World War II to Rohwer, Arkansas, as were almost all Southern California Japanese Americans, my mother started her formal schooling in an internment camp. My grandfather was drafted from camp and became part of the Military Intelligence Service. He was sent to Fort Snelling in St. Paul, Minnesota, to translate documents from Japanese into English for the U.S. military.

Although my grandmother was relocated to St. Paul at the end of the war, she left her husband and he returned to the family business in Gardena. Toshi proceeded as a single Japanese American woman and raised her two daughters on her own until she married a Japanese American veteran of the 442. Although their house on Race Street and subsequent education at University of Minnesota High School made my mother and my aunt into "true Americans," they always felt a tie to Gardena (and their father), where they made occasional trips in the summer.

My parents met at Carleton College in Northfield, Minnesota, and my mother became the first of her generation in our extended family to marry out to a *hakujin* (white) man. My dad, born in Borger, Texas, never could get his family to participate in our lives, and I was born into a family with two very active sets of Japanese American grandparents (one set in California and one in Minnesota) and a vague notion that my dad was different. Growing up in a small and dispersed Japanese American community in Chicago did not prepare me for my eventual journey backward along my mother's, grandmother's, and great-grandmother's pathways.

I, too, went to college in Minnesota, barely surviving the broomball and eyelash-freezing winters to be near my grandmother, now living in White Bear Lake. After college and teacher training, I moved to Japan and was sent to—of all places—Kumamoto prefecture, ten miles from where my great-grandmother was born. After teaching English in Japan, I went on to study sociology at the University of California at Berkeley, which brought me full circle back to California, where it had all begun for my mother and her mother before her.

My move to Japan was considered strange by my grandmother, who had worked so hard to get away from her own mother and from a "parochial" Japanese American community in Gardena. "Why," she complained, "would you want to go to Japan or California?"

As a mixed-race Japanese American woman, I was always aware of myself and my appearance. My great-grandmother's preoccupation with her daughters' appearance transferred down into an obsession with clothes, shoes, and handbags in my own mother (and, dare I say it, myself). While my grandmother was meant to "look well" to advertise her mother's sewing abilities, she was also trying to become more American, more middle class.

In a Chicago suburb surrounded by whiteness and Jewishness, I knew I was Japanese American and didn't know that much about "being white." I just knew that we went into the city to buy Japanese food at Star Market, collected Japanese dolls (my dad's passion, not Mom's), and met other Japanese American families for New Year's celebrations. I was just like them, Japanese American.

When I went off to college in Minnesota, however, I was clearly not Japanese enough. The ASIA student club was dominated by first-generation Koreans and Chinese, with a few Japanese Americans from Hawaii. As one of a small number of students of color on campus, I knew I wasn't Asian enough to be in the club but knew also that my Japanese-language-studying boyfriend didn't just see me as white either.

Teaching in the JET program in Japan, I was a *gaijin* (foreigner) along with all the other foreign English teachers imported to bring internationalization and English to our Japanese secondary students. When I met the "long-lost family"—my great-grandmother's youngest sister and her family—I retied the links in our family between the United States and Japan that had been broken during the war. But despite my Japanese family, name, and some language skills, I was not, nor would I ever be, really Japanese. I was too washed out, too far culturally from the "real Japanese" of Japan. Even so, my colleagues in the Japanese secondary school treated me differently from my predecessor, a white man from Washington State. I was often told that "I should know better" about cultural norms that I had no idea I was violating. Why? Because down inside they considered me to be Japanese. The harshness of the cultural judgments, made differently in different eras and places in my life, have come to inform this book in subtle and important ways.

In California I encountered racial eligibility rules for the first time. I joined the Hapa Issues Forum at UC Berkeley, and for the first time had friends and colleagues who were also mixed Japanese American, fighting misunderstanding and discrimination not only in the white mainstream but also in the Japanese American community. I learned much from them about the right to stand up and say that we are mixed and yet have rights to be accepted. We were welcomed as mixed-race

Japanese Americans into a declining community structure by forward-thinking community leaders who could see our energy and enthusiasm for Japanese Americanness as new life blood for the community. As one of my HIF friends put it, they "have to accept us or there will be no community left to speak of—plus, we know more about what it means to be Japanese American than they do!"

The shifting nature of my own racial, ethnic, and gender identity development changed much over these time periods in my life, but also reflects the changing contexts in which I lived. It shaped whether I asserted my identity and was rejected or accepted. My claims to racial identity in particular meant that I was both fascinated and reviled by formal rights of rejection based on blood quantum amounts (e.g., you had to be 50 percent to run in the Cherry Blossom Queen Festival Pageant). Cringingly, my past history as a high school homecoming queen made me highly aware of the gendered nature of these titles and the behavior that was expected to accompany them. It also made doing fieldwork in beauty pageants eerily familiar, throwing me back to the big hair, tiaras, and sashes that made up my own teenage years in the 1980s.

All of this is to say that racial and ethnic identity does develop over time, but individual identity development is strongly influenced by the social context in which it takes place. The Japanese American community, first in Chicago and later in California, profoundly influenced which racial and ethnic identities were available and which were claimed or rejected. The ongoing visitation and sponsorship relationships of the pageants with Japan highlight the community and social network ties with the "homeland," the supposed provider of "real and authentic" Japanese culture to the hybrid Japanese American culture now struggling to redefine itself.

This is a trip forward and back through shifting notions of Japanese Americanness in relation to the United States and Japan, paying attention to how community beauty pageants give us a way into the discourse that constitutes one part of Japanese Americanness. The book focuses on how the "doing" of race by candidates in community beauty pageants takes effort and work which they hope will accomplish their social and cultural acceptance as the queen of a racial/ethnic community.

The writing of this book has taken the better part of a decade, which included the birth of two children, a transcontinental move, several dual academic couple job searches, and the death of a parent. In the end, the analogy to childbirth is apt. The creation, gestation, and delivery of the manuscript were enabled by the labor of many people.

First and foremost, thanks to all of the queens, princesses, and court members past and present who gave generously of their time, photographs, and documents to make up the data for this book. For the most part their names do not appear in the book to ensure confidentiality. Great thanks to the Cherry Blossom Queen Pageant Committee in San Francisco, which served as my home base during and after the fieldwork, and their counterparts in Honolulu, Seattle, and Los Angeles. Indebted thanks to Chris Aihara, Sandra Fernandez, Eric Inouye, Mitch and Ann Inouye, Mike Matsuo, Tosh Mitsuda, Earl Mostales, Behn Nakajo, Terry Nakano, Hamilton Niwa, Stacey Nolan, Miki Novitski, Allan Okamoto, Glenda Okamura, James Okazaki, John Saito, Jamie Tamura, Grant and Tobin Tsujii, and Alan Yamada. Thanks also to Japanese American community leaders: Gary, Lynn, and Erin Barbaree, John Esaki, Steve Nakajo, Allen Okamoto, David Omori, Dean Osaki, Paul Osaki, Walter Saito, Jill Shiraki, Kenji Taguma, John Yamada, J. K. Yamamoto, and Mike Yoshi.

At UC Berkeley, I was blessed with a vibrant intellectual community both within and outside the sociology department. Special thanks to Michael Burawoy, Troy Duster, Evelyn Nakano Glenn, Michael Omi, Ron Takaki, and Barrie Thorne. Colleagues Kim McClain Dacosta, Kaaryn Gustafson, Cindy Nakashima, Stephen Small, Caroline Streeter, and Kendra Wallace provided much needed love and wine. My dissertation group is the reason the project got finished at all; thanks to Kamau Birago, Robert Bulman, Pam Perry, and J. Shiao.

I had the honor of being on the faculty at the University of San Francisco, initially hosted by the Irvine Foundation and then by the university itself. The faculty development fund at USF made most of this research possible, and I am forever indebted to USF's keen understanding of the crucial importance of supporting junior faculty members' research. Gratitude is also extended to my much beloved colleagues at USF who created an intellectual and teaching community where this type of project was possible. Thanks to Yoko Arisaka, Kevin Chun, Shona Doyle, Bill Edwards, Eileen Fung, Josh Gamson, Jay Gonzales, Anne Hieber, David Kim, Lois Lorentzen, Gerardo Marin, Eduardo Mendieta, Julio Moreno, Vijaya Nagarajan, Nikki

Raeburn, Anne Roschelle, Cecilia Santos, Stephanie Sears, Jenny Turpin, Mike Webber, and Steve Zavatoski.

I have been equally blessed with terrific colleagues on this side of the Atlantic Ocean. As a relative newcomer to the Republic of Ireland, I received amazing support from my colleagues during the last phase of the manuscript preparation. Thanks to the sociology department here at the National University of Ireland, Maynooth: Aine Breen, Anne Coakley, Mary Corcoran, Colin Coulter, Laurence Cox, Tony Cunningham, Honor Fagan, Jane Gray, Deirdre Kirke, Peter Murray, Michel Peillon, and Eamonn Slater. A particular thanks to Ronit Lentin at Trinity College Dublin for not only welcoming me to the race/ethnicity scene in Ireland and Europe more generally but also for providing, with kindness and friendship, cultural instruction on how to navigate unfamiliar waters.

Thanks to many colleagues who have read drafts of this work and offered needed comments: Raphael Allen, Rick Bonus, David Brunsma, Heather Dalmage, Reggie Daniel, Shilpa Dave, Yen Espiritu, Tim Fong, Steve Fugita, Laura Grindstaff, Brian Hayashi, Emily Ignacio, Nazli Kibria, George Kitahara Kich, Ben Kobashigawa, Lon Kurashige, Joane Nagel, Wendy Ng, Leilani Nishime, Jon Okamoto, Gary Okihiro, Kristen Peterson, Kerry Rockquemore, Maria Root, Steve Ropp, Larry Shinagawa, Vicki Smith, Miri Song, Ranier Spencer, Paul Spickard, Jere Takahashi, Linda Vo, Teresa Williams-Leon, and Chris Yano.

Archival access and support was provided by Karl Matsushita of the Japanese American National Library and Susan Fukushima of the Japanese American National Museum. Research assistance was provided by Brooke Ogawa, Kortney Okura, and Kristy Yasunari. Thanks also to Celia Kehoe of the Russell Library at the National University of Ireland, Maynooth, for photography assistance.

My labor as an academic was made possible by the many people who provided childcare and love to our children during this project. My love, affection, and appreciation to Maria Miller, Jennifer Meisner, Patricia Robles, Sharon and Yvonne and the crew at Kindercrescent, Annette Wilson, the Laird-Benner family, the Carty-Galvan family, and the Ó Foghlu/Reynolds family for loving support for myself and my kids in collaborative child-rearing.

I would like to thank Doug Armato, Carrie Mullen, and Jason Weidemann at the University of Minnesota Press for their comments and support. Also, thanks to the anonymous reviewers and to Rona Tamiko Halualani for their comments and suggestions.

Finally, the love and support of my extended and immediate family is why this book is here. To the Kobata, Hagio, Fujii, and Shigaki clans, thanks for the futons, maps, and Gardena Bowl fried rice. Thanks also to the Burns family, Bates Cook, my sister Debbie, her husband Bob, and their son, Evan, for all their love and support. To my in-laws, the ÓRiains, for their love and support. For Aidan Toshio and Aisling Keiko, during your entire lives I have been working on this book. I am sorry for the times it has taken me away from you, but I hope you will see yourselves and my love for you reflected in this work. For Seán, for reading draft after draft, you know that the project would not have happened without your love and support. You are, without a doubt, the world's Irish expert on Japanese American beauty pageants. This book is dedicated to Toku, my great-grandmother, who dared to venture to America; to Toshi, my grandmother, who dared to live through it all; and to my mother, JoAnn Chiyoko, who dared to allow me not to forget what came before.

Introduction
Negotiating Racial Hybridity in Community Beauty Pageants

As the Cherry Blossom Parade makes its way down Post Street toward the Buchanan Mall in Japantown, San Francisco, the thrumming of the taiko *drums gets more furious and the scent of the sake being thrown from the* Mikoshi *(traveling shrine) starts to burn in our noses. I am walking alongside the "Queen's float" at the end of the parade and have been trying for the last mile or so to help prepare the queen and her court for their "crowning moment"—when the float pulls up outside of the Union Bank (one of the largest sponsors) and they bow to the dignitaries and VIPs in the glass-enclosed viewing area.*

As we near, I see a pointing finger and hear a voice from the crowd: "Where is the queen? I can't see her!"

"There, on top of the float," another replies.

"But she doesn't look Japanese, she can't be the queen."

Then I am off in my own world again, wondering, "How, with all this hoopla of the kimono, the parade, the float, and the dignitaries, can you not see? She is the queen!"

—From the author's fieldnotes

Increasing hybridity within community boundaries is changing what it means to be Japanese American. This book examines how that meaning is being negotiated and renegotiated in Japanese American beauty pageants. While the construction of Japanese Americanness has never been static and continues to change within a monoracial framework, a particularly significant shift from a primarily monoracial to a more multiracial understanding of the community occurred after the 1960s. This demographic shift has carried with it a cultural challenge to the biological definition of race, which we will see in the time periods covered in this book. The traditionally held belief that race signifies presence of ethnicity and therefore membership in the Japanese American community is shifting. Fifty years ago membership was based upon being 100 percent racially Japanese, and it was taken for granted that being Japanese American meant being monoracial; blood quantum rules masked race's conflation with ethnicity. Many of my Japanese American interviewees argued that the community in the past was "more pure" and had less mixing than other groups. They argued that Japan, as a nation, had a very isolationist history and strong racially pure understandings (Dower 1986). Furthermore, before 1960 Japanese Americans had very low "outmarriage" (marriage to non-Japanese American) rates. These two factors combine to create a sense that this isolated history may have contributed to an understanding of the concept of "Japaneseness" as a racial concept and one that was considered to be more pure than other groups (e.g., African Americans, who recognize a long history of racial mixing). Alongside the trope of purity existed a postwar Japanese idealization of Westerners, which may have led to an increasing obsession with Western looks and possibly to increasing rates of intermarriage with white men (Simpson 2002).

Today, satisfying membership criteria is a dynamic process often based on geographic residency, community service, and culture, as well as racial eligibility rules. However, race still has a cultural conceptual primacy and connection to the body and physical appearance that is difficult for people to undo. In community beauty pageants, and in other community institutions, such as basketball leagues, the continued insistence on racial (ancestry-based) eligibility rules (i.e., a participant must be 50 percent of Japanese ancestry) highlights the grasp that *race* has on community definitions of Japanese Americanness, as well as access to cultural institutions and social networks. By contrast, in various Japanese American cultural events, mixed-race Japanese

Americans have used their ethnicity as a tool to claim a racial identity and membership in the community. In doing so, the mixed-race interviewees have challenged not only the criteria for membership (*content* of racial categories), but also the very definition of membership (*form* of those same racial categories). I examine how the increased participation of mixed-race Japanese Americans in traditional Japanese American institutions has motivated a private and public discussion of *who* is Japanese American and how this relates to changing meanings of race, ethnicity, community, and gender. But to analyze this as a collective process one needs to analyze a specific racialized field or project.

Ethnic beauty queens are contested symbolic representations of their local communities and touchstones for racial/ethnic community issues. When racial eligibility rules are added to the mix, community beauty pageants become highly racially charged arenas in which debates about authenticity and representativeness abound. In 1998 when the Honolulu Japanese Junior Chamber of Commerce voted to change its racial eligibility rules from 100 percent to 50 percent "Japanese ancestry," some felt the "softening" of the racial rules signaled an erosion of racial thinking and a decline in the community. Some critical race theorists have welcomed these types of changes as they argue that we need "to free ourselves from the bonds of 'raciology' and 'compulsory raciality'" (Ali 2003, 18; see also Gilroy 2000). Ali argues that society should shed racial thinking, deconstruct it, and move into a postrace society. She argues that one of the spaces where this is likely to happen is in the lives of mixed-race people.

The mixed-race body becomes a focal point, then, where we can call into question the singularity of race and herald the "end of race as we know it." But do mixed-race bodies really call into question racial concepts? Do they actually transgress racial boundaries and the materiality of race? If it is true that mixed-race people can lead to the undoing of race, one place that we would expect to see this is in the Japanese American community, which has grappled recently with increased multiraciality. Japanese American beauty pageants bring together the embodiment of race and ethnicity, community representation, racialized gender meanings and bodily deportment, and ploys aimed at accomplishing what I call *race work*. This takes the understanding of "doing" race as an accomplishment of social interaction (West and Fenstermaker 1997), but it moves beyond the symbolic interactional understandings of "doing" to argue that the doing of race happens within realms of power that are deeply controlled by ideas and institutions. Race then, is not just a free-floating "doing," but instead it is "work"—an accomplishment that takes bodily, cultural, and political effort by social actors to assert, maintain, and challenge racial meanings.

Shifting Demographics in the Japanese American Community

With low rates of immigration, an aging population, and high rates of interracial marriage, Japanese Americans are seen by many to have successfully assimilated into American society.[1] Within Japanese American communities, collective anxiety about overassimilation, or "out whiting the whites" (Omi 2000), has led to an individual and collective search for cultural reassurance that a Japanese American community will continue to exist. This is readily apparent in the cultural institutions of the community, one of which is the Japanese American community beauty pageant.[2]

The Japanese American community has one of the highest ethnic and racial outmarriage rates, at 52 percent, and is the Asian ethnic group with the largest proportion of mixed-race members (31 percent) (Barnes and Bennett 2002, 8). Postrace theorists would therefore predict that Japanese Americans will place a decreasing importance upon race and, in fact, will allow race to disappear into the ether without a backward glance. But even the most assimilated (by measures of social class, geographic neighborhood, and levels of education) mixed-race Japanese American women in the beauty pageants that I studied were working hard to maintain the primacy of race as a legitimate criteria for community membership.

Instead of "doing away with race," both as concept and lived experience, these demographic shifts have propelled a racialized debate about what it means to be Japanese American and about the future of the Japanese American community. An important underlying issue is the impact mixed-race Japanese Americans will have on collective and community racial and ethnic meanings. Those who assume that mixed-race Japanese Americans will not be a part of the Japanese American community argue that "the Japanese American community . . . thriving today 'will be no more in 2050'" (Hirabayashi 1993, B-15) or that these shifts have created a "major ethnic disaster" (Inouye 1977). They do not see mixed-race Japanese Americans as part of the community and a resourceful group of potential community members. Others have taken a more dynamic stance and argue that the Japanese American community is changing, but that this doesn't mean that the community will cease to exist. They see the community as evolving to include "an ethnically diverse Yonsei generation" (Osaki 1995, 1) and envision themselves "coloring the future multicultural" (Honda 1995, 9).

Japanese Americans are also an interesting case of racial change because (a) they have been in the United States for over one hundred years, (b) have long-standing cultural and community institutions that are well documented, and (c) may provide insight or a model for how other racial/ethnic groups may fare in similar circumstances. These factors allow us to see how one racial/ethnic community has grappled with change over time. This is a particularly good time to look at Japanese Americans because a significant number of mixed-race "kids" are coming of age and having an impact on the leadership structures of the community. Looking at this community now, during its current transition, may shed light on a larger process of racial and ethnic group formation and reformation.

Brief Comment on Methodology

I employed three complementary research methods, often referred to as a "triangulation" to better cross-check qualitative findings and increase confidence in the findings themselves (Bryman 2004, 454). By combining documentary and archival research with intensive interviewing and extensive participant-observation, the book presents new empirical research on the topic of race/ethnicity, the body and beauty, and beauty pageants. It forges new empirical ground on Japanese Americans and enhances other studies into the community with theoretical richness. I conducted archival research at the Japanese American National Library (San Francisco), the Japanese American National Museum (Los Angeles), and the Japanese American History Archives (San Francisco). Through participation and observation, I performed ethnographic fieldwork in Japanese American community beauty pageants from January 1995 to April 1996 and periodically in 2000. I also conducted sixty in-depth interviews with pageant candidates, queens, and committee and community members in Seattle, Los Angeles, San Francisco, and Honolulu.

For archival research, I reviewed all of the Japanese/English newspapers in Los Angeles *(Rafu Shimpo)* and in San Francisco *(Hokubei Mainichi* and *Nichi Bei Times)* and read the articles pertaining to the community queen pageants in their local settings. At the historical archives, I also reviewed newspapers from Hawaii and from the internment camps. At the Japanese American National Museum, I viewed photographs, program booklets, mementoes, and various other documents. Much of my archival research actually took place in interviewees' homes as they would often drag out a large box of photos and mementoes as we were speaking. This type of data is important and groundbreaking, but at times piecemeal. It was important for me to understand the historical context in which these Japanese American beauty pageants were created and how they have changed over time. This allowed me to situate the Japanese American pageants in relation to the greater society and historical time period in which they took place. It revealed change over time and when and why changes were made to the pageant.

To complement this archival research, I also interviewed people who had been involved and were presently involved with the pageant to see how the "oral historical" version of the pageants fit with the documentary accounts of them. Interviewing sixty participants, committee members, chaperones, and organizers in four different cities allowed me to gather data that revealed individual level data about racial identity dynamics and thus allowed me to probe particular individual perspectives and individual reflections about how the pageant and the community represented changing notions of race, ethnicity, and community. Interviewing was a nice complement to participant observation because it also allowed me to "unpack" more tacit knowledge gained from the fieldwork of individual social actors and the motivations for their actions in terms of the race work that they engaged in.

Finally, I jumped in and participated in the pageant, not as a queen, but as a committee member in San Francisco. I did intensive fieldwork for fifteen months in the mid-1990s, which included shadowing the candidates and queens on all their appearances, visitations, and duties as well as the time-consuming training and preparation for the pageant. I followed the queen and her court for more than a year, driving, chaperoning, helping backstage, walking the parade route, doing hair, and watching rehearsals and the pageant itself, from the audience, as a judge, and backstage. This allowed me a unique perspective on the pageant, not just as a consumer of the pageant as a text, but also being privy to the "backstage" chaos of the pageant and its production. The rehearsals, or "training sessions," to become queen were particularly revealing. I also traveled as a part of the entourage with the queen and her court to all of the other cities where I conducted research. This placed me in the pageant world for an extended time/space and put me at the mercy of the pageant organizers and queens themselves. While the breakneck pace of the visitations was exhausting, it did allow me to observe how people behaved over a long period of time. This allowed unique insight into the social contextual effects on racialization. This differs from previous studies of pageants that read them as a "text" to be analyzed (Banet-Weiser 1999). Using participant observation allowed me to capture the production of racialized bodies in action and not just as flat images to be deciphered.

Ultimately these three methods allowed me to develop a unique and detailed analysis of Japanese American community pageants which is comparative across space (places and locations) and time (historical changes).

Community Beauty Pageants as Racialized Projects

Racialization studies (Banton 1987; Miles 1982; Small 1994) argue that race is not just a category to be studied, but in fact is a process by which racial meanings gain content and power. The process of racialization, then, is embedded in certain racial projects where the main goal is to determine the content and form of racial categories and meanings. Racial and ethnic community beauty pageants are prime examples of a racial project in action. Japanese American beauty pageants that have racial eligibility rules based on percentage of ancestry are fundamentally racial projects and as such are "[s]imultaneously an interpretation, representation, or explanation of racial dynamics, and an effort to reorganize and redistribute resources along particular racial lines. Racial projects connect what race *means* in a particular discursive practice and the ways in which both social structures and everyday experiences are racially *organized*, based upon that meaning" (Omi and Winant 1994, 56). In this case study of Japanese American beauty pageants and their racial rules in four Japanese American communities, it is the multiracial population that problematizes race and prompts the renegotiation of individual and collective racial meanings.

Other studies of mainstream beauty pageants have focused on the construction of gender, morality, and nation in pyramidal, national beauty pageants (Banet-Weiser 1999) or in non-U.S. settings like Thailand (Callahan 1998) or Venezuela (Guss 2000). These studies read the pageant as a symbolic text for debates around nation, race, and globalization. Unlike mainstream pageants, Japanese American beauty pageants are primarily local, festival events that tend not to be a stepping stone to bigger pageants, prizes, and media coverage. There are exceptions, such as the Greater Seattle Queen being eligible to participate in the all encompassing SeaFair Queen contest, and Nisei Week queens and Cherry Blossom queens who have participated in the Miss Nikkei International pageant in Brazil, but even these larger-scale pageants do not lead to broader pageants. Also, unlike Miss USA or even Miss America, there is no official "beauty" component in the judging criteria of the pageant. Japanese American pageants are different because they are produced, viewed, and supported by local Japanese American communities; they are supposedly not primarily or even secondarily about beauty, but instead about community service to the Japanese American community; they do not have big prizes or lead to massive media coverage, which means that the participants do not commodify themselves in the same way that they might in a mainstream pageant. Finally, they are not mainstream pageants, but are for Japanese American women, with the audience of the Japanese American community foremost in the minds of the producers of the event. Pageants are spaces in which Japanese American women and communities can assert their votes, standards of beauty, and cultural norms on a public stage. Because the pageants are "of the community" they are one of a number of places where one can see public conversation about what it means to be Japanese American.

There were, of course, many conflicting and uncertain definitions about who should be queen and how Japanese she should really be. This debate about the criteria (both real and imagined) for judging and the characteristics of the queen allowed me to tap into ideas about what it means to be Japanese American today. In addition, it allowed me to explore the redefinition of the relationship between race and ethnicity in practice. I examine the analytic distinction between race and ethnicity further, but some examples may illustrate the point. One racially mixed queen (her mother was from Japan) was born in Japan, could speak Japanese, and was very culturally Japanese, but she didn't "look it." She had ethnicity, but not the race to back it up. On the other hand, another candidate was monoracial, but many called her a "cultural impostor" because she knew nothing about Japanese American culture, language, values, or the community that she claimed to represent. This candidate had the race, but not the ethnicity to back it up. She—with race but no culture—was still considered to have "something" that the first did not. The continued salience of physical appearance (of course amplified in beauty pageants) supported the claim that race as physical embodiment mattered, even when the conditions were ripe for its extermination. This is just one example of how I found people doing race and ethnicity through the defining and refining of racial identities.

This research, while prompted by an interest in race, also offers insights into gender. Fundamentally, the pageants offer a way for Japanese American men and some women to try to control Japanese American women—particularly controlling their bodies to try to shape their roles as representatives of the race. With interracial-marriage rates soaring in the community, the finger of blame and shame has been clearly pointed at Japanese American women. Women outmarry almost two times more often than men (Shinagawa 1994) and are often blamed for the demise of the community. The pageant, then, is a way to control women in order to control racial boundaries. By rewarding women who are ideally Japanese American, whatever that may mean at the moment, there is control over who is and who is not Japanese American through the racial rules. The importance of the racial rules is to control who can make legitimate claims to Japanese Americanness.

Women in the pageant do emotional labor in order to "sell" Japanese American culture. In Japantown, San Francisco, and Little Tokyo, Los Angeles, pageants were developed as a ploy to bring more business into these ethnic enclave areas. The creation of the pageant as an "event" to draw in people and their money uses the women for the economic gain of others, in the process of using them to hawk culture as well. They are often labeled as ambassadors of culture and are asked to get others interested in Japanese culture through their wearing of the kimono, participation in cultural events, media interviews, and the like.

Finally, the pageant "objectifies" the queens throughout the process of the pageant. She is a symbol and often is treated as such and not as a person with feelings, political commitments, and a brain. I often heard queens complain about the photo-op or "eye candy" appearances that they were required to do. Usually, this entailed getting "dolled up" in kimono or, more often, nice street clothes, with tiara and sash, makeup and hair, and driving two to three hours to do what they called the "Vanna White thing" of posing for photos and cutting the ribbon on a new store for five minutes. Often, the women were not required to say anything or speak to anyone (many times because of the language barrier between Japanese businessmen who spoke no English and the queen who often spoke no Japanese). Nor were they asked to sit, eat, or rest. Clearly being the symbol wasn't that much fun and the objectification was considered one of the downsides of representing the Japanese American community as queen. The pressure to be the ideal Japanese American woman was difficult for many and the formal and informal rules around sexuality (the myth of virginity), appearance (no tattoos), and class and educational expectations were too much to bear.

The research in this book does not support postrace social interactions, but instead argues for the fact that although race has become more subtle, complex, and unspoken, it remains as significant and powerful as ever. The intertwining of gendering and racialization lay at the heart of many of the flashpoints and conflicts that emerged within the pageants themselves.

The Evolution of Japanese American Beauty Pageants

The cities I studied (Los Angeles, Honolulu, San Francisco, and Seattle) each had a Japanese American community queen pageant, which was shaped uniquely by its location within the nation, geographic specificity and cultural values. Each pageant, while similar in form (i.e., held on a stage with an audience and with similar parts such as evening gown, kimono, and speeches), was situated differently historically because of how and when the pageants were started. Pageants did not necessarily "resolve" their own struggles with national issues, but instead these issues were layered over one another, shaping future struggles in the pageants.

Los Angeles

Nisei Week, the first Japanese American festival with a queen pageant, was started in 1934 in "Lil Tokyo" near downtown Los Angeles. Today it continues to be a lively cultural festival celebrating the Nisei (second-generation Japanese Americans) and presenting Japanese American culture to both the ethnic and mainstream communities. The festival has included Japanese dancing *(ondo)*, flower arranging *(ikebana)*, tea ceremonies, martial arts, calligraphy, a parade, and talent programs with the highlight being the Nisei Week Queen Pageant and Coronation.

Los Angeles' geographic dispersion and proximity to the "entertainment" industry of Hollywood influenced the type and style of the Nisei Queen pageant. Its location near the entertainment industry meant that Nisei Week was a flashier style of pageant: big Hollywood-style dance numbers, hip designer outfits and gowns, celebrity judges, and a golden circle of beautiful people, those who could afford to pay more to sit closer to the stage at the pageant, which mirrored the Academy Awards. Because there were satellite Japanese enclaves for food and goods, and since the 1992 riots it was considered "too dangerous" to go downtown, downtown events held out of doors in Los Angeles, like the Nisei Week parade, had relatively low attendance.

While all of the pageants in the four cities had their own unique flavor reflecting their cultural, geographic and historical specificity, they all developed relationships to each other and all had sister city ties to communities in Japan. So while they were certainly not the same, they did develop common issues that served as a challenge in terms of gender and race. The pageants, and especially the queens, came to represent the informal ties and networks that developed between the pageant organizers in many cities. This developed into hospitality committees who worked hard to "out-host" the visitors from the other cities when on their home turf, including sightseeing, free meals, shopping, and entertainment.

Hawaii

Akira "Sunshine" Fukunaga, the first vice-president of the Honolulu Japanese Junior Chamber of Commerce (Jaycees), was visiting a buddy in Los Angeles in 1949 when he attended his first Nisei Week Festival. Thinking the festival an ideal way to "help to perpetuate and promote the Japanese culture in Hawaii, as well as provide members with the opportunity to gain valuable leadership skills," he returned to Honolulu to start planning the first Cherry Blossom Festival in Hawaii.[3] Fukunaga followed the assimilationist tendencies of Nisei Week and adapted the queen pageant to mirror the growing economic and political power of Japanese Americans in Hawaii. Reflecting its sponsorship by the Japanese Junior Chamber of Commerce, the Hawaii pageant is the largest and the best marketed, but tends to emphasize, due to geographic closeness to Japan and dependence on Japanese capital, traditional Japanese cultural dress and values.[4]

San Francisco

In 1968, in the midst of the civil rights movement, the Northern California Cherry Blossom Queen Pageant was started to choose a queen to reign over the Cherry Blossom Festival held each April in San Francisco's Japantown. As neighborhood reorganizing in Nihonmachi (Japantown) finished, modernizing the area and making it into a primarily commercial rather than residential area, the festival was created to bring people into Japantown to patronize the local businesses. The pageant also gave Japanese American women a chance to claim that "Japanese American is beautiful," following from the civil rights "Black is beautiful" theme that women of color should be found beautiful in their own right and not just compared to white standards of beauty. The original organizers saw this as a way to increase business in Japantown as well as share Japanese culture, not only with other Japanese Americans, but with the larger society as well. It was decided that a queen should be chosen to reign over the parade and festivities and to make visits to other cities representing the Japanese American community of northern California. The queen became a focal center of the festival. She drew raffle tickets, walked through Japantown in kimono, and greeted important visitors from Japan. The San Francisco pageant also reflected its more liberal community. In San Francisco, the first and only attempt to try to ban pageants altogether on feminist grounds occurred in 1988. There was such an outcry that the pageant was reinstated the next year but was altered by eliminating beauty-based judging criteria and astrological signs and adding "service to the community" as a judging criteria.

Seattle

Although the Seattle Japanese American community had a few pageants throughout the 1940s and 1950s, the current one was not started until 1960 when Nancy Sawa was crowned the Greater Seattle Japanese Community Queen. The Seattle pageant, like Los Angeles and Honolulu, has undergone changes over time and is reflective of the local social context in that it seems to have done away completely with racial rules and instead substituted community and geographic rules about who is eligible to participate. It is also distinctive in the way that it has dealt with the increasing number of mixed-race candidates and is yet another model for how Japanese Americans are dealing with this issue of community membership.

The Seattle Japanese Community Queen Pageant is the only pageant that is a scholarship pageant. While this difference may seem subtle at the outset, it has had a profound impact on the type of queen the pageant chooses and also who in the community would come forward to be involved in the pageant. Contestants' grades constitute 20 percent of their scores. Given this orientation, Seattle's pageant has a reputation as having intelligent queens.

Creating Community

Since the queen is a representative of a local Japanese American community, I was surprised to find that some of the candidates I interviewed were not originally from the area where they were running for queen. Yet they still had a desire for "connection" to the local Japanese American community. Tori, who is originally from Honolulu, came to Los Angeles to attend the University of California at Los Angeles.[5] She ran for Nisei Week Queen and explained her reason for doing so. "This was a wonderful way to meet lots of people. I was very active in the Honolulu Japanese community. My parents were very active. But you come here [Los Angeles] and you don't know anybody. I really enjoyed getting involved in something again."

Tori recognized that running in the pageant would put her more in touch with other Japanese Americans in Southern California. Another queen remarked that the best thing about doing the pageant and reigning as queen was "You have a connection with the community. It is a cool thing to have a community involvement thing, and a lot of cultures don't. I've found that many of my friends, especially the white ones, don't have anything like that. They say they are jealous."

Part of the outcome, then, of the pageant and, to a larger extent, the festivals themselves is the feeling of unity between Japanese Americans. The queen partly helps to create, as well as symbolize, the Durkheimian collective consciousness of this racial/ethnic group. I wrote about this feeling in my field notes when I recounted walking along side the queen's float in the San Francisco Cherry Blossom Festival Parade: "Along the parade route the surge of energy and pride that accompanied the queen's float down the street was almost palpable at times. Japanese Americans of all types were waving frantically at the queen and her court and burst into spontaneous applause as she drew near—the pride they felt at seeing her." This bond among people of Japanese ancestry during the pageant makes them feel a connection that is to be envied, particularly by white people who often describe themselves as just white, as if whiteness was a vacuous state of non-ethnicity. In contrast, Japanese Americanness was something to hold onto and the basis of connection with others.

The pageant also allowed very practical connections to be made within Japanese American communities. One participant described it as "a bridging of the generations. It's a vehicle in that it's a way for parents to teach their kids. It's not like we can all afford to send our kids to Japan and show them what Japan is like. We can at least show them what the traditional music and dance is."

The intergenerational nature of the participants, committee members, and community members brought diverse types of Japanese Americans together in a collective activity around the festival and pageant. The queen was supposed to represent this diverse set of community ideas and interests. Some of the groups involved were Japanese businessmen from Japan who didn't see the queen as representing them; Japanese American business owners who saw the queen as a local girl; parents of pageant participants who saw the queen as a status to aspire to; committee members who saw the queen as a true representation of the community; sponsors (community organizations/individuals) who saw the queen as a way to get business; and other attendees who saw the queen as the archetype of Japanese Americanness. Community participation ranged from ads from Japanese American businesses in the program, invitations throughout the year from various community organizations to do appearances, and donations of prizes, floats, and so on, from Japanese-owned banks/companies. All of this activity connected the queen to many people in the Japanese American community and to Japan. Many of these interest groups also had very different agendas, and the conflicts over the pageant reflected some of the positions of the people involved.

The queen was the focal point of many conflicts. She was oftentimes the center of discussions about the community and what that means to various social actors. I do not mean to say that there is only one community, nor do I intend to essentialize the Japanese American community into a monolithic concept. However, it is a worthwhile exercise to oversimplify difference, just for the moment, in order to understand the community as the distillation of the participants' understandings of what they think it is. This will tell us what they considered to be Japanese Americanness and will highlight the most salient differences within the category of "Japanese American community." The queen is seen as a link between people, but because they feel they have a stake in what is being portrayed and because she represents them, they feel they have a say in what she does, who she is, and how she is seen by others. This could be seen in the particular conflicts in Los Angeles over mixed-race queens and in San Francisco over the pageant and sexism.

Some people argue that the benefit of this connection to the community entices some women to become involved in the pageant in the first place. For example, some argued that Heather, a candidate in the early 1990s in San Francisco, used the pageant as a forum to promote her film about Japanese Americans. They claimed that she needed the legitimacy of being recognized as truly Japanese American in order to sell her film, which is about Japanese American ethnic identity. One of the pageant candidates explains:

> I think she wanted to be queen. If she were queen it would look a lot better and it would seem like she was really a part of the community. . . . So, maybe she needed it to make her film seem really valid and give her that sense that she really is a part of the community so she can tell about this because she knows what she is talking about. But she isn't. It really comes through that she is using the community to promote her film.

Therefore, links were not just limited to the Japanese American community. Many women participated in order to "get to know" the Japanese American community better, but others did it to make connections with those outside the Japanese American community. Many tell of meeting famous actors, politicians, and even the emperor and empress of Japan, as well as several local and national officials and businessmen. More than one job has come from these outside connections. Each city, though, has its own unique twist on this. In Los Angeles with the entertainment industry nearby, many of the Nisei Week queens have used their title and the connections that followed as a stepping-stone into modeling and acting careers. Others, as in

Honolulu where the Cherry Blossom Queen is perhaps most in the broader public eye due to the large population of Japanese in Hawaii, used their positions to find jobs in politics or newscasting.

Studying Japanese American Beauty Pageants

Festivals in the Japanese American community have been around since 1934, beginning with Nisei Week in Los Angeles, and have become institutions within the various Japanese American communities (Kurashige 2002). Festivals "persist, in part, because they help communities maintain themselves . . . they are believed by their participants to help the community function" (Ashkenazi 1993, 146.) While analyzing festivals and pageants is not a traditional way to study issues within racial/ethnic communities, these events do provide a window into the complex negotiation at the heart of the making and remaking of collective racial/ethnic, gender, and class identity. Pageants are racialized projects and in many ways are a litmus test of what is going on in the larger local Japanese American community. In one of the first scholarly books on beauty pageants, *Beauty Queens on the Global Stage*, the editors write, "By choosing an individual whose deportment, appearance and style embodies the values and goals of a nation, locality, or group, beauty contests expose these same values and goals to interpretation and challenge" (Cohen, Wilk, and Stoeltje 1996, 2).

Beauty pageants make a good example when looking at the redefinition of race and ethnicity because the explicit goal of the pageant is to select a symbolic representation of the Japanese American community. Again, this does not mean that the queen represents the entire community or even a portion of it, but she does represent the production of some sense of Japanese Americanness. Mixed-race Japanese Americans are simultaneously inside and outside racial boundaries and thus jar people to change the way they think about race and ethnicity when they assert their right to represent the Japanese American community. The most surprising finding in this study was that race (albeit in a slightly different guise) continued to play a huge role in maintaining definitions of who was and was not Japanese American.

This dynamic process of collective Japanese American self-definition is mapped out in the selection of the queen and in debates about her ability to represent the community. She is a symbolic representation of the community, but her body is also the field on which Japanese Americanness is debated. Therefore, beauty standards are not all that are at stake here, but so are the Japanese American community's definition of itself and its future trajectory as a racial/ethnic community. The fact that many of the participants in the pageants (and a majority in some cities) are now of mixed descent signals a change, not only in the definition of Japanese American, but also in the basic definitions of race, ethnicity, and community membership. In fact, race, which one might think would not be a criterion given the high levels of mixing within the community, persists, and people work hard to maintain its preeminence.

Beauty pageants are a good way to study collective racial/ethnic identities for four reasons: they are symbolic; they are open, public, performative events; they are racial projects; and they involve a particularly explicit intersection of gendering and racialization. First, the pageant is not just the sum of the Japanese American individuals who participate in it. Because the queen is a symbol of a larger community, she is a collective racialized, ethnicized, and highly gendered and classed symbol. There is evidence in many forms that the queen represents more than just herself. The queen is visible in the ethnic newspapers. Because she is a figure in the community and its representative, she is expected to behave a certain way and to be open to almost everyone. This also leads people to feel that they can be critical of her as their queen. In fact, the proof that she is a symbol can be seen in pageant detractors like Mei Nakano, who was quoted in *Asian Week:* "I think it is far out to say that the queen represent and speaks for the community. When people say the tradition promotes solidarity and is good for the community, I want to say 'give me a break.' Is Miss America good for America?" (Tanner 1998, 12–13). The fact that they feel that she is even worth commenting on focuses attention on the queen within the Japanese American community. In drawing the analogy to Miss America, Nakano implies that the pageant is not good for Japanese America and is a trivial and offensive practice that should be abandoned. It is precisely the symbolic nature of the pageant queen that makes her worthy of analysis as a site where there is a deliberate attempt to create and recreate Japanese Americanness. Nakano clearly recognizes that the symbol does not make the community what it is, and that there is not agreement over the symbol, but her focus on rejecting the symbol proves that this, too, is a part of the discourse about Japanese Americanness. This visible challenge from Japanese American feminists is present in the pageant each year as the women participating carefully negotiate the tricky issue of not wanting to buy into feminism so much as to jeopardize their winning of the pageant. It matters tremendously that the queen is a woman and that issues of gender and gender roles are appropriated and controlled, as a mechanism for racialized social control. The queen pageants not only consist of individual racial projects, but also reflect and constitute a collective racial project, including the debates and disagreements that they signify. The acceptance or rejection of mixed-race women as queens and candidates is interesting, but their mere presence brings the issues of racial challenge, change, and renegotiation into the public sphere.

Pageants are also suitable for study because they are public; they are openly accessible to anyone who wants to attend. This is convenient for getting access in research, but, more important, it means that the pageant is open for the community and others to view for the price of a ticket. It is difficult to do research on collective racial identity construction. Collective identities are often felt and forceful, but intangible or "imagined" forms of identity that make them difficult to tap into and study (Anderson 1991). The pageants, then, were also ideal because they were public events in the sense that they were on stage and made overt manifest issues of collective identity that are often not discussed. They were performative in nature and therefore easily observed and absorbed by the audience who attended them. Ethnography allowed me to see both the "frontstage" and the "backstage" parts of the production of the pageant.

> When an individual presents him*(her)*self before others, his*(her)* performance will tend to incorporate and exemplify the officially accredited values of the society. To the degree that a performance highlights the common official values of a society in which it occurs, we may look upon it . . . as an expressive rejuvenation and reaffirmation of the moral values of the community. (Emphasis added; Goffman 1959, 35)

Both the presentation of self to the audience and the presentation of the self to the judges, pageant committee, and those backstage are recorded in my ethnographic study of these pageants.

Third, the pageant is a suitable site of study because it is an openly racial project—it is guided by racial rules (i.e., one must be of 50 percent Japanese ancestry to even be considered for participation). Participation itself is premised upon belonging to the racial/ethnic community and that belonging is dictated by racial eligibility rules. In this case, the racial and ethnic rules and the debates about them provide us with a look at how collective racial membership is being defined, enforced, and legitimated. It makes visible the racial and ethnic boundaries of the community, pointing out who is and who is not truly or legitimately Japanese American and therefore creating a hierarchy of authenticities. While other racial/ethnic groups base membership on parentage, place of birth, or race, the Japanese American communities I studied still used racial rules to determine membership. However, they were also beginning to use ethnicity as an equal way to determine community membership. The process of choosing and producing the queen each year is a dramatization of sorts of the collective myths, values, and selves in local Japanese American communities.

Finally, these local racial/ethnic queen pageants are ideal for exploring how collective racial projects intersect with processes of gendering. Because it is largely a community spectacle and one that is based on performativity—meaning that the process of the pageant is largely in the public eye—it provides many with the ability to observe the spectacle in action. Judith Butler explains,

> Acts, gestures, and desire produce the effect of an internal core or substance but produce this *on the surface* of the body, through the play of signifying absences that suggest, but never reveal, the organizing principle of identity as a cause. Such acts, gestures, enactments generally constructed, are *performative* in the sense that the essence or identity that they otherwise purport to express are *fabrications* manufactured and sustained through corporeal signs and other discursive means. That the gendered body is performative suggests that it has no ontological status apart from the various acts, which constitute its reality. (Butler 1999, 136)

Likewise, this same body, which is constituted of these fabrications, can be "done" in relation to race. These racialized gestures and acts, such as "walking Japanese" in kimono, reveal the process of expressing these fabrications—and are intentional. These actions take effort and work to perfect and perform. In addition, all of the pageants are exhibitions and therefore are performed on stage, with an audience, and with judging taking place at the time of performance. This sense of the public display and the controlled exhibition makes the pageant a very visible and therefore unique social act.

Conclusion

Japanese Americans are thinking about mixed-race issues. As this moves from being just an individual or family issue, the community is adapting to the presence of mixed-race bodies and the problematization of the racial underpinning and definitions of Japanese Americanness. This can be seen in the shifting notions of who is Japanese American enough to represent the community through the expanding racial eligibility rules that incorporate mixed-race female bodies as possible representations of the local community. As an analytical object, eligibility rules also draw us into the intersections of race, ethnicity, gender, community ties, the body, and collective symbols. We become voyeurs in the world of beauty pageants and local community parades and festivals—into the action and interaction of creating cultural meanings with racial connotations.

Community pageants are just one instance where we can see shifting demographics highlighting the issues surrounding the increasing tensions around mixed-race members within the Japanese American community. This has larger theoretical implications to tell us about how mixed-race people neither bridge (mend) or blend race but become a site for the contestation and redefinition of race. But in looking at Japanese American beauty pageants, questions remain: How is the discourse about race and ethnicity changing within the Japanese American community because of the presence of mixed-race bodies? How are mixed-race Japanese Americans seen by others racially? How does that come to impact concepts of race, ethnicity, culture, and gender? It is clear that through "race work" social actors, mono- and multiracial alike, try to link gender, the body, and sexuality in the pageants in an attempt to control racial boundaries. As the book moves from the micro level of intra- and interpersonal interaction, up to a more macro level, race work becomes more and more intense to maintain race as a concept hardwired into community boundaries, culture, and gender.

The beauty pageant provides a case where meso-level discourses can be revealed and analyzed for normative notions of beauty, culture, and community. Through a close examination of individual and collective as well as institutional negotiations of race/ethnicity on the body, we will see that this does not paint a picture of a "postrace" world with mixed-race bodies leading us into a world of fewer racial meanings, but instead into a world of increasing "race work" that aims to prop up racial concepts using culture, gender, and community networks as a scaffolding.

1   Race Work and the Effort of Racial Claims

The pink delicate Cherry Blossom Trees bloom in early April. They are beautiful, but very fragile. They peak quickly and soon blow away with the breeze.
The trick is to get the photo for the cover of the program booklet with the
Queen candidates in their kimonos before all the pink willowy blossoms hit the
ground. The race against time to capture the photo rushes the kimono-clad
women to—quick—strike a pose before the rain comes and the wind whips
their "Japanese hair," piled high upon their heads with the help of cotton
stuffing and a million bobbypins, into a tangle of momentous proportions.
    —From the author's fieldnotes

Mixed race does not mean the end of race as a concept or as a product of biological race thinking, where racial meaning is congealed and
tied through its supposed association to the body to biology. Indeed
the mixed-race body invites us to examine more carefully *race work*—
people worked hard around the pageants to keep the biological notion
of race (typically references to looks or physical appearance) in line
with their thinking about culture (i.e., full-blooded people of color
have culture, whites don't). In order to shed light on how race is socially and politically constructed in a world where race as a concept has

gone underground and is more difficult to detect and trace—a world where there can be "racial intent without race" (Ignatiev 2004)—I will look at multiple levels of social interaction. Eduardo Bonilla-Silva (2002) writes that the world is becoming more racially blended and that race, on the surface, is mattering less and less. He argues that the United States increasingly will follow a Latin American model of racial stratification, where ancestry matters less than color and society is divided roughly along the lines of white and nonwhite. The mixed-race trend of blending exists alongside and is often mobilized in support of this softening of race thinking, but this does not lessen the importance of race. Just because race has become more subtle and clever does not mean that it is less significant. The mixed-race body then does not destroy race, but leads to a repoliticization and problematization of race. Races and mixed race have been studied in a variety of institutional arenas—family, state, social movements, cultural products, the law, for example—but not in terms of race's power to transform existing racial/ethnic communities and the ways in which people do race work.

By "race work" I mean that social actors exert extreme efforts in their social actions to sustain the belief that biological notions of race (how one looks physically/phenotype) determine ideas about culture. The link between biological characteristics and cultural action is the essence of "race thinking." I found this process at play in my fieldwork in almost all everyday interactions at different levels. In my research, multiracial people didn't particularly dissect biological race from culture, but instead tried hard to reinforce the dynamism of the connection between the two by doing "work" in their behavior to keep them together. Race was work. It took effort and support via interaction to make and substantiate racial claims. As with all work, some people—for example, mixed-race people—were made to work harder than others. Like emotional labor (Hochschild 2003), race work means laboring with and through race for a purpose, in this case community acceptance and access to social networks. By using race in interaction, the women I studied propped up the concept of race as useful and socially "real" and then proceeded to use it to accomplish the goals of community acceptance and access to social networks through social interactions. Some would argue that whites do not have to work hard at race at all, where mixed-race people may work harder at race. They are made more aware of their racial difference, work hard to make any racial claims, and may often transgress boundaries to do so, thus creating more boundary work for themselves. Race work is the bodily labor that social actors perform in deportment, dress, action, language, food practices, accent, and a range of other ways in order to make claims to a physical appearance or phenotype associated with biological notions of race.

The process of race work involves self-reflection and the internalization of racial meanings in order to take action to bolster social race in social action. In this case, there is activity and action in the creation and maintenance of race done by real people. This action is both focused on a specific physical and cultural body and imbued with collective and symbolic meaning.

Multiraciality and the Socially Constructed Nature of Race: Blending or Amending Race?

Multiracial people are one of the quintessential examples, often used by social scientists, to illustrate the social constructionist view of race (Cornell and Hartmann 1998, 237). I use the word *race* to mean a social construct, which is composed of the legacy of biological notions of race thinking as well as social race meanings. The goal of this book is to work out the relationship between the legacy of biological race and social race and how they are related to ethnicity and gender. (I do not mean to reify race by using it as a term, nor do I think if I didn't use the term *race* that racism would cease.)

The mixed-race case within communities of color provides a particular challenge to the grounding of the concept of "race."

> To group formation, racial characterization adds the fabrication of naturalism, the fixed and fast insinuation of community insider and outsider. In qualifying hybridity, it delimits the (al)chemical dynamics of cultural transformation by giving in to the racializing presumptions of ownership and selectivity, of purity and homogeneity, of the dangers of pollution. At best then, the condition of mixed race formation constitutes an ambivalent challenge to the racial condition from within the fabric of the racializing project. (Goldberg 1997, 76)

Mixed-race people and studies, then, have moved into the realm of attempting to undo race not only as a concept, but also as a political base around which collective identities are formed.

This challenge to race by mixed-race people, both conceptually and politically, has also arisen in the literature written by mixed-race people themselves. Early studies of multiraciality (Root 1992; Zack 1993) examined how mixed-race people negotiated the monoracial terrain they encountered in their everyday lives on a micro/individual level. Focusing mainly on identity construction in relation to communities both of color and of whites, this early writing contained tremendous optimism about the ability of mixed-race people to be bridges between communities, mending racial fences along the way. Early studies of multiraciality argued for doing away with the false sense of race as an untrue biological fact. Zack (1993) in particular argued for antirace, that is, doing away with race as a concept because of its dubious origins in biology. Unfortunately, recognizing the false biological origin of race did not undo race as a concept or the racism that flowed from it. Ropp (1997) argued that although mixed-race people did draw attention to the socially malleable nature of race, there was scant evidence that mixed-race people could undo racial thinking on a large scale.

More recent studies of multiraciality, while still focusing on identity (usually black : white identity), have moved to a more macro level, using newly available census data and other large data sets to study mixed-race identity choice and how it is shaped by social factors such as affiliation with racial groups, parents, and levels of education (Harris 2002; Herman 2003; Rockquemore and Brunsma 2001). While improving the generalizability of mixed-race identity studies, many of these studies have struggled with the issue of the changeability of race over time and from context to context. It is almost too complex to capture and "[t]he practical implication of this realization *(of the complexity)* is that analysts must think critically about what they mean by race, design surveys that more precisely measure race, and be aware of the implications of mismatches between available and ideal racial data" (emphasis added; Harris 2002, 625).

These types of studies may not be the best way methodologically to capture the process of racialization since they do not have the all-important "face-to-face" interactive, contextual data on identity formation. The survey designers formulate a question that is not asked within a constant social context and it takes for granted the subjects' racial identifications and objectifications of themselves. Often these surveys were not designed solely or even primarily to collect multiple racial data. As such they may find it difficult to account for contextual factors such as physical appearance—one of the most important factors that seems to shape the mixed-race experience. Some work has been done on regional differences (Brunsma 2003; Gallagher 2002), on racial group differences (Williams-Leon 2001), and on sexuality (Williams 1997; Kitahara Kich 1996). There have also been excellent qualitative, small-scale studies of youth (Wallace 2001). The research on multiracial families in different settings has helped us to understand the foundation for the multiracial movement (DaCosta 2000) and how it challenged the color line in racial politics in the United States (Dalmage 2000, 2004). These studies of family help us to better understand race relations in the United States.

> Both interracial families and multiracial individuals will maintain cultural importance in America as long as race is understood as a biological reality. . . . Thus the very act of defining which groups make up an interracial family or multiracial individual is shaped by who we think belongs to different races and implies that we believe that there are qualitative differences between individuals in those groups. (Yancey 2000, 205)

Mixed-race people, then, are shedding light on one part of the process of racialization rather than being responsible ontologically for "undoing" race at its biological core or politically for bridging racial groups. It is through analysis of their experience, particularly through their bodily experience (i.e., their bodies being taken as racial subject/object at the same time) that we can reveal the beliefs and processes that are the basis for the dividing of people into racial groups in the first place. For this reason the multiracial body is a perfect way into looking at changing notions of racialization.

Perhaps the most widely studied area within mixed-race studies has been the change in the way the U.S. Census allowed people multiple racial choices beginning in 2000. Many have heralded this change as the beginning of the end of race as we know it. While some books have analyzed the movement and its contradictions (Spencer 1999), others have tried to contextualize it through comparison with other understandings of the mixed-race experience in South Africa and Brazil (Spencer 1997; Nobles 2000). The availability of hard data generated by the census has moved demographic studies of multiracial people into the mainstream of sociology. This has changed the nature (from personal life history and small identity studies to large-scale quantitative studies) and the voice (mixed-race personal experience at the grassroots level to well-funded, prestigious, predominantly white scholars) of the types of research getting done and questions asked (Perlmann and Waters 2002). A clear political agenda underpins much of this new work on the Census, and organizations like the NAACP and the National Council de Raza worry out loud that mixed-race people's claims to make race multiple and flexible will mean the "end of race." They argue that mixed-race research and activism may have gone too far and will now threaten civil rights achievements in law, housing, education, hate crimes, and employment. The multiracial movement was used by the ultimately defeated Racial Privacy Initiative in California in 2003 to argue that if race is multiple, it loses meaning and therefore there should be no collection of racial data at all.

While these studies of the census tell us much about the macro and even state levels of racialization, traditionally the subject of study in racial formation studies (Omi and Winant 1994), it may be that micro and qualitative research can tell us more about the process of self-identification within specific social contexts by mixed-race people. To date, however, many of these studies (DuBose and Winters 2002; Penn 1998; Williams-Leon and Nakashima 2001) have examined the mixed-race experience in relation to traditional racial/ethnic groups, that is, what it is like to be mixed-race black/white in relation to the black/African American community. Rarely, if ever, do they go beyond how the traditional community impacts mixed-race people to give agency to mixed-race people to see how they, in turn, affect the traditional communities of color that they belong to. It is this relationship between mixed-race people and assumed monoracial people of color that seems to be the crux of this issue. This book takes the mixed-race experience and tries to understand how it impacts racial/ethnic groups that mixed-race people are affiliated with, not just in relation to the Census or to self-identity.

> [Sociologists] know relatively little about the social processes at work when an individual reports himself or herself to be a member of a particular racial or ethnic group. For decades social scientists have taken such reports at face value with little careful consideration about how they are produced. What is the calculus used when an individual chooses to report a racial identity? . . . Why do some individuals with relatively little American Indian heritage nonetheless claim this for their racial identity? These and many other related questions need to be answered to make the interpretation of racial data more meaningful. (Snipp 2003, 583)

For the NAACP, one of the largest fears in the quest to change racial/ethnic enumeration on the Census was that while mixed-race people were busy pursuing their right to recognition on the Census form, they were unwittingly (if one is kind) or purposefully (if one is not) attacking the basis of civil rights claims and recognition for "true" minority groups. This pitted the identity politics claims of mixed-race people against the lived inequalities of more traditional groups of color based on perceived race. Critics of the collection of racial/ethnic data in education, contracts, and employment assume that people can and do check multiple race boxes. This, they argue, makes it difficult to determine if a mixed-race black/white person was discriminated against because of his or her ambiguous appearance. Because of this racial and assumed physical ambiguity, it may not be possible to attribute any discrimination as a racially motivated incident and therefore worthy of civil rights protection or compensation. The critics see no need to collect racial data at all. The assumption is that with people more racially mixed and the world more racially equal, the boundaries between black and white will become heavily blurred. In this sense, the argument for a postethnic America (Hollinger 1995), where we all wear racial identities like "Kiss me, I'm Irish" buttons on St Patrick's Day (Waters 1990), seems to have progressed to a post–civil rights society where race doesn't matter anymore. Multiracial people, then, in many descriptions are leading the way in deconstructing race into a postrace society (Ali 2003). However, key in all of these predictions is the importance of not visually sticking out and being able to blend in with whiteness as the basis of equality. Physical appearance/phenotype (race) and others' perceptions of it are central to these arguments and remain the lynch pins of the whole process of racialization.

Making Mixed-race Bodies

Intermarriage has long been an interesting field to study because it is the place where two, assumed to be separate, racial/ethnic groups come together in a close and intimate way.

> Intermarriage is, at one and the same time, a sensitive barometer of the acceptability of an ethnic group . . . a reflection of the state of contacts across ethnic lines and the ethnic context in which the next generation will be raised. On average, persons with mixed ancestry are much less exposed in their upbringing to ethnic traits. . . . [T]herefore, as . . . a group is increasingly composed of those of mixed ancestry, the group as a whole will become less and less ethnically distinctive. (Alba 1996, 179)

In this line of thinking, mixed-race people are not as full of culture as full-blooded, or unmixed, members of the community. Culture and ethnicity in this formula are indivisible, but race and culture are—half the race, half the culture. The disintegration of the community is largely caused by intermarriage. Intermarriage and mixed-race people are the point at which we should see huge change in definitions of culture, race, and community membership. Because of high intermarriage and an increasing number of mixed-race Japanese Americans in the community, this is an important time and place to watch race and ethnicity change before our very eyes. This potential change from being a distinct racial/ethnic community to being part of the mainstream (white) society can be analyzed by looking at the relationship that the Japanese American community has had with itself and other outside communities and how that has changed over time. Even with the changing of racial meanings, however, race itself is hardly questioned at all and much individual and collective race work is done in order to reinscribe the concept of race, as physical difference, with meaning. In addition, within the Japanese American community the focus has been on intermarriage rather than other demographic shifts such as low immigration. This is due in part to the fact that women are seen as important procreators of the race and teachers or maintainers of culture and they have been the ones to marry out.

Theories of a colorblind society predict mixed-race people will blend race into oblivion and mend racial divides (Ali 2003; Nakashima 1996). In this line of thought mixed-race people are either prime examples of the future of race relations or the downfall of people of color, but very little research actually studies how mixed-race people affect groups of color, both those they belong to and those they don't. The above studies, both small and large, rest on an interesting set of assumptions. First, mixed-race people are seen to be a fairly separate community, with separate concerns from communities of color. However, mixed-race people are also seen as having the agency to bring communities together. Yet analysts are not sure what the basis of this "community" is and if they have their own mixed culture or not (Aspinall 2003). Second, mixed-race people are taken as the object of racial change—either for better (building bridges) or worse (challenging much needed racial categories to track discrimination). They are not seen as active agents in the process of racial change. Finally, mixed-race people's physical nature and appearance are often the focus of these two types of articles (The new face of America, *Time* 1993). How they are perceived by others, through visual contact, is important as it shapes how they see themselves through interaction with others, and how others see them in relation to privilege. Mixed-race people may be seen as "kinder, gentler, more privileged" people of color or assumed to be middle class and privileged in larger white society because they are whiter/lighter (Streeter 1996).

It is important to understand, then, how mixed-race people actually and empirically relate to and affect communities of color, how they see and are seen within communities of color (are they respected/resented or both?) and how their physical bodies come to problematize concepts of race for communities of color. Do they get rid of race? Reinscribe it with different, but still powerful meaning? While these studies focus on the deconstruction of race (Ropp 1997) or promote living in a postrace world (Ali 2003) through mixed-race people, they do not look outward at the larger impact that multiraciality has on those who are not "mixed race." Other than to anger groups of color, mixed-race bodies have been little examined to understand how they lead us to the need to examine how individuals and collectivities do race work in an attempt to rescue the concept of race in their everyday lived experiences. Clearly, if critical mixed-race studies illustrate one thing, it is that the continued existence of bodies of mixed race does not deconstruct or do away with race. On the contrary, race still constrains social action by all people, mixed or not.

While people (particularly mixed-race people) realize that race is socially constructed, they still continue to shore up the idea of race as biological (through ancestry rules) and relate it quite strongly to ethnicity and even gender. Both racial meanings, such as blood quantum rules, and the actions and interactions around race that I term "race work," keep the believed biological basis of race alive. These links are strengthened in race's assumed connection with ethnicity and culture, and are used to maintain community borders through racialization and to keep gender intact via racial control of the reproduction of the community (i.e., those who can pass on culture to future generations.) All of this is observed through the physical embodiment of racial interactions. When the embodiment of racial meanings is in flux, it also makes all of these related concepts—ethnicity, culture, and gender—

in flux. The mixed-race body, while it problematizes race and opens the door for more flexible understandings of race, does not, inevitably, do away with race.

Why then is race still such a powerful social concept, even in the multiracial case? I found that mixed-race women in the beauty pageants were "raced" by others as non–Japanese Americans. In this sense, the discrimination they may face both from within the Japanese American community and from whites means that race is something that they cannot escape—as either whiteness or Japanese Americanness. Alternatively, even though some of them who were half white could pass, they chose not to but instead identified themselves even more strongly with the Japanese American community. I argue that they see the racial passport of Japanese Americanness as allowing them entry into an ethnicity (cultural capital) and network of social relations (social capital) to which they didn't have access before. In this sense, it is the combination of blood quantum rules (ancestry), social ties, and cultural knowledge that they seem to crave by participating in the pageant. This craving is caused by the upwardly mobile move of most Japanese Americans to dispersed geographic areas (suburbs and rural), among other racial/ethnic groups (i.e., not a Japanese American ethnic enclave), with high exposure to non–Japanese Americans via school and work, creating a need to connect with Japanese American communities and other Japanese Americans. Perhaps there was an inherent and continuing need for racial/ethnic community connection.

This project takes an empirical case of one community of color and looks at the mixed-race experience in it. It looks not just at the mixed people themselves, but at relations within the communities they belong to, and how and if they change those relations. In the end, this is accomplished by centering the embodied nature of race to include the formative interactions between individuals and collectivities where racial labels are made. The conclusion then goes beyond strict claims that "race is socially constructed, but racism is real." It explores how, while race is socially constructed, social actors work hard doing race work to hang on to and reinvigorate the concept of biological and embodied race in order to shore up the link to the connected concepts of ethnicity and culture.

It may be that the embodiment of race and the social interaction that shapes interpretations of that embodiment is the key to understanding both individual and collective mixed-race identity processes.

In taking for granted the identity formation process, many mixed-race studies are interested in the factors that shape identity but can't tell us much about the process of how that happens or why choices are made the way they are. This study contextualizes the process of individual and collective identity formation, not by focusing on the census or other static data sources, but instead within a specific social context with specific focus on the agency of the multiracial women themselves.

The Larger Field of Race

Studies of mixed-race people have had tremendous impacts on racial theories that try to connect race as a concept with ethnicity, culture, and gender.

> One of the first things we notice about people when we meet them (along with their sex) is their race. We utilize race to provide clues about *who* a person is. This fact is made painfully obvious when we encounter someone whom we cannot conveniently racially categorize—someone who is, for example, racially "mixed" or of an ethnic/racial group we are not familiar with. Such an encounter becomes a source of discomfort and momentarily a crisis of racial meaning. (Omi and Winant 1994, 59)

The mixed-race beauty queens in this study are not just symbolic representations that cause crises in racial thinking when people encounter them as "representing" the Japanese American community. They also signify the larger structural shifts going on in the economic, political and social integration of Japanese Americans into the U.S. racial order. They call into question the salience of race itself and the relationship of race to ethnicity and culture. "The notion of ethnicity experienced as culture—the culturalization of ethnicity—is in important senses different from the experience that involves notions of race or genophenotypical and ancestral differentiation—the racialization of ethnicity" (Spickard and Daniel 2004, 9).

My research contributes to Spickard and Daniels's understanding that culturalization and racialization are processes that are or can be done to other social phenomena. Ethnicity, in the case of the mixed-race beauty queen, is clearly made cultural. However, it is at least as often made racial and assumed or affiliated with phenotype. For example, racial eligibility rules assume in the first place some correspondence of race with ethnicity because of the implicit claim that one can't be an authentic ethnically, culturally informed Japanese American without 50 percent or more Japanese ancestry. Now, of course, there are exceptions. The queen who is racially Japanese but is adopted into a white family has no cultural authenticity, but has the required embodied race. The white person raised in a Japanese American family has the culture, but is less likely to be deemed authentic because she doesn't have the racial body recognized as Japanese American. The first can be queen (a symbol of the community) and the second can't, thus reinforcing the racial underpinning of ethnicity.

Miri Song also highlights the relationship of race to ethnicity in her discussion of "ethnic options" available to people of color and their relationship to race. "Rather than adhere to overly neat analytical distinctions between racial and ethnic identities, future studies concerning minority groups' ethnic options need to examine the variable and complex intertwinings of racial and ethnic identities as experienced by disparate ethnic minority groups" (2001, 76). In other words, even mixed-race, half-white, middle-class Japanese Americans have constraints placed on how wide their "ethnic options" can be. They may be constrained in their identification as Japanese within the Japanese American community, not being seen as legitimate queens, but also from outside, not being seen racially as Japanese at all.

Audrey Smedley argues that one of the main goals within the multiracial movement—to better recognize and understand both parental "cultures"—is misguided. Mixed-race people "fail to realize what anthropologists have long known, that there is no relationship between one's culture or lifestyle and one's genes or biological features" (1995, 697).

According to Smedley, "The racial worldview, with its emphasis on assumptions of innateness and immutability, makes it possible to interpret all forms of human behavior as hereditary" (1995, 697). She believes that, basing their claims of "mixed-race" on racial foundations, mixed-race people reify rather than problematize "race." Mixed-race people also perpetuate the racialization of ethnicity and culture when they make the "recognize the culture of both parents" argument.

For these reasons the labor (both emotional and physical) of maintaining the ideal Japanese American woman creates a need for the women in the pageants, and particularly the mixed-race women, to "work" to maintain their racial claims. In doing so, this race work reinscribes the concept of race with meaning in the Japanese American context. They work to keep race and culture aligned through bodily practices. They work hard to keep their bodies and selves in line with racial and cultural expectations and thus reinforce the race/culture nexus.

Race Work in Japanese American Beauty Pageants

I found that in beauty pageants the presence of multiple mixed-race beauty pageant contestants caused a crisis in individual and, particularly, collective racial thinking about ethnicity. For example, it was assumed that if a contestant was racially of 100 percent Japanese ancestry that she would have the corresponding ethnic and cultural knowledge *because* of her racial background. Even though many of the contestants realized that race was socially constructed, it was not until they were face to face with a mixed-race contestant who was deemed to have more Japanese culture (e.g., spoke Japanese, knew cultural traditional arts, and so on) but less racial claim to it that they started to realize how tightly coupled they believed race and ethnicity to be.

Edles (2004) describes this relationship as being between ethnicity, race, and culture. She applies this to local Hawaiian identity to flush out not only racial identity (What are you?), but also ethnicity (Where are you from?) and adds in culture (What do you know? How do you act?). Edles's formulation allows us to think not only about the social perception of physical appearance (race) highlighted in the pageants and the corresponding "ethnicity" of the community that supposedly goes with it, but the cultural (such as language, food) practices that go with both. While Edles's model is conceptually helpful, I focus on the processes that connect these three concepts in social action. They are so closely related that claims in one sphere are typically connected intimately with claims in another. Claims to ethnic identity can even win recognition of "racial" identity where it is seen to be lacking (as in the mixed-race case) above. This is often done by "working" with cultural objects and practices to make expressly racial claims.

Even in cases where there would be great structural advantages to "passing" in white middle-class culture, in the pageant setting mixed-race Japanese Americans and others went to extreme measures to work to maintain race's importance in the race : culture relationship. In this sense, race is not just a subcategory of ethnicity but often dominates ethnicity—it was, in fact, their phenotypical "race" that mattered. Within the racial project of the racial/ethnic beauty pageant, the pageants themselves "work" to make the links between race and culture and between representations and structural meanings of race.

The Process of Race Work

In order to provide a processual model for understanding a microlevel racial project such as the Japanese American beauty pageant, I use an analytical method that divides the race-work process into multiple conceptual levels (King 1997).

Level 1—Individual Negotiations

On level 1 I borrow from ethnomethodology (Garfinkel 1967) the idea that race, like gender, is something that one "does" (West and Zimmerman 1991). People actively practice it in their everyday lives. But "doing race" happens on two distinct levels; within individuals and between individuals. While George Herbert Mead did not theorize explicitly about race, his theory of the self as the "ability to take oneself as an object" and thinking as "the internalized conversation of the individual with himself via significant symbols and gestures" lays the groundwork for thinking about race as an identity within an individual (1934, 47). Although this identity process happens within individuals, it remains social in nature because it is the internalization of the dispositions of the generalized other (society) that creates the ability to take oneself as an object. For race theory, this means that individuals can be self-reflexive about what race they identify themselves to be, but that they cannot choose without restriction. For example, a mixed-race person could identify him- or herself as such (i.e., both white and Japanese), but the current racial frameworks constrain this identification. Most mixed-race people know this and think of themselves in social life not as they are, but as the current racial frameworks will allow them to be. Asserting a mixed-race identity, that one can be two races at once, becomes a challenge to existing racial frameworks.

Level 2—Interpersonal Negotiations

This leads us directly to the second level, where people present their racial identity in interaction with others. Erving Goffman argued that the self is not a possession of the actor, but instead is the product of the dramatic interaction between the actor and the audience. Racial identity in this sense becomes situational and impressions need to be managed differently from context to context (see Goffman 1959; Lyman and Douglass 1973; Okamura 1981, 458). Lyman writes, "From the ethnic actor's perspective, ethnicity is both a mental state and a potential ploy in any encounter, but it will be neither if it cannot be invoked or activated" (Lyman and Douglass, 1973, 349). Thus, a mixed-race Japanese American can think she is Japanese racially and can use this to strategize to get what she wants, but this will be limited if others do not "legitimate" or "authenticate" her racial identity. For example, if a mixed-race Cherry Blossom Queen candidate thinks of herself as Japanese American, but because of her phenotypical characteristics doesn't "look Japanese" to others, her racial/ethnic identity is not legitimated by others and she may not feel she can be a "good queen," that is, representative of the community. Mixed-race Japanese American women may then use "markers" or "cues" such as language, behavior, or dress as a way to convince people of their racial/ethnic authenticity.

Level 3—Collective Negotiations

These interactions typically occur in a context of wider collective identities, networks, and solidarities. Therefore, race is interactively created not only by individuals but also by groups. Groups legitimate certain modes of interaction, and race in this sense is "done" collectively. Blumer and Duster argue that racial groups create images of their own group and others via complex interaction and communication among the group's members. They interpret their "runs of experiences" and form "judgments and images" of their own group and others (1980, 222.) Here the very presence of mixed-race people, who actively identify as mixed, and their interactions with monoracials redefine through interaction what it means to be Japanese American, both individually and collectively.

Level 4—Hierarchical Negotiations

But these racial groups do not exist in isolation from other groups. Racial/ethnic groups are relational and hierarchical. Race is relational in that racial categories are usually seen as mutually exclusive, that is, a person can belong to one and only one of the categories "that are positioned, and therefore, gain meaning, in relation to each other" (Barrett 1987, as quoted in Glenn 1992.) This means that the experiences of people in the different racial groups are "not just different, but connected in systematic ways" (Glenn 1992, 34). In addition, racial groups exist in a hierarchy of differential power, and their actions around race will be shaped by the arenas in which they have power and whom they have the right to exercise power over. The pageants were initially very much in response to being shut out of whiteness as a small minority ethnic group with little economic, political, or racial power.

These levels are visible in the pageants that I studied. The presentation of self is clear and the women had to think about their appearance and presentation at every turn. Each "practice" brought the women closer to the ideal they thought the judges and audience wanted to see. The presence of an audience and the public nature of the pageants meant that collective norms and discourses about race, ethnicity, and culture (as well as gender) were to the fore.

Conclusion

Through the levels, I examine race work in each chapter as a strategy to understand how race, ethnicity, culture and gender get linked together in social practice. In the next chapter, I describe the demographic shifts that have impacted the changing nature of Japanese Americanness by focusing on the increasing number of interracial marriages and multiracial people within the communities. Chapter 3 gives a historical overview of the different eras through which the pageant has evolved and the different struggles over membership in the nation, feminism, and mixed-race queens. In chapters 4 and 5, I examine how claims to membership in the Japanese American community were mediated through race and produced, controlled, and legitimated. On the most macro level, I examine in chapter 6 how the struggles to legitimacy are shaped by broader discourses of multiculturalism and larger structural forces such as economic and political power. Finally, chapter 7 examines these claims in light of the community's larger collective struggle over the definition of Japanese Americanness and criteria for membership in the community. In the conclusion, I focus once more on the concept of "race work" and how it can be the basis of new approaches to the study of racialization.

2   *The Japanese American Community in Transition*

The Cherry Blossom Queen and her court are walking in their kimonos through Japantown accompanied by the flap-flapping of their feet against their zori (slippers) before the raffle drawing. Surrounded by throngs of people, they slowly make their way down the food booths, smiling and chatting with various people and trying not to get anything sticky on the expensive silk kimonos. As they make their way to the teriyaki booth, a voice from the crowd asks one of the mixed-race princesses, "Are you Japanese?"

There is dead silence among the court and then a sigh with the answer, "Yes, I am."

The voice continues unabated: "You don't look Japanese!"

"I am," she responds. "My name is Erica Takahashi."

The older man who asked the question seems satisfied with the answer, and the queen and court continue on their way. Why does this man not see the princess as Japanese American? Why did he feel the need to question her and ask her for proof, and why was her answer treated as sufficient "proof"?

    —From the author's fieldnotes

This questioning of mixed-race people as to whether or not they are Japanese "enough" is an issue for mixed-race people within the Japanese

American community. Paul Spickard in his book, *Mixed Blood*, examined how the offspring of Japanese women and American men, both black and white, were often harassed and faced racist treatment not only from white and other racial/ethnic groups, but also from within the Japanese American ethnic group. In particular, if Japanese women had married African American servicemen, their children were treated with disdain and cast out from Japanese society (1989, 148; Williams 1991).

Similar racial hierarchies still exist in the Japanese American community, which has become home to many of these mixed children. The idea of racial hierarchies perpetuated by the Japanese American community is evidenced in the community beauty pageants. For example, there have been few if any African American/Japanese American mixed-race queen candidates and none has been successfully chosen to be queen. With a historical legacy of stigmatizing mixed children in the community, particularly those who are part black, it is significant that recently there has been an increasing acceptance of mixed-race people in the Japanese American community. Movement of mixed Japanese Americans into the community and their acceptance have brought a reconsideration of concepts like race, ethnicity, and community in institutions such as pageants and has revealed the large amounts of race work done at the community level to maintain racial membership rules.

The recent social history of the Japanese American community provides a good example of how racial and ethnic meanings change over time for both individuals and ethnic groups. With low immigration, an increasingly elderly population, high outmarriage, and an increase in mixed-race members, the Japanese American community is wrestling with complex issues. The community is shrinking relative to other Asian American communities (Chinese Americans have larger populations in three of the four areas that I studied—Los Angeles, San Francisco, and Seattle/King County) and the larger society (Asians were less than 15 percent of the total population in each area except Hawaii, where they make up 55.9 percent of the population, according to 2000 U.S. Census data). Therefore, mixed-race people make up a much bigger part of the younger Japanese American community. This has changed the dynamics not only of community membership, but also of community understandings of race and ethnicity. In this chapter, I discuss the current demographic shifts, give a brief historical overview of what factors may have affected these shifts, present a summary of research done on Japanese American intermarriage patterns, and provide a critique of that literature. I present an account of how mixed-race Japanese Americans have been affected by and have come to affect definitions of race in the larger Japanese American community.

Japanese Americans Today

The demographics of the Japanese American community have changed radically in the last fifty years and leave the community struggling with new issues. The four main demographic shifts have been low immigration rates from Japan, an increase in the percentage of Japanese Americans over sixty-five, an increase in interracial marriages, and a smaller proportion of monoracial Japanese American babies being born.

Recent immigration from Japan has been much lower than from other Asian countries. Immigration from Japan remained at approximately 5,000–6,000 people per year throughout the 1980s and 1990s and is relatively small compared to Filipino and Chinese immigration (see Table 1). The fact that there are few new immigrants from Japan has made the Japanese American population "shrink" relative to other Asian American groups (see Table 2).

Where Japanese Americans used to be one of the biggest and oldest Asian American groups, they now negotiate political control within the pan-ethnic Asian American community with other bigger, younger, and more newly arrived groups, such as Koreans, Filipinos, Indians, and Vietnamese. Asians are also one of the smaller racial/ethnic groups within the United States, so that mixed-race Japanese Americans make up a larger percentage of that community faster than they would in other, larger communities of color.

The Japanese American community is also increasingly elderly. This is divergent from other Asian Pacific Islander groups where in 2000 "Asians had a median age of 33 years in 2000, 2 years younger than the national median of 35 years. By far, Japanese was the oldest of the detailed Asian groups with a median age of nearly 43 years." The Japanese community was found to have 12.1 percent of its population under 18 years of age, 67.5 percent between 18 and 64 and 20.4 percent

Table 1. Immigration by region and selected country of last residence

Years	Japanese	Filipino	Chinese	Korean	Vietnamese
1861–70	186	—	64,301	—	—
1871–80	149	—	123,201	—	—
1881–90	2,270	—	61,711	—	—
1891–1900	25,942	—	14,799	—	—
1901–1910	129,797	—	20,605	—	—
1911–20	83,837	—	21,278	—	—
1921–30	33,462	—	29,907	—	—
1931–40	1,948	528	4,928	—	—
1941–50	1,555	4,691	16,709	107	—
1951–60	46,250	19,307	9,657	6,231	335
1961–70	39,988	98,376	34,764	34,526	4,340
1971–80	49,775	354,987	124,326	267,638	172,820
1981–90	47,085	548,764	346,747	333,746	280,782
1991–2000	67,942	503,945	419,114	164,166	286,145
2001	10,464	50,870	50,821	19,933	34,648
2002	9,150	48,674	55,974	20,114	32,425
2003	6,724	43,258	37,396	12,177	21,270

Note: *Historical data compiled from Barringer et al. (1993, 39). Data from 2000 from Reeves and Bennett (2004), table 1. See also http://uscis.gov/graphics/shared/aboutus/ statistics/IMM03yrbk/IMMexcel/Table 2.xls.*

aged 65 and older. This contrasts widely with other Asian communities in which approximately 8 percent are 65 and older (Reeves and Bennett 2004, 6).

Japanese Americans are also significantly older than all other groups in the United States. Anecdotally, this is evidenced by the Japanese American Citizen's League member average age of 65 (Odo 1994). The community is depleted when new immigrants and births do not replace dying community members.

Higher outmarriage rates in the Japanese American community mean a more multiracial immediate future than that of other Asian groups and groups of color. This is readily obvious when attending any community event. For example, the faces of the participants are decidedly more mixed at the Cherry Blossom Festival parade than at the Chinese New Year's parade in San Francisco. Japanese Americans

Table 2. Population of Asian Ethnic Groups in the United States during the Twentieth Century

Year	Japanese	Filipino	Chinese	Korean	Vietnamese
1900	85,716	0	118,746	—	—
1910	152,745	2,767	94,414	5,008	—
1920	220,596	26,634	85,202	6,181	—
1930	278,743	108,424	102,159	8,332	—
1940	285,115	98,535	106,334	8,568	—
1950	326,379	122,707	150,005	7,030	—
1960	464,332	176,310	237,292	n/a	—
1970	591,290	343,060	436,062	69,150	—
1980	716,331	781,894	812,178	357,393	245,025
1990	847,562	1,406,770	1,645,472	798,849	614,547
2000 (alone)	795,051	1,864,120	2,422,970	1,072,682	1,110,207
2000 (in combination)	1,152,324	2,385,216	2,858,291	1,226,825	1,212,465

Note: *Historical data compiled from Barringer et al. (1993, 39). Data from 2000 from Reeves and Bennett (2004), table 1.*

Table 3. Median ages of American populations, 1980

Ethnicity	Total	Male	Female
White	31.3	30.0	32.5
Black	24.5	23.5	26.1
Japanese	33.6	31.4	36.2
Chinese	29.6	29.4	29.8
Filipino	28.6	27.9	29.1
Korean	26.1	23.3	27.1
Vietnamese	21.2	20.3	22.3

Note: *Data from Berringer et al. (1993, 91).*

in this sense are dealing with different demographic pressures than other Asian American communities. Their ties to mainstream white America are stronger and closer, although not always characterized by cultural appreciation or a lack of racism.

The total number of interracial marriages in the United States in

1990 was 1,493,725. While some people think of interracial marriages only as blacks married to whites, in reality Asians marrying whites make up 31.2 percent (by far the biggest proportion) of interracial marriages (Bennett, McKenney, and Harrison 1995, Table 1).

Historically, Japanese Americans had very low interracial-marriage rates, and usually men were the ones to marry out. In 1973 the Japanese American interracial marriage rate was 50 percent (Kikumura and Kitano 1973). In 1980, according to an analysis of census data, the interracial marriage rate was 47.7 percent (Shinagawa 1994). In 1984 43.4 percent of Japanese males and 56.6 percent of Japanese females outmarried. Between 1977 and 1984 intermarriage rates dropped from 63 percent to 51 percent (Kitano 1993). In 1990 interethnic and interracial marriage rates show whites (at 2 percent) and blacks (4.7 percent) far behind Chinese (26.1 percent), Mexicans (28.4 percent), Filipinos (43.3 percent), and Japanese (47.7 percent) (Shinagawa 1994). Although overall interracial-marriage rates continued to decline slightly in the 1990s, those in the Japanese American community continue to be quite high (around 50 percent) and much higher than other groups. Only Native Americans marry out more than Japanese Americans.

Using U.S. Census data from 2000, more recently C. N. Le found that an Asian American group's length of time in the United States increases the likelihood of group members marrying someone of a different race. He found that "those who are US-raised are much more likely to outmarry with either whites or other Asian Americans (pan-Asian)" (Le 2004a, 3). Since Japanese Americans are one of the longest established groups in the United States, it isn't too surprising that outmarriage rates are so high.

Outmarriage is highly gendered. Shinagawa found that "[b]y 1980, in the state of California, for every Asian male who had intermarried, there were now 1.8 Asian women who intermarried. . . . Roughly 1 in 4 marriages involving Asian Americans were the result of marital relationships between Asian women and non Asian men" (Shinagawa and Pang 1988, 272, 273). Other sources using the 1990 census found that "12 percent of married Asian men and 25 percent of married Asian women have wed a person who is not Asian" (Holmes 1996, A10).

Japanese American women lead the way with a 37.1 percent rate of outmarriage to whites (see Table 4). "Somewhat surprising is the fact that Japanese husbands have relatively high endogamous (same ethnicity) rates, since Japanese Americans are in many ways the most assimilated

Table 4. Intermarriage percentages among Asian American ethnic groups

Ethnicity	Spouses	
	Husbands	Wives
Asian Indian		
Asian Indians	89.7	92.0
Other Asians	1.5	1.2
Whites	6.3	4.1
Blacks	0.6	0.7
Latinos	1.4	0.8
Chinese		
Chinese	89.5	83.0
Other Asians	4.1	3.3
Whites	5.1	12.0
Blacks	0.1	0.3
Latinos	1.1	1.0
Filipino		
Filipinos	83.1	62.7
Other Asians	2.5	2.7
Whites	10.1	27.3
Blacks	0.2	2.8
Latinos	3.3	3.9
Japanese		
Japanese	69.2	50.9
Other Asians	8.8	5.4
Whites	17.4	37.1
Blacks	0.3	1.7
Latinos	2.7	2.4
Korean		
Koreans	93.1	69.4
Other Asians	1.9	2.8
Whites	3.9	24.3
Blacks	0.0	1.7
Latinos	0.9	1.4
Vietnamese		
Vietnamese	92.4	86.4
Other Asians	3.7	3.3
Whites	2.7	9.0
Blacks	0.1	0.3
Latinos	1.1	1.0

Source: Le 2004a, 1–3.

of all Asian American groups so we might expect them to intermarry with non-Japanese more" (Le 2004a, 4). The main coupling we see in the Japanese American interracial-marriage statistics, therefore, are Japanese American women and white men. Unlike the early 1900s, when Japanese men might have been the ones to outmarry, now decidedly Japanese American females are doing so.

In addition, more mixed-race Japanese American children are being born in the United States. "Since 1981, the number of babies born with one Japanese and one white parent has exceeded the number with two Japanese parents" (The numbers game, 1993). The difference in these birth rates is not because interracial couples have more children (thus higher fertility rates), but instead because there are simply more interracial couples (i.e., outmarriage rates are higher). The net effect is that more mixed-race Japanese American children than monoracial ones are being born. The number of multiracial Asians (1,655,830) by racial/ethnic combinations in 2000 were predominantly part white and part other combinations with Asian.

The outmarriage rate to whites is particularly impacting the Japanese American community. "Between 1968 and 1989, children born to parents of different races increased from 1 percent of total births to 3.4 percent. There has also been an increase in births to Japanese and White parents. There are now 39 percent more births to Japanese-White parents than births to Japanese-Japanese parents (in the United States). By 1989, for every 100 births in which both parents were Japanese, there were 139 births where the parents were mixed" (Kalish 1993, 54). C. N. Le also found that "multiracial Asians constitute 7.3 percent of all Asian Americans. The 2000 Census further shows that 30.7 percent of those who identify as at least part Japanese are multi-

**Table 5. Number of multiracial Asians
by racial/ethnic combinations, 2000**

Ethnicities	Number	Percentage of all multiracial Asians
Asian and other race	1,655,830	100.0
Asian and White	868,395	53.4
Asian and Native Hawaiian	138,802	0.84
Asian and Black	106,782	0.64
All other combinations	755,415	45.6

Source: Le 2004b, 3.

racial, the highest proportion among the six largest Asian American ethnic groups" (2004b, 5).

What effect is this high outmarriage rate and the emerging racial and ethnic identities of mixed-race Japanese Americans having on the definitions of *community*? Kitano argues that the mixed-race progeny of these interracial unions are non–Japanese Americans and therefore that the community will "be no more" by the year 2050. In contrast, it might be more interesting to ask if the community did continue to exist, what changes would happen in the definition of an authentic member of the community? From the above statistics it is clear that the future of the Japanese American community is decidedly multiracial. This does not necessarily mean that the community will crumble and cease to exist or that it will be absorbed into white mainstream society.

A review of Japanese American history helps to trace historical trends in outmarriage, the gender balance or imbalance in outmarriage, and the causes behind these trends. It is important analytically to understand what effects interracial-marriage rates are having on the individual and collective constructions of Japanese Americanness and the context in which this distillation of race in race work is happening. Is it proof of assimilation that Japanese Americans are "out whiting the whites" (Omi 2000)? Or is a "transracial ethnic" model in action where mixed Japanese Americans are given membership in the community over and above other racial groups (King 2002)? In order to answer these questions, it is important to place the contemporary quantitative data in a historical context.

Japanese Americans of Yesterday

Some scholars argue that the presence of women made the Japanese in America successful where the Chinese erred by encouraging only men to immigrate to the United States (Glenn 1986; Takaki 1989). The Japanese were quickly able to marry, have American-born children with citizenship rights, and establish informal and formal ties to one another that created a much more permanent and stable community within the United States. "As maintainers of the family they [Japanese women] were active in the creation and perpetuation of group culture, and their labor was an important resource in the effort to secure a viable position within the dominant society" (Glenn 1986, 6). The presence of some women in the middle stages of Japanese immigration (1908–24) actually meant that Japanese American intermarriage rates were quite low. Darrel Montero found that outmarriage for the immigrant Issei (first generation) was less than 1 percent; for the Nisei (second generation) in the 1930s the outmarriage rate was 10 percent; and for the Sansei (third generation) in the 1960s, it was 40 percent (Montero 1980). In Hawaii "4 percent of Nisei men and 6 percent of Nisei women were interracially married in the 1930s" and by 1970 "25 percent of Sansei men and 42 percent of Sansei women were interracially married" (Tamura 1994, 238).

Unlike Japanese men in America, who had no problems finding Japanese women, many Chinese and Filipinos found themselves a part of "bachelor society" made up mostly of older men. Although interracial marriage was illegal in California until 1948, when Asian Indians or Filipinos wed in California they often fled to Washington and married white or Mexican women (Leonard 1992). Japanese men, on the other hand, married Japanese women in Japan and brought them to the United States or used the picture-bride system, where women in Japan and men in the United States wrote to each other, exchanged photos, and were wed by proxy before meeting, often for the first time, when the women stepped off the boat in the United States (Takaki 1989, 406).

Japanese women were allowed to emigrate because the status of women in Japan was quite favorable, unlike in China. During the Meiji restoration, it was decided that education would be universal for *all* people in Japan. Japanese women could study, travel, and work. In China most women were not allowed to travel, were certainly not encouraged to travel to the United States, and were often bound by obligation to their husbands' families. Japanese women, on the other hand, came to the United States either with their husbands or to meet their husbands, and they worked alongside them in the fields in Hawaii or California, as well as tending to what small, modest homes they were allowed to rent. Many Hawaiian sugar-plantation owners also encouraged the immigration of Japanese women for a time in order to keep the men in check and to use the wives' labor as well as their husbands' in the cane fields (Ogawa 1986). Early on in Japanese American history, it was rare for Japanese Americans to have an interracial marriage; if they did marry out, it was more likely a Japanese man marrying a non-Japanese woman. "Issei separatism and anti-miscegenation laws limited the first generations exogamy rate to 1.5 percent despite a shortage of women" (Woodrum 1981, 160). In addition to legal barriers and social separation, the racialized, sexualized image of Japanese American men as a threat to white women inhibited their rates of interracial marriage. Antimiscegenation laws in places like California limited Japanese men from marrying interracially, in particular with white women. The supposed sexual threat of Japanese men to white women caused great concern in the early 1900s and became an integral part of the rationale for anti-Japanese sentiment which culminated in the Gentlemen's Agreement. Negotiated in 1907–8 between President Theodore Roosevelt and the Japanese government, the Gentlemen's Agreement allowed Japanese schoolchildren to attend "mainstream" white schools and not segregated "oriental" schools as long as Japan would voluntarily limit immigration of laborers from Japan. This "agreement" cut off much of the immigration from Japan and prevented many Japanese American men from returning to Japan to seek a wife. Instead many opted to use the *shashin kekkon* or picture-bride system to get married.

Newspapers like the *San Francisco Chronicle* and patriotic organizations like the Native Sons joined in the anti-Japanese exclusionist clamor by rhetorically asking, "Would you like your daughter to marry a Japanese?" (Takaki 1989, 201). The Exclusion League in San Francisco in the early 1900s capitalized on this idea and emphasized the menace that older, full-grown Japanese men posed for white schoolgirls when they sat next to them in public classrooms. In reality, the contact at that time between Japanese and non-Japanese was limited at best. However, the perceived lack of women, perceived lack of conjugal families, and antimiscegenation laws created the stereotype of Japanese men as sexually aggressive and a threat to white womanhood. In addition, the early immigration from Japan was still primarily male and there was a ratio of 11:1 (men to women) until the Gentlemen's Agreement (Modell 1977). Thus, an integral part of the push to limit immigration from Japan was premised on the idea that there were too many sexually aggressive Japanese men already in the United States.

Ironically, while the Gentlemen's Agreement cut off the immigration of laborers from Japan, it also increased Japanese female immigration to the United States via the picture-bride system, thus almost ensuring that families would thrive and a second generation of Japanese would soon be born on American soil. "As a result, the sex ratio among

Japanese in America began to change from one that was overwhelmingly male to one that by 1924 was beginning to approach a balance (in California the rate went from 5.4 percent women in 1900 to being 36.9 percent women by 1920)." The Chinese had a much smaller increase in the same time period and went from 5.0 percent women in 1900 to 12.6 percent women by 1920 (Daniels 1988, 69, 126–27). It appears, then, that Japanese men were considered a sexual threat to white women and were therefore not allowed to marry them legally. Often, though, they did not desire to do so because they brought their wives from Japan, married Japanese women already in the United States, or found a wife through the picture-bride system. The building of families with American-born citizen children fueled anti-Japanese feelings, and the Immigration Act of 1924 effectively cut off immigration from Japan. Even so, with balanced gender ratios, the Japanese American community began to grow.

Explaining Changes in Outmarriage

A number of influences are mentioned when discussing the significant increase in interracial marriages for Japanese Americans, including the effects of World War II both in the United States and in Japan, the upward mobility of Japanese Americans, and the racialized images of Japanese American women and men.

After World War II, many American troops residing in Japan had Japanese girlfriends and wives who eventually came to the United States as war brides. The post–World War II Japanese American interracial-marriage rate, therefore, includes a large number of Japanese women who married American men associated with the U.S. occupation of Japan. By 1990, of the 400,000 war brides from countries all over the world, a significant number who had married American men came from Asia (Shinagawa and Pang 19987, 273). Some of these American men stayed in Japan, but many returned to the United States with Japanese wives and mixed-race Japanese children. This trend may contribute even now to the persistent stereotype that mixed-race Japanese American children are the products of illicit unions where the mothers were war brides and fathers were military men. While initially American men and their war-bride wives were not well received, films such as *Sayonara* and *Tea House of the August Moon* illustrated American perceptions of war brides, and eventually these types of interracial marriages gained a level of acceptance (see Marchetti 1993).

Within the United States as well, World War II affected the intermarriage rate of many Japanese Americans. Once concentrated on the West Coast, after the internment experience the marriage pool of available Japanese American men and women was scattered all over the United States. "By the 1960s most Japanese Americans in southern California did not live in any of these clusters (of Japanese Americans); they lived near no other Japanese at all" (Spickard 1996, 136). Likewise, many young unmarried men who had served gallantly in the war did not return, which led to a slight gender imbalance in the Japanese American community after the war.

During the war Japanese Americans were accused of being disloyal Americans. After the war, they tried to be "110 percent American." Many saw becoming assimilated or acculturated into white, mainstream culture as a way to achieve this goal. Issei parents thought they could insure their children would be considered Americans if their children spoke English and were culturally "American." Some people have gone so far as saying that the internment experience *caused* the increase in the outmarriage rate of Japanese Americans where interracial marriage is purely a symptom of internalized racism (Inouye 1977). They believe that Japanese Americans were so ashamed to be Japanese during the war and internalized that hostility so much that after the war they tried as hard as possible to disassociate with things Japanese.

If it is true that World War II was responsible for the demise of the Japanese American community by increasing interracial marriage, what solutions would those who believe that the Japanese American community has been damaged by outmarriage and needs to be rescued propose? First of all, Japanese Americans would need to be taught to not necessarily be "110 percent American," but instead to have pride in their culture and want to preserve it. Some have responded by establishing cultural schools to teach children about their heritage (e.g., Daruma No Gakko in the Bay Area).[1] If geographic scattering after the war increased interracial marriage, developing Japanese American neighborhoods (like Gardena in Los Angeles County) would reverse this trend. But cultural schools and Japanese American enclave neighborhoods do not seem to have decreased the interracial-marriage rate.

By the late 1940s the interracial marriage rate was 8.8 percent (Woodrum 1981, 158). Even so, there was not that much public concern about interracial marriage in the ethnic presses, at community meetings, or in community groups. Many of the blood quantum eligibility rules, which now guide Japanese American activities such as the community pageants and basketball leagues, did not exist then. For the most part, most Japanese Americans were monoracial and married other Japanese Americans. It was not until the 1960s and 1970s when interracial marriage rates soared and there were many mixed-race children that the Japanese American community started to struggle in earnest with the issue of race and membership.[2]

The upward social socioeconomic mobility of Japanese Americans after World War II, rather than the war itself, might be the crucial factor in the increasing outmarriage rate. For many, with upward mobility came increased intimate contact with Caucasians. Many of the Sansei went to school, worked, and worshiped with Caucasians. It was not a huge leap, then, to marry one. In addition, the legal barriers (anti-miscegenation laws) that limited interracial marriage were lifted in 1967 with the *Loving v. Virginia* case, which ruled interracial marriage to be legal in all states.

Many Sansei who came of age in the 1960s were active in the civil rights movement and truly felt an increasing interracial tolerance. This is not to argue that all or even most interracial marriages of Japanese Americans to non–Japanese Americans took place under the same conditions. Clearly, a war bride from Japan is very different from a Sansei Japanese American woman marrying a college boyfriend during the 1960s, but both have contributed to the outmarriage rate of the Japanese American community and both have produced mixed-race children.

This discussion would not be complete without a discussion of the images of Asian men in this time period as well. Some argue that the images of Asian men as sexist, wimpy, or simply too demanding has sent Japanese American women out looking for white men to marry. Shinagawa and Pang (1988) have argued that Asian American women chose white men to marry precisely because of the white man's position of power and the assimilation that he could bring to her. They argue that Asian women are marrying not only *out* but also *up* in terms of socioeconomic status and prestige. What they can't explain is why the outmarriage rate is so much higher for Japanese American women over other Asian ethnic groups. If it was purely a "power grab" wouldn't all Asian women have the same outmarriage rates?

Others argue that it has been the "images" of Japanese women that have increased the interracial marriage rates (Hamamoto 1994). Ogawa states that it is because the "Japanese woman has been stereotyped quite differently. She has been stereotyped in a manner unique to non-white women. She is graceful, delicate, a cultured woman of the Orient. She is infinitely more refined than the black female. Furthermore, she is not merely a temporary sexual outlet; she is a prospective bride, a woman to be married" (1971, 59). If it is the "images" of Japanese American women and men that are causing high interracial-marriage rates, then according to this point of view the solution would be to change and make more positive the media and other images of Japanese American men and women.

Japanese American Intermarriage:
Assimilation or Persistence of Community?

Perhaps the largest number of monographs and articles ever written about Japanese American intermarriage came out of the Japanese American Research Project (JARP) based at UCLA in the 1970s. Many important works came out of this project about Japanese American socioeconomic mobility (Levine and Montero 1973; Woodrum 1981), economic and political accommodation (Modell 1977), generational change (Levine and Rhodes 1981), and ethnic affiliation (Montero 1980). Using quantitative data, these studies gave important primary data on the status of Japanese Americans. For the first time, Japanese Americans had data about themselves to examine demographic and social trends in their community. Many of these studies focused on intermarriage. Furthermore, most were premised on the idea that Japanese Americans were assimilating structurally into the mainstream and that intermarriage was proof of their success. The up side of these studies was to show how well economically, politically, and socially Japanese Americans were doing, but many of them argued that the cost of this assimilation into the mainstream was a disintegrating community. They argued that structural change caused Japanese Americans to marry out and that this was a natural process that happens to any group over time.

Structural theorists such as Milton Gordon have argued that interracial marriage is the normal outcome of groups who are becoming upwardly mobile and assimilating into mainstream American society (Feagin and Feagin 2003). While Gordon and others have defined assimilation through social measures like intermarriage, they overestimate how much this tells us about the process of assimilation. The assumption is that when one marries a person of a different race, one does so only to gain access to the mainstream. These claims about interracial marriage rely excessively on an overly rational view of racial and ethnic identity and marriage decisions. To my knowledge, there has been no research that proves Gordon's theory that people who interracially marry (particularly to a white person) consider themselves to be assimilated, or that people who do marry "out" and "up" do so only for that reason. They fail to consider other factors that come to play in the choice of a marriage partner. Also, none of these studies try to investigate how the mixed children of these marriages racially/ethnically identify. The underlying assumption is that mixed children automatically identify with their non–Japanese American parent and not their Japanese American parent. Although Gordon was studying primarily white ethnics, the researchers in the JARP studies seemed to take Gordon at his word and thought of outmarriage as proof of acceptance and assimilation into mainstream white society. They argued that the following factors increased Japanese American integration:

1. Dispersal of Japanese American community; living instead in a white community
2. Loss of language: speaking English and little or no Japanese
3. Emphasis on education: higher educational attainment levels
4. High number of outmarriages, high intermarriage rates with whites
5. Peer group containing primarily non–Japanese American friends
6. Professional jobs in a non–Japanese American work atmosphere
7. Low participation in Japanese American groups/events.

Interestingly enough, even though upward mobility, higher educational attainment levels, and geographic dispersement also led to the changing demographics of the Japanese American community, interracial marriage became the target for much debate and was and still is often considered *the* reason why the Japanese American community may become extinct.

Consider the following predictions from the JARP studies:

Given the dramatically increasing trend of out marriage among the Sansei, with its concomitant diminution of ethnic ties and affiliation, we are justified in wondering whether a Japanese American ethnic community can be maintained into the next generation—the Yonsei. (Montero 1980, 88)

The predilection of the Sansei to choose Caucasian mates spells disaster for the passing on of traditional ways. (Levine and Rhodes 1981, 153)

This [interracial marriage] rate will continue to grow with each new successive generation so that in time there may no longer be a pure Japanese American group. (Kikumura and Kitano 1973, 79)

Or in the local vernacular press of the *Pacific Citizen:*

What is the greatest threat to our race here in the US? Is it the FBI? White Racism? Is it the media? The intermarriage problem is by far the worse threat to our existence than a hundred million Manzanars, Tule Lakes [both internment camps], or Pearl Harbors. (Inouye 1977, 9)

Through quantitative research, Levin and Rhodes (1981) show that indeed Sansei do in fact marry out more than the Nisei did. However, the authors do not try to test the persistence of traditional ways. Their book contains no empirical data that show the disaster for the passing on of traditional ways or that intermarriage causes people to lose their traditions. One of the main issues in all of the JARP studies is that they assert that factors like interracial marriages will lead to a dilution of culture/traditional ways, but do no consistent testing of the children of these interracial marriages. To my knowledge, there has been no study that irrefutably concludes from direct research that mixed-race Japanese American children have no "traditional ways" because their parents were interracially married. This is an important assumption in past research, which must be examined carefully.

A Threat to the Community?

Why was outmarriage the focus of claims that the community would cease to exist? Several factors placed interracial marriage at the core of people's worries about the future of the community. First, interracial marriage is the most visible and open target for criticism. Who in the Japanese American community would criticize getting a good education, a good job, or living in a good neighborhood? Second, outmarriages in the Japanese American community had been long in coming, in particular due to the unique experiences of Japanese Americans during World War II. There is also a sexist undertone to much of this research in that the blame lies clearly on Japanese

American women since they are the ones now participating most often in interracial marriage. By focusing on interracial marriage and ignoring the role other demographic factors play in the dissolution of the community, these studies imply that it is acceptable to get a good job, but not acceptable for Japanese American women to marry whomever they choose. Interracial marriage in this case is given all the power to destroy the community, while attracting attention away from other, in some cases more powerful, factors like educational success. This may be because many Japanese Americans are now solidly middle class.

Early studies also focused on outside forces such as discrimination and its effects on Japanese Americans. They did not see Japanese Americans and the Japanese American community as agentic creative actors capable of maintaining and creating racial meanings themselves; instead, they saw Japanese American attitudes as either adopted from whites or in direct reaction to whites.

Saenz, Hwang, Aguirre, and Anderson were the first to tackle this problem with their quantitative study of the children of intermarried couples using 1980 U.S. Census data to discuss the ethnic identities of these children. While their results show a tendency toward Anglo conformity, they also found that a significant part of their sample (38 percent) also viewed themselves as Asians (not white), a result unanticipated by the JARP researchers (1995, 189). However, they caution that there are problems with using census data to understand ethnic identity of mixed children for the following reasons:

1. Parents (which we know is more likely to be the "husband" and "white") fill out the form, not the children themselves (not self-enumeration).
2. The census only allows one racial/ethnic identification (mixed identity not allowed).
3. There is no information on phenotype, which some authors assume strongly influences ethnic identity.
4. The contextual and sometimes changing nature of ethnic identity cannot be adequately captured in survey research.

The researchers conclude that "ethnographic research should be pursued to more fully observe the essence of the manner in which multiethnic people construct their ethnic identities" (190). It is precisely this ethnic identity of multiracial/ethnic people that is at the core of this book. Assuming that mixed-race people automatically identify with the majority parent may be a serious weakness of assimilation theorists like Milton Gordon and the JARP sociologists. Past research, such as edited collections like *The Multiracial Experience* (Root 1996), have explored this by looking at individual multiracial people (Hall 1996; Iwasaki Mass 1992; Root 1996; Thorton 1996; Williams 1996). However, this book examines primarily how multiracial people collectively negotiate and impact racial/ethnic identities and the concepts of "race" and "ethnicity" in their everyday lives.

In fact, some argue that while Japanese Americans have assimilated in some ways, they still retain much of their racial/ethnic identification on a more symbolic level. Stephen Fugita and David O'Brien have shown how persistent and resilient Japanese American ethnicity still is, much more so than their European American counterparts. Fugita writes, "Thus even with changes in the geographical distribution and intermarriage rate of Japanese Americans it is still likely that there will continue to exist a Japanese American community which can rely on the contributions of its members to collective goals" (Fugita and O'Brien 1991, 126). So, though there may be high intermarriage, these rates do not tell us about how Japanese Americanness is played out in those marriages/families and in fact, it may be the case that even the intermarried still identify as Japanese American and participate in the community as such. Even in small communities Japanese Americans try to hold onto communal ties. "Most striking is the fact that Japanese American involvement in ethnic voluntary associations is actually higher in areas with a lower density of fellow ethnics. This suggests that in places where they are found in small numbers Japanese Americans make a special effort to create organizations that encourage community involvement" (102).

Indeed, many of the people in my research had strong, if not exclusive, identification with being Japanese American and many had commitment to maintaining, if not increasing, their Japaneseness. Fugita and O'Brien are less clear, however, about what has *caused* this persistence of ethnicity. They seem to imply that in fact it may not be ethnicity but race that has caused many Japanese Americans to continue to have ties to community organizations. It may be that structural assimilation only goes so far until race constrains how American Japanese Americans can really be. When Japanese Americans realize this, it forces them to recognize their need for racial/ethnic ties. In this instance, race may force them to cultivate a primarily symbolic ethnic identity. Mia Tuan has argued that these structural constraints make Japanese Americans, like other Asian Americans, foreigners and not honorary whites (1998).

Conclusion

Japanese American history shows us that initially interracial marriage was quite low (1880–1908), followed by a period of increasing immigration by women which gave no reason for Japanese American men to marry out. During and after World War II, outmarriage increases, mostly for Japanese men, and later for Japanese American women. Today these gendered outmarriage rates seem to have slowed, but remain quite high in comparison with other groups. This book builds on the research on intermarriage in the Japanese American community to examine the impact that mixed-race people, particularly women as symbolic representatives of the community, are having on Japanese American collective definitions.

As we saw, some community members feel that outmarriage is genocide and worse than the internment camps of World War II. However, other community members realize that the outmarriage rate is not going to change, and that these mixed-race offspring are potential members of their organizations. To this end, some have increased outreach efforts to mixed-race Japanese Americans, although there is a feeling that they are being forced to do so due to dwindling membership. Nonetheless, there is an organizational imperative for them to incorporate mixed-race Japanese Americans into their rapidly falling membership.

Some staunch purists would rather see Japanese American organizations expire before they see them opened up to mixed-race Japanese Americans or other Asian Americans. Others would rather have mixed-race Japanese Americans than other Asian groups. Still others have tried to recruit newly arrived Japanese immigrants (Shin Issei) in order to boost membership in their organizations and bring "Japan Japanese" racial understandings into the community. A multiplicity of racial/ethnic tactics are being explored and advocated within the Japanese American community.

Many of these discussions depend heavily on the definition of who exactly is a Japanese American community member. In defining community membership, most assume that race and ethnicity go hand in hand, believing that if one is half Japanese racially, one will at best be half Japanese ethnically/culturally. Many of the mixed-race Japanese Americans that I interviewed were out to prove specifically that race does not equal culture. They felt committed to being able to participate in the Japanese American community without having to prove themselves or authenticate their right to participation. Many argued that although they are racially "half," they are culturally "whole," meaning they are more Japanese culturally than the monoracial Sansei. Indeed, for some this is true. They are the children of the Shin Issei. Many are born in Japan, speak Japanese, choose to live their lives here as Americans and yet feel they were raised in a Japanese way in a Japanese household. This confrontation of the image they have of themselves versus the image that others have of them gets renegotiated over and over when they interact with the traditional Japanese American community.

In this sense, mixed-race Japanese Americans have a different experience than many other mixed-race people. They are quickly becoming the majority of the community and therefore have more power to be heard within the community. They are also concentrated and, like many Japanese Americans, live on the west coast of the United States or in Hawaii. Many have Japanese American mothers, which has large implications for how they are raised and their socialized gender identity. Some may be proud of their Japanese heritage and some may simply pass into mainstream society trying to forget their Japanese heritage.

Many mixed people actually probably do this "passing," and it is not my claim here to speak for all mixed-race Japanese Americans. There is no scientific way to randomly sample mixed-race Japanese Americans, and I am not trying to make generalizations about every experience here. I am not even trying to assert that all mixed-race Japanese Americans recognize their Japanese heritage. I intend to illustrate how many mixed-race Japanese Americans choose to participate in the Japanese American community and how their presence has forced a redefinition of what it means to be Japanese American. Because there was an understanding, primarily before the 1960s, of the Japanese American community as monoracial, the shift in the late-1960s community has had significant impact on community organizations, individuals, and racial definitions. Looking carefully at these organizations and how they have been affected by this shift may help us to understand how the meanings of race and ethnicity can shift from one historical period to the next.

The visibility of these mixed-race women in beauty pageants and people's personal experience with them highlight their presence and brings this issue to the fore. Most Japanese Americans have a family member who married out, so they are less and less able to exclude mixed-race Japanese Americans from their social circles and the community at large, even though in the past this pattern of exclusion was widespread.

With racial and ethnic theories in mind and the history of the Japanese American community as a context, the next five chapters examine the effects of increasing intermarriage and multiracial people on Japanese Americans by examining their beauty pageants in four spheres: gender, social class, the body, and race. By looking at the debates over Japanese American beauty pageants, we will be able to see how Japanese Americanness itself is being made and remade along these lines.

3 Japanese American Beauty Pageants in Historical Perspective

I represented Orange County in the Nisei Week Queen Pageant.... This was back in the 1950s–60s... and Orange County was still a farming community back then. We were the country hicks... the city folks and the country folks, you know? I was a country girl, very sheltered. Some people asked my parents if I would run for Nisei Week Queen. To them it was a great honor even to be asked. To me, I thought, Oh gosh! It was quite overwhelming... not like today.
—Nisei Week Queen Pageant participant

Throughout the years, Japanese American beauty pageants have revealed the challenges of community definition, gender, and racial identity politics being played out in the name of the local Japanese American community in their pageants. The historical context of the evolution, change, and persistence of Japanese American beauty pageants in the four cities I studied illustrate their role as the touchstones for the community. In each of the eras discussed, it is clear that the beauty pageants reflect larger anxieties present in the community about feminism, nationhood, and multiraciality. While all the communities examined are Japanese American and all had community institutional histories of beauty pageants, the analysis serves to show how race work is shaped by historical and geographic contexts.

Internment and Beyond, 1935–1950s: Debates about Nationalism and U.S. Citizenship

In 1935 the Nisei Week Festival organizers in Los Angeles were looking for a way to raise attendance at the Japanese American festival. They decided to add a Nisei Week Queen Pageant, which reflected the larger goals of the festival, namely, easing mounting economic and social tensions between Japanese Americans and the larger, white community. At the same time, Little Tokyo merchants wanted a way to bolster the Depression-era ethnic economy and bring business into downtown, particularly encouraging Nisei Japanese Americans to shop in and maintain ties with their ethnic community. In the first Nisei Week Queen contest, votes for potential queens were based on ballots gained when merchandise was purchased in Little Tokyo establishments. This cleverly combined commodifying the women in the pageant to drum up business as well as using them to symbolize the Japanese American community to the larger, white, community as "not a threat."[1]

Los Angeles' Nisei Week Queen Pageant was primarily focused on representing the Japanese American community to itself under a predominantly white hegemonic gaze. This meant that the Japanese American women in the pageant were race-working with white standards of beauty pageants in mind, recreating them with a Japanese American twist. The rationale was that if Japanese Americans, symbolized in the queen, were seen to be truly American, they could make claims that they were good and loyal Americans.

The Nisei Week Queen Pageant and Festival marked the beginning of Japanese American beauty pageants in the United States. Nisei Week Queen Pageants became an important space for Japanese American women to make claims in relation to hegemonic femininity. Even though they were not allowed to participate in mainstream pageants such as Miss America, they could at least be Nisei Week Queen. The goal was clearly to recreate for the Japanese American community some elements of mainstream pageants such as the question-and-answer and talent sections from the Miss America Pageant, while at times forgoing others, such as the bathing-suit competition (San Francisco only had it once, in 1972).[2] These local Japanese American pageants were separate, but parallel in form and in some content to mainstream pageants in terms of the process of claiming the nation. As a queen from the early 1950s said:

> We always had to appear dressed very dressy, in suits and stuff. I made my dress out of a yard and a half of fabric with a pattern I copied from the Sears catalogue. They gave us nothing from the committee. I was very naïve. I just thought that is what you did. I joined a sorority and went to college. I wanted to be accepted and I wanted to be very Americanized.

She presented herself in symbolic ways in order to be seen as American. Her behavior as well as her dress focused on acceptance, for herself and—through her—for the Japanese American community, into mainstream America by playing down race and playing up the loyalty to America that they had in common with mainstream society. Claims to the nation came through deracializing Japanese Americanness in the pageant. These strategies of dressing the queen in Western garb and promoting her keen and usually native-born ability to speak English helped to highlight the Americanness of Japanese Americans, whose push for citizenship and inclusion in the nation of the United States was paramount in this era. If the queen looked, spoke, and carried herself as an American, it was hoped, she would be seen as such by others. This would then allow Japanese Americans acceptance in a cultural sphere where they had first experienced rejection as "unassimilable aliens" (Takaki 1989). They, too, could claim that they were "All American girls" by mimicking and adopting hegemonic American cultural values such as innocence, sexual purity, honesty, and caring. "My dad always said to me, 'Sit with your legs crossed and always put your best face forward. You are representing the Japanese American life. If you say anything wrong, if you are rude or ungainly or sit with your legs apart, people will think poorly of us Japanese.'"

As a symbol and representative of the Japanese American community in the wider society, a participant's behavior was subject to social control by Japanese Americans in the name of assimilation. In addition, she was likely to be viewed by the larger society as a typical Japanese American girl. Ironically, the creation of separate pageants for Japanese Americans meant that they were separating themselves further from the mainstream culture in which they sought to gain acceptance. This isolation may have encouraged the exoticization and objectification of Japanese American women in the minds of white America.

However, were the Nisei Week Queens typical Japanese American women? The pageant may have overrepresented the Japanese American desire to be assimilated and American. It naturally drew women who were more acculturated and who idealized American cultural forms of beauty, especially those forms that manifested themselves publicly in the local pageant. The ballot voters, on the other hand, were primarily patrons of Japanese American businesses in Little Tokyo. They may not have been as assimilated as the pageant participants and may have been socially oriented to the Japanese American community first and foremost as residents or shoppers in Little Tokyo. The pageants claimed membership in the nation selectively at times—apparently it was not necessary to wear bathing suits to be American—but the pageants themselves were an acceptable strategy to make the claim. However, these selective appropriations only reinforced the desirable innocence and virtue of good American girls of Japanese descent. This presents a dilemma for race work in the Nisei Week Pageant as these women were racially excluded from the white mainstream images of beauty and pageants, but also were trying to bring versions of white beauty and culture into the Nisei Week beauty pageant sphere.

In the early days it was clear that the primary audience of the pageant and festival was internal to the Japanese American community: "In the beginning, they [the festival organizers] wanted everyone to come to Little Tokyo. They have always wanted people to come to Little Tokyo. It is just that there weren't a lot of non-Asians that came to Little Tokyo. Before it was all Japanese people at the pageant/festival, now it is half and half."

Before World War II Japanese Americans in the pageant tried to display a bicultural association with both the United States and Japan and bring whites into Little Tokyo (Kurashige 2002). The Issei, first-generation Japanese immigrants, had been denied the chance at U.S. citizenship by the 1790 Naturalization Law and land ownership by the Alien Land Law of 1913. What they couldn't gain in the legal sphere, they tried to gain in the sphere of culture by mimicking and adopting some American culture including mainstream popular events such as beauty pageants.

Figure 1. The 1938 Nisei Week Queen Margaret Nishikawa and her court touring Los Angeles. They are dressed in kimonos and are chauffeured in a convertible car decorated in red, white, and blue striped bunting. Photograph courtesy of the Japanese American National Museum (93.102.252), gift of Jack and Peggy Iwata.

The pageants were discontinued during World War II internment and started up again shortly after the end of the war, but the postwar stigma and the isolation of the community still bore its mark on the pageant and those who participated in it. A queen from the early 1950s said:

> When I came out of [the internment] camp I had the same problems as many in high school and college, the la-la kind of idea that we really wanted to become American and fit in. Live the American dream. You really wanted to be like a blonde-haired blue-eyed kid. It is a real heartache when you think about it now. But this is what happens when you are discriminated against so much, you just want to be assimilated.

The pageants became a site where Japanese Americanness was collectively produced. However, one outcome of the pageant was that Japanese Americans created their own images of beauty and deportment, such as "walking Japanese" with small steps while in kimono, which competed with mainstream images such as "walking American" while in evening gown, with long wide strides and pivot turns. The pageants therefore combined Japanese and American cultural forms, although white American culture clearly dominated. The women in the pageant were supposed to perform both cultures well, but the emphasis was on the evening-gown portion and speaking in good, unaccented English. Most covers to the program booklets that advertised the pageant/festival and its activities consisted of the queen in Western clothes, usually an evening dress with her crown, sash, and smile in tow. The style of the cover is glossy and colorful, much like the *Life* magazine covers of the time, and bouffant hairstyles and clumpy false eyelashes reflect some of the mainstream beauty standards of the era.

The Battle over Feminism, 1970s–80s

In the 1970s Japanese American beauty pageants became an arena in which larger battles in mainstream society, this time about feminism, were fought and contested. In response to widening awareness of feminist values, Japanese American pageants in more liberal places like San Francisco did away with the bathing-suit and fitness competitions after one year. They also eliminated many of the beauty-related judging criteria. Started in 1968, the San Francisco pageant was able to sidestep elements of the 1950s patriarchy that had shaped Nisei Week. A Nisei Week queen from Los Angeles in the late 1980s said:

> I would never have become involved if they had had bathing suits. I think half my court would not have become involved had there been bathing suits. I think they did away with it the year that Lila won. Lila—she was the one that is credited with being the vocal spokesperson in getting rid of the bathing suits. I don't know what year that was. It must have been the late '70s, early '80s. The whole women's movement happened in the early '70s in the rest of the U.S. and we sort of came along later. You also have to look at who was in charge then—mostly middle-aged men . . . bathing suit was their favorite part.

Interestingly, the largest and most serious challenge for change, in terms of actually affecting the pageant, came from within the pageant set. Often the participants themselves were the most vocal about no bathing suits, measurements, or anything to encourage objectification by what the girls called the *skebe* (dirty old) men who were organizing or judging it. The interviewee above recognized the Japanese American patriarchy that these middle-aged men represented, but the women themselves are credited with being strong enough to stand up to them and eliminate the bathing-suit section of the pageant as unnecessary and sexist. This also reflects the small, community-based nature of the pageant so that participants were able to mobilize and apply pressure on organizers to change. Notice, though, that they didn't want to get rid of the pageant altogether. They may have seen the pageant as serving an important outlet or forum for Japanese American women to speak out.

The most serious feminist challenge came in San Francisco, where the pageant was discontinued for one year in 1988 because the festival chair felt it was outdated and sexist. However, there was such an outcry from the community that it returned in 1989 in a new format with no beauty judging criteria, career goals as part of the candidates' biographical statements, and no height, weight, or body measurements. Due to increasing awareness of feminism both inside and outside the Japanese American community, the focus in the pageant judging criteria was shifted to community and professional service and away from beauty per se.

Through these challenges to the pageant, Japanese American women didn't just replicate white, mainstream, feminist views. Many could not relate to radical Japanese American feminists and felt they were too demanding and therefore not culturally sensitive enough to be considered Japanese American. They referred to feminism as the "f" word and wanted to act *like* a feminist but not *be* a feminist—because feminists were ugly and white. These pageant candidates racialized feminism and gender roles. In their minds, to be Japanese American meant something very different, perhaps being less outspoken than white feminists.

Of course, some of the most offensive aspects of beauty pageants— such as the bathing-suit competition—were never that prevalent in Japanese American pageants. In this sense, the pageants may have ironically been a place where feminism of a sort developed. The pageant allowed a networking opportunity for Japanese American women not only to be heard, but also to rub elbows, even if only during a short dinner reception, with dignitaries from Japan, politicians, and high-level business people, as well as the media and the entertainment industry. These networks helped them to assert their ideas, but also to further their own professional careers. In this sense, they took it upon themselves to promote Japanese American women and the opportunities provided in the beauty pageant.

From this, a form of liberal Japanese American feminism developed in the pageants. The long history of Japanese American women's presence in athletics and political positions took a new and more public form in the pageants. Adopting American outspokenness, Japanese American beauty queens began to push their issues as women to the forefront within the community and challenge the mantra of toeing the "racial" line in order to work for Japanese American progress. Pageant participants now aspired to attend law school and business school, to obtain political careers, and to speak publicly for social and Japanese American causes. Many of the women who participated in the pageant in this era describe the pageant as a platform for centering Japanese American women, allowing them to speak out publicly (older community members might have felt was contradictory to Japanese American values of modesty) and to show themselves publicly, which could be considered very *hazukashii* (embarrassing/immodest) especially if they didn't win. A new type of Japanese American woman was evolving both within the pageant and outside of it. Again, it was a blending of Japanese American cultural values and practices in a Western, some would say uniquely American, form of the beauty pageant.

Many Japanese Americans outside the pageant were, and still are, strongly critical of the message that Japanese American pageants send to the rest of society and to the young Japanese American women within and outside of them. This feminist critique was most clear in San Francisco and Hawaii. In Hawaii Terri-Ann Shiroma of Moanalua High School wrote about pageants for a high school journalism contest. Her winning essay stated, "Beauty contests continue to erode years of progress toward achieving sexual equality. Providing pageant winners as standards for young women to emulate and admire encourages them to focus on outward appearances rather than inward cultivation. Eradicating pageants would serve as a momentous step toward ensuring the future health and success of all America's women." A journalist responding to the piece, published in the *Honolulu Star-Bulletin*, added, "Contestants are rewarded for pleasing via talents and interview responses deemed to be appropriately feminine. In short, they are reduced to actresses portraying an expected role" (Chang 1996, 1).

In San Francisco, too, critiques of the pageants came from within the Japanese American community. Mei Nakano and the Women's

Concerns Committee (WCC) lobbied hard in the 1980s for the Japanese American Citizen's League (JACL) to stop sponsoring pageant candidates. Their argument was that the JACL, as a civil rights organization, should have a more progressive view of not only race, but also gender. The WCC campaign failed to end support for the pageants as other community members emphasized the importance of the pageants as a place for Japanese American women to honor alternative models of beauty. Even if Japanese American women couldn't be Miss America, they could be honored here. It was a chance to celebrate the beauty and accomplishments of Japanese American women.

Feminism was also affecting Nisei Week in Los Angeles. The bathing-suit portion of the pageants was removed in the 1970s and the impact of larger, white feminist understandings was undermining pageant participation. One past participant explained,

> Feminist criticisms of the pageants have made it more difficult to get candidates to run. Fewer women are interested in doing this. A lot of times they are reacting to what they think it is rather than what they will find out it really is. They don't know. And they aren't going to find out because there is a stigma attached to the word *pageant*. You think of a bubble-headed ditzy actress-wannabe. Some people said to me, "I'm surprised you are interested in that sort of thing." "You are Phi Beta Kappa so why are you running in this pageant?" What does that have to do with anything? I think if someone thinks it is going to help them, it is worth pursuing. For me, my goals were to meet more people in the community and develop more poise and grace. I asked my department chair, who was a woman, "If I participate in this pageant, will people question my academic integrity?" and she said, "Not if they are smart. Other people are involved with their church or sports groups. What is the difference?" It is an interest of mine, but it isn't my life.

Feminist critiques were clear in the criticism and treatment of the queens in this story recounted by a Nisei Week Queen from the 1980s:

> I was with a group of Asian American actresses and they starting teasing me about it. "Is it just thrilling to be Nisei Week Queen? Is it everything you've ever dreamed of?" and I was like, "Excuse me?" They were all laughing; they thought they were so funny. I said, "No, it was something I got involved with because I thought it was interesting and it has been." Then they said, "You must have had so much fun going to all those parties and wearing your crown," and I thought, You all are really rude. What gives you the right to judge? Like I am not smart enough to know that they were being facetious. That was a pretty negative experience.

It is clear that feminism created a struggle within the pageants and the Japanese American communities at large. The pageants became a logical focus of feminist critiques, but surprisingly also became a place where a Japanese American feminist ideology of sorts developed. The banning of the listing of bodily measurements and zodiac signs was prompted by the women themselves, as was a change from identifying the women as "contestants," which promoted the idea of a contest or competition. In San Francisco the new word was *candidates*, so that like political candidates each woman was running a campaign for herself and, in theory, creating a competition against herself and not against other women. In reality, the stigma of the pageant as anti-feminist was clear both inside and outside the community, but all of this happened through a process of racializing gender roles, norms, and visions of feminism. The act of participating in the pageant was framed as in the above quote, as making a bold, and some would say feminist, move to stand up and participate when there are such strong norms not to do so.

In the end, both gender roles and feminism came to be racialized by the women in the pageant and the pageant organizers. These Japanese American women saw themselves as upholding community norms in their own assertive ways, but they did so in a forum that was and continues to be deeply shaped by hegemonic gender ideologies. It is important to remember, though, that these community beauty pageants, with the possible exception of Los Angeles, were less commodified and provided a better access point to community networks than mainstream pageants. Participants also had more power to shape the pageants. The Japanese American community was a small pond where the participants became big, publicly known, fish. They spoke publicly and made network contacts with many elite members of the community.

Multiculturalism, Multiracialism, and Globalization, 1990s

In the post–civil rights era of race relations, the certainties of ethnic identity were fading as the 1990s brought increasing attacks on multiculturalism as the foundation of ethnic identity politics. This was most clear in debates about the increasing numbers of multiethnic queens and their authenticity and legitimacy as representatives of their local Japanese American communities. These reflected larger debates about the declining significance of race (Wilson 1978), overrepresentation of Asian Americans in higher education (Takagi 1993), racial privacy laws (Millard 2002), and multiple racial responses on the 2000 U.S. Census (King 2000). The debates in the community pageants focused primarily on the racial eligibility rules, which until recently limited participation to women who were of 50 percent or more Japanese ancestry in San Francisco and Los Angeles and 100 percent in Hawaii. The increasing incorporation of mixed-race queens was a touchstone for increasing anxiety in the Japanese American communities over increasing assimilation.

In the 1980s and 1990s, the pageants became a central venue for debates over loss of culture and over assimilation in the Japanese American community, which was attributed to the increasing number of multiracial contestants. Mixed-race people started to make up a bigger part of the Japanese American community and this changed the dynamics of community membership and understandings of race and ethnicity. Multiracial women embodied this tension between shifting Japanese American identities and the norm of whiteness and sparked heated debate over racial eligibility rules for pageant participants.

This debate over racial rules began most publicly in Los Angeles in the local Japanese/English newspaper, the *Rafu Shimpo*, which debated about the increasing number of "half" Nisei Week queens in 1982. One participant from that era told me,

> We've had some girls who are half Japanese and half various other things. Some of them have been more trained to all the Japanese culture—more exposed to Japanese culture than some of the girls who are biologically all Japanese. The Posey sisters are both bilingual, but they are half Caucasian. Are they more Japanese than me because they speak Japanese or are they less because both my parents are Japanese? Their mom is from Japan and I am third-generation.

This interviewee questioned, like many, how definitions of Japanese American authenticity were shaped by the relationship between ancestry (race) and culture (ethnicity). The presence of multiracial queens, like the Posey sisters, highlights the question of who has the right to represent the community as queen. This question had never been asked before because there had never been a large number of multiracial women participating. With the increase in multiracial participants, attention was drawn to the issue of who, racially, could claim to speak for or to represent the community as a whole. The assumption of the link between culture and ancestry was questioned and challenged, if not broken, by the increasing presence of multiracial queens.

However, it also took effort to maintain the race : culture nexus in the pageant setting. If a majority of the community was ever to become multiracial, then it would be more acceptable for the queen to be multiracial because then she would physically and therefore racially resemble the average Japanese American. One participant from the 1980s said, "They were saying in the papers, 'Are we choosing queens based on a Western standard of beauty?' and that whole thing. I don't know if it is ethnic integrity or sour grapes." The racial appearance of the queen was highly correlated in her mind with ethnic integrity and authenticity. The debate, then, about mixed-race pageant candidates illustrates the growing anxiety about Japanese American assimilation and cultural preservation. As we will see in the next three chapters, the accurate physical appearance (being monoracially Japanese) and conformity to the racial ideal were paramount to who could be eligible to be considered Japanese American.

Ironically, community concerns have come full circle from the 1930s, when the pageants were a strategy for assimilation, as contemporary Japanese Americans debate whether assimilation has gone too far and whether there is now a need for Japanese American cultural preservation. This argument is based on a race equals culture equation, meaning that to be a member of the community one must be 100 percent racially Japanese and then the culture will follow. However, multiracial participants challenged the "either Japanese American or not" dichotomy. Multiracial participants developed their own strategies and conduct as well as identification, which problematized the race : culture nexus. A Cherry Blossom queen from San Francisco in the 1990s said:

> I think if the community wants to survive it's going to have to learn to take in people that maybe it would not have previously. They have to be flexible. A lot of people who are biologically Japanese don't care to be a part of what we call the Japanese American community. They don't attend a Japanese church. They don't shop in J–town. They don't eat Japanese food, the whole bit. There are people who are half or a quarter Japanese, not even Japanese, and they want to be part of that. I think you have to be a little less ethnocentric and say if you are interested, we are interested in having you participate.

In Los Angeles a 1990s Nisei Week queen said,

> I think they would shut down Nisei Week first though before they would let just someone of any race be queen. Not even thinking that they were

being racist or anything. It would be like, "Oh, darn, we ran out of candidates. We faded away." Maybe that would be the time for the pageant to fade away.

This changes the shape of the community when borders are opened and the criteria for authenticity is challenged and changed. This was most clear in 1998 when Hawaii (the last bastion of racial purity) changed its racial eligibility rules from 100 percent Japanese ancestry to 50 percent. Keith Kamisugi, the Honolulu Jaycees president, changed the rule, but he received much criticism for doing so. He said:

> [O]ne of the reasons why we have the Queen and Court is to represent the Japanese American community. And so, to be true to that, I think that we needed to set different standards for who these women are, who the Queen and the Court are. And also that if we are asking women to represent the Japanese American community, that we accept the broadest spectrum of women who are Japanese American. And if the definition of Japanese American means more than full-blooded Japanese American women, then that's what we need to strive to. I actually picked 50/50 just because I think at that time that I proposed it, I thought it was a moderate step. (Quoted in Yano 2006, 312)

The issue of authenticity in terms of race and culture continued in Hawaii. In 1999 one participant was part Chinese. In 2001 the first queen with a non-Japanese surname (who was multiethnic) was crowned, and in 2002 the queen was part–Native Hawaiian.

Conclusion

Over time, Japanese American beauty pageants have not just mimicked mainstream culture or created a totally new cultural form. They have reappropriated a mainstream form in a context where this form has been controlled and debated by Japanese Americans with influences from both within and without. Fundamentally, Japanese American pageants illustrate the struggles within Japanese American communities from 1935 to today over national citizenship, gender, and race.

The struggles in the early era, both before the war and directly after it, focused on moving away from the experience of ethnocentric and racist exclusion by trying to claim membership as Americans. By looking like Americans (whites) in cultural forms such as beauty pageants, Japanese Americans selectively appropriated Americanness to further their own inclusion in the nation. Doing so, though, meant embracing

Table 6. Primary concerns of Japanese beauty pageants since 1950

Years	Struggle	Strategy
1950s	Ethnocentric/racist exclusion vs. citizenship (assimilation by mimicry)	Selective appropriation of the "Nation"
1970s	Patriarchy vs. feminism	Claiming public space for women within patriarchal constraints
1980s–1990s	Racial purity vs. porous definition of community/ multiculturalism	Relaxing the race–culture nexus

Western dress, the English language, and mimicking some, but not all, of the components of mainstream American pageants. The queens in this era served as symbols of Japanese American abilities to assimilate into white America. A determined ethnic strategy was pursued to overcome the obstacles posed by race.

In the 1970s the struggle facing Japanese American communities was how to integrate feminism, particularly mainstream feminism, into a heavily patriarchal society as evidenced by the mere existence of beauty pageants. I argue, though, that even in this patriarchal cultural form, there was room for some women to make feminist claims to a voice for women. It was, in fact, the combination of their exposure to feminism and strong commitment to the Japanese American community that made them stay within the pageant but assert new, feminist notions of womanhood.

Finally, the struggle in the most recent era has been over racial purity rules and who constitutes an authentic member of the community and is therefore a worthy symbol. This debate has created more porous community definitions and community boundaries. Conceptually, it also prompted a strategy of dealing with racial community change by recognizing that the race equals culture nexus must be questioned and challenged. Chapter 7 examines the specificity of these racial eligibility rules in more detail. All of these issues have been present in the pageants, thus proving that they are semiautonomous spaces for strategic action and cultural production. Pageants, while public in nature and despite the restrictions on this kind of space, can be a venue for public and, perhaps, challenging discourse about the nation, gender, and race. The issues surrounding Japanese American beauty pageants have continued to deepen in contemporary times. But race has always been an issue, and seen through this brief history of Japanese American beauty pageants, it is clear that changing racial and gender meanings in the pageant are produced by historical struggles over racialization. It also confirms that the queens have long been, and continue to be, a focus of struggles to maintain community through a policing of racial/ethnic boundaries. These have typically happened through using racial/ancestry eligibility rules and their related ideas about the claims that racially grounded identities can make to ethnicity, community membership, and social networks.

4   *Cultural Impostors and Eggs: Race without Culture and Culture without Race*

The sense of competition is clear. When the Cherry Blossom Queen winner is announced, the tension in the room is almost palpable and I can hardly contain myself. I hold my breath without realizing it, waiting for the name to be read. Even as a judge, I have no idea who will win since the other titleholders of Miss Tomodachi and the First Princess are not ones that I have chosen. I am struck by how enticing the sense of competition can be and realize that the whole pageant season and particularly this evening has been leading up to this one moment. I lean forward in anticipation of the announcement. We can delay the gratification no longer. As the name of the queen is read, she gracefully steps forward as she has been told to do, but makes a crucial mistake in pageant etiquette. She does not hold hands with the other girls in anticipation and does not hug them or get hugged by them when her name is announced. She just stands up tall and receives the adoration of the crowd as the crown is placed on her head. She is later criticized as being a self-directed queen who doesn't think of others first and I wonder if her "racial credibility" will be questioned, as she is not considered to be "fully Japanese American."

—From the author's fieldnotes

Within the context of Japanese American beauty pageants, mixed-race Japanese American women neither destroy the concept of race

74

nor bridge the Caucasian and Japanese American communities. In fact, it is clear that these particular Japanese American mixed-race women worked quite hard and quite deliberately to reproduce race as a concept and to legitimate themselves as racial subjects even as they were arguing for multiple racial identities. Mixed-race women, then, in this instance problematize the relationship between race and ethnicity/culture. They don't just destroy this assumed relationship, but instead reinvigorate it in their race work.

The Queen as a Racial/Ethnic Ideal Type

Pierre Van den Berghe argued that most people have an ideal type of each ethnic group inscribed in their way of thinking about ethnic groups (1967, 68–75). Drawing from Weberian notions of ideal types, Van den Berghe argued that social actors have a picture in their heads of how an ideal Japanese American would look and act. Beauty pageants are just one social context in which we can see racial/ethnic ideal types defined, challenged, and changed.

Past studies of the history of beauty pageants (Banner 1983) show us their continuing historical importance for understanding the construction of the nation (Banet-Weiser 1999), or ethnic groups within a nation (Callahan 1998), by using women's bodies as symbolic representations. While these women may not have the power that they portend to represent, they do claim a cultural space by linking bodies (and women's agency to work with them) to assumptions of character (Gimlin 2002).

Guss (2000) argues that these festivals and pageants are important cultural phenomena above and beyond their textual contributions to collective identity. They are performances that "are clearly framed events set off from what might be considered normative, everyday reality"; "are important dramatizations that enable participants to understand, criticize and even change the worlds in which they live"; are "a profoundly discursive form of behavior because actors use these events to argue and debate, to challenge and negotiate"; and have "the ability to produce new cultural meanings and relations" (Guss 2000, 8–11).

Gimlin (2002) adds a bodily dimension to this analysis of beauty practices as more than just oppressive of women. She highlights the agency women have in their beauty practices (hair salons, cosmetic surgery, working out, and the like) that seek to reassert the link between body and character. In Japanese American beauty pageants women are working hard to resist hegemonic mainstream beauty norms and exercise agency by claiming counterhegemonic beauty norms and practices, ones that are racialized as alternative or different to mainstream white beauty (King 2001). They are also actively involved in rescuing race as a concept in their race work within the pageants and thus producing new cultural meanings not only for the Japanese American community, but also those images and cultural practices that are put on stage and projected for those outside the community.

Racial and ethnic beauty pageants are by definition about embodied practices (Butler 1999). Like Emile Durkheim's symbol or totem of a collective community, the queen is the active creation and embodiment of the ethnic community that she claims to represent. Her body is a field on which Japanese Americanness gets "done," and her body becomes inscribed with racial and ethnic meanings both through the process of the pageant and through people's gaze on her. First, the queen symbolically represents the community as an ideal type of Japanese Americanness. While many Japanese American women aren't ideal in appearance or behavior, like most ideal types the queen has unattainable and unrealistic characteristics that define her. Some of these characteristics are set forth in the formal rules of the pageant, such as her racial ancestry (typically she must be of 50 percent Japanese ancestry), her marital status (she must be unmarried and have never been married), and her sexual experience (she must not be a mother and have never been a mother). Others are more informal issues of pageant etiquette, such as always giving the right *omiage* (gifts), bowing correctly, and never drinking or smoking while in kimono. The production of the queen as an ideal type means that the product, the queen, is the final stage of a negotiation that is shaped by the power of the factions within and outside of the Japanese American communities. The findings show how cultural knowledge and ethnicity can be used to make racial claims on behalf of the queen pageant participants.

Racial and ethnic beauty pageants highlight how race is about the process of marking the body as different in terms of physicality, for example, skin color, eyes, hair, and body shape. The often-heard argument that the queen must have a Japanese backside (flatter than other groups) in order to look good in kimono is an example of bodily racialization within the pageant. Ironically, Hall (1996) found that mixed-race people are more likely to notice physical difference, perhaps because they live in a world of heightened awareness of the physical body due to their own perceived ambiguous bodies. Race in the pageant setting then leads to a hyper embodiment as the racial nature of the pageants places increasing significance on physical characteristics. The pageant, in the end, is in large part about judging appearance, in which race plays a large role, and not necessarily the person in her entirety.

> Race is an embodied identity, that is, one is considered a member of a race because of the physical appearance or the genetic make up of one's body. . . . Since race is constructed as an embodiment identity, challenges to racist hierarchies are often expressed as contests over the representation of racialized bodies. . . . Images of beauty practices can serve as a focal point for viewing the complex project of racial rearticulation. (Craig 2002, 12, 14-15)

This racial rearticulation in the case of Japanese American beauty pageants has not meant the disappearance of race, biologically or socially. The examples that follow illustrate how race is redone in relation to ethnicity, language, culture, and gender, but not in ways that seriously challenge racial thinking into a postracial world. These examples challenge past literature that sees race and ethnicity as separate phenomena (Cornell and Hartmann 1998) or as subcategories of each other, for example, race as a subcategory of ethnicity (Loveman 1999).

Defining Japanese Americanness

I wanted to find out how people involved in the Japanese American community pageants defined Japanese Americanness. To establish this, I asked my interviewees (mostly participants, past queens and princesses, organizers, and community members who attended the pageant) to define what they felt made someone Japanese American. Most of the pageant participants responded that it was not only one's appearance that made someone Japanese American, but also that there was something "inside." It mattered how one appeared physically, but personality also mattered. They identified certain cultural values such as *Shikataganai* (It can't be helped) or *gaman* (perseverance) that they said were instilled from their parents that made them uniquely Japanese American. They said, stereotypically, that most Japanese Americans understood discipline, respect for elders, a sense of obligation to others, and the concept of saving face.

According to one past princess: "A white person who has lived in

Japan their whole life and knows how to act in those situations, even if they are not Japanese themselves, at least they understand. They feel it in their heart. They know when something is taboo." She does not emphasize race, but instead the feeling inside of a person or their values. Not very many people went this far to say that they would consider a white person to be Japanese because of their *kokoro* (inner feeling), but many mentioned that they did feel that this was a core part of being Japanese American often expressed in bodily terms. One participant defined it:

> How you carry yourself, that is a Japanese thing, too. Because the American way of walking is like the American way of thinking, very individual, like how you strut, that is your walk. Traditionally, in Japanese culture you have to be the same as everyone else, but if you can walk evenly, balanced . . . that is the Japanese way of walking.

Interviewees emphasized thinking of the community as an extension of their family.

> It means valuing family, community. That is what we are saying. I think it is something we do in our heads. We say it's because I am Japanese. Now there are little things . . ., like omiage, that are tangible. We use them as markers of who we are and to remind ourselves, to feel good about belonging to something.

Many of these comments reveal the group orientation and collective sense of Japanese Americanness, which in these passages is deemed a cultural value. This is supported by similar findings by Fugita and O'Brien (1991), who found relatively high levels of social capital among Japanese Americans. These connections and commitments to the community are heightened in the pageant setting through the construction of collective racial/ethnic claim-making and the challenges to those claims.

Certain cultural markers signify people as Japanese American and connect them to both a historical narrative of past experiences and to other individuals of a similar heritage. These are both tangible cultural practices like omiage and girls' day/*o-bon* (holidays), and the intangible things that they "do in their heads." There seem to be two levels at which people were referring to Japaneseness—the inside (or personality of a person) versus the outside (or display of that person's personality traits). This seems to correspond roughly to delineations that they were making between race as the outside part and ethnicity as the inside part. But the outside and inside were clearly related. For example, it was of no use being completely Japanese inside if the candidate couldn't let people know that she was indeed Japanese American or if others (both inside and outside the community) didn't see her Japanese Americanness (often referred to as "race") as a part of themselves. Hence, the pageant context highlighted that the exterior presentation of self was constantly enacted in a bodily manner and was an important way to relay information visually to others. Likewise, even if people think someone is behaving in a way that is considered Japanese American, if that person couldn't back it up with the cultural characteristics (knowledge of the language, arts, foods), that person was perceived to be not authentically Japanese American. One mixed-race candidate from San Francisco discussed the contradiction that she faced in the pageant in terms of varying definitions of Japanese Americanness.

> I think some of the candidates do Japanese talents because they can't speak Japanese. They think, Let's stick something in there that is something to do with Japanese or they look like I don't have any aspects of Japanese culture in my whole presentation. I think that has something to do with it. The candidates that are half Japanese—the only difference is visual in some cases. Someone who is full Japanese ancestry, whose culture is American, I think they kind of have to strive to prove that, too, but maybe they don't have to prove it as much as someone who doesn't look Japanese.

The work, then, that the half-Japanese has to do to unhitch race from cultural practices (such as Japanese talents) is clear. Because the queen is a living symbol of a collective identity, she must embody the collective she wishes to represent. In this instance, since the community is a racial/ethnic community, it weaves race into the equation so that the symbol (queen) must also be racialized. When the queen is multiracial not only is the race of the symbol shifted, but so is the symbol itself. The mixed-race queens I interviewed didn't want to disrupt the symbol/race connection. Instead, they climbed into the race/ethnicity/body/symbol equation and worked from within it to make racial claims from a mixed-race position. The perceptions of Japanese Americanness then form both micro- and more meso- (group) level hierarchies of authenticity that produce racial claims, some of which are accepted and other rejected.[1]

Racialization of Looks

The participants that I interviewed, particularly those who were mixed-race, were keenly aware of being accused of being closer to the white

Anglo model of beauty, but they didn't always agree that looking more white was better or made their chances of winning easier.

> The community wants a representative who can say they're Japanese American without raising a controversy about what is Japanese American. Then if it [the blood quantum rule] becomes 10 percent, you could have a blonde-haired, blue-eyed woman . . . and they don't look Japanese American. They could identify as Japanese American. They could grow up in Japan for all we know. But to the community, they are going to look at her and say, "Cherry Blossom Queen? No way!"

The queen "looking Japanese" signals to the Japanese American community that this is what "we," the collectivity, are. This is what *we* look like. It is a touchstone for the community and debates are triggered when people see the effect that interracial marriage is having on the Japanese American community through the participation of mixed-race women in the pageant. This is not just a debate about the pageant, then, but more important, about the community as a whole. Thus, even if a woman feels totally Japanese American, she still needs the acceptance of others in order to assert that. If she doesn't look Japanese American, the community may and probably will question her ability to represent the community. One pageant participant explained that this happened within her own family. She explained,

> It is hard for my own mother. I have to remind her sometimes that I am Japanese. So I know a lot of it has to do with appearance. It is very visual. Even if my mom is speaking to someone in Japanese, she will automatically translate into English for me even though she knows I understand. She just can't help it. As far as the judges were concerned, I think that physically not looking Japanese has a little bit of bias. I wouldn't say prejudice . . . kind of like . . . not being able to absorb that fact that this person will represent the Japanese American community. If you look more Japanese then it is okay. My brother looks Japanese and he would be able to be Cherry Blossom King, or whatever. It shouldn't matter. People should know that there are mixed Japanese people and they may look different, but basically what they are looking for is the black hair and almond eyes, but if you don't have that you don't quite fit.

Her own mother forgets that she is Japanese American because she doesn't "look" that Japanese. In the minds of people putting on the pageant there is a Japanese American model, which recognizes what it means to look Japanese. It is an unspoken part of the criteria used to select the queen. Different people interpreted the unspoken nature of Japanese Americanness in different ways: "If it is based on how well they understand Japanese culture and how well they are able to communicate. Then I would say just anyone would be a good queen, but if the important thing is what you look like then it has to be a Japanese person. You can't really get away from the visual aspect of it." And it seemed that the criteria that people used to judge was very different. "I don't think I look that Asian unless I am sitting around other Asians. I notice when I am sitting with the people from the pageant I look Asian then." Even though they are not trying to create a look, it matters how they look to others.

Others, like Linden Nishinaga, who wrote a letter to the editor of the *Rafu Shimpo* newspaper in Los Angeles in 1982, argued that it isn't fair that mixed-race women get to run in the pageant because they have an unfair advantage. He wrote:

> This disproportional selection and seeming infatuation with the Eurasian looks not only runs counter to what I consider pride in our Japanese ancestry but also to the very idea of the Nisei Week Queen tradition. . . . Since the Nisei Week Queen is supposed to represent our Nikkei community which is still large, viable and strongly identifiable, our beauty representatives should at least be representative. (Nishinaga 1982, 3)

He argued that since we are raised on images of white dominant society, we become infatuated with Eurasian beauty and associate it with whiteness. He clearly felt that since the community was still predominantly monoracial so, too, should be the queen.

However, I found that when the candidates did try to alter their physical appearance it was to make themselves look more Japanese. They were not trying to look whiter. For example, one candidate revealed that she dyed her hair a darker color (from dark brown to black) to look more Japanese. Another used eyeliner to make her eyes more almond-shaped. Even so, some of the older Nisei still felt that mixed-race women clearly had an advantage. Ironically, it was these Japanese Americans who most clearly accepted Anglo norms of beauty. "A Eurasian woman is much more attractive than the plain Japanese. Unless they are looking for a Japanese looking girl, but the Eurasian is usually better looking because she is taller, slimmer."

This queen from the 1950s recognized that there were different standards of beauty. Is the pageant for the Japanese American community to choose a Japanese girl and to reaffirm Japanese women as beautiful? If this is true, then the Japanese American pageants, particularly early on when Japanese American women could not compete in the

Miss California or Miss America contests because of racial discrimination, can be seen as reactions or resistance to dominant forms of beauty. This could be viewed as taking control of notions of beauty in a racially discriminating society, but it also illustrates a continuing belief in race, not an attempt to destroy it.

> If you think about thirty or however many years ago, pageants might have been a way for young Japanese American girls to get involved in pageants. When you are obviously not going to be Miss America or Miss California, but hey, you want to be the prettiest Japanese American girl around . . . do this.

One candidate described the debate in Los Angeles in the 1980s about mixed-race queens:

> They were saying . . . are we choosing queens based on a Western standard of beauty and that whole thing. I don't know how much of it is sour grapes and how much of it is ethnic integrity.
>
> It is what you see in the media. You see European Americans . . . white people. Blonde hair, blue eyed, big busted, tall . . . you don't see many Asian American women portrayed in a positive light. I think the image of the queen is a little of both because you have the image of what is out there in the media and then you have the community one. They have to intermesh somewhere.

These two definitions are definitely in competition with each other. On the one hand, there is the community definition—she must look Japanese (be short, small, not a big chest, dark hair and eyes)—in order to be a good queen.[2] On the other hand, there is the outside media image of beauty—blonde hair and blue eyes. Mixed-race women, then, bring up the interrelationship of the two images in their own, often blended phenotypical appearance.

Are the mixed-race women the ideal interplay of these two images? It may be in the eyes of the beholder. If so, then it matters who the judges are. Caucasian judges can affect the outcome. Often the judging panel is a mix between Caucasian judges and Asian American (primarily Japanese American) judges. Sometimes the judging panel contains a past queen and someone from the entertainment or beauty industry. However, there are never more white judges than Japanese American or Asian ones and the committee strives to have half men and half women on the panel.

> I know we had two actors who were judges. I thought they swung away from that because these Caucasian judges didn't judge what they considered classical Japanese traits . . . having brown eyes, a slim body. . . . I thought

they pulled away from that [having white judges] to feature Japanese features.

Another said:

> When you have celebrity judges or people who are involved in movies or TV . . . you usually get a more glamorous looking queen. When you get judges who are more local . . . personality . . . you are going to get someone who has been involved in the community as queen. It is just natural that the people who are judges on the panel . . . they don't know any of these girls. It is natural that their personal biases or priorities are going to become involved.

> Look at the judges. . . . [Ray Mancini] was a great guy, he's funny and personable, but what they heck does he know about Japanese culture? If you look at the people that they chose, they are all from the entertainment field. So you're going to get someone who has their biases going in, even if they are not thinking who is the prettiest. They are surrounded by people who look a certain way and that influences people's evaluations of beauty and attractiveness.

In this context, with white judges, who have white standards of beauty as their bias and who don't know anything about Japanese culture, people assume they are judging for a more mainstream-looking queen. Having said this, though, most people concluded that the white judges had very little impact on the total outcome because of their small numbers. Many people thought that this was acceptable because they realized that the Japanese American pageants are based on different standards than a mainstream pageant. Most recognized the cultural nature of the pageant and thought that different, more–Japanese American beauty standards were appropriate in this context and that it was a way for Japanese American pageants to set themselves apart from other more traditional-type pageants.

Because it is a cultural pageant, many people argued that even though looking Japanese was not among the set scoring or judging criteria, it helped. In many cases, it was not looking white that mattered, but looking Japanese that did. Some people hypothesized that if there were a majority of Japanese judges that they would choose a Japanese-looking girl. Even a mixed-race candidate admitted that "Japanese people look more natural in a kimono than *hapa* (mixed) people."

The pageant, then, is a place where Japanese standards of beauty were affirmed and even enforced. For example, the Los Angeles pageant had a no-tanning rule; they asked the participants not to get too dark. It was rumored that some women in past pageants had been disqualified for tanning. Once again, a Japanese sense of beauty (not being too dark because it means being lower class or working outside for a living) was valued over the more popular Western belief in a tanned body. Many people told me that being too dark makes the candidates look bad in kimono and that lighter skin is "better for Japanese." One candidate, who was naturally very dark, was warned to be especially careful about tanning. She tried desperately to make her skin as light as possible and told me that she had rubbed lemons on her face at one point to try to lighten her skin.

> They told us not to tan. [Why?] Because dark in Japanese means . . . you are the peasant class. You work in the fields. In American society the darker you are, the fuller your lips are is what you really want to look like. It hasn't moved into the Japanese community. They still want you to be very fair and light.

In addition, the negative association with darkness is probably also related to the attitudes to dark skin found in Japan; for example, Okinawans were considered "darker" and associated with being inferior or less Japanese. This is probably reinforced by the assumption that lighter skin is associated not only with higher racial status, but also higher class status. One candidate from Los Angeles explained:

> But that's the Japanese way of thinking. The more beautiful, the more white you are. The ones in the northern area are more white and considered more beautiful. They probably had that a long time ago. If you saw a picture in the paper and you had one dark girl, and the rest were white looking . . . well, they wouldn't want that. They want good publicity shots.

Japanese Americans had their own colorism standards and did not just adapt majority standards from a white dominant society. They were not just blindly mimicking white standards of beauty. This emphasis on lighter being better by Japanese standards, however, did not mean that the half-white candidates did better. In fact, many found that, indeed, they were too white.

Some went even so far as to imply that in the pageant a bias existed toward Japanese-looking or even Asian-looking women. "It is sad, but if you are half Chinese and half Japanese, it is still better than being half Japanese and half Caucasian. You still look Japanese technically so it is better." It was important to look Asian, not just Japanese

American. The visual nature of the queen as a symbol makes it important to be able to visually peg her as the symbolic representative of a
racial/ethnic group. In order to represent a Japanese American group,
she must look Japanese and be seen as such by the community she represents. If not, then she has to convince them (the Japanese American
community and the judges) that she is Japanese American enough to
represent them. She must gain their acceptance to be authenticated by
them as a representative of the community. One monoracial candidate
explained why she thought a mixed-race woman didn't do well in the
pageant: "Her age (being young) hurt her—that and the fact that she
is half held her back. She is just too white looking!"

Another noted that the context matters as well as how a person
looks:

> I have a friend who is Chinese and Caucasian. She speaks Mandarin fluent-
> ly and she looks Mexican. When you see her you would not think she was
> even mixed, but she totally identifies with her Chinese side. She has never
> been in the situation like a pageant or a job interview that was requiring an
> Asian ethnicity. If she went to a job interview, and they were looking for a
> minority . . . they would probably turn her out. Her last name is white, too.

Again, what a person *looks like* is not necessarily what that person *is*.
However, there are clearly contexts in which it is better to have Japanese American looks and the pageant is one of them. If a participant
doesn't look Japanese and wants to, she changes her appearance or gives
other outward signs. There was tension between the assertion that light
was better and and the belief that looking more Japanese American was
better. Mixed-race women then had to negotiate between these two
standards of beauty.

Cultural Impostors: Race, but No Culture

Some monoracial candidates had the race but not the culture. This
was true for most younger Japanese Americans (although less so for
Japanese nationals and older Japanese Americans) and created a problem when the committee and other candidates believed the winner
knew nothing about the culture. In many cases I observed, it was someone who was monoracial who was being called a "hollow bamboo," or
cultural impostor. Those who were labeled as cultural impostors explained that in the pageant they needed to pretend, for the sake of the

pageant, to be more culturally Japanese than they really were. For example, one candidate changed her name from a Chinese to a Japanese name and seemed to be at a loss for common cultural phrases. Others felt she didn't know anything about being Japanese American. This seemed to imply that there was a limit to how much one could present herself as Japanese American even if she was monoracial. If the culture was too "put on," then it was inauthentic; embodied racial claims were made but not authenticated by cultural performance. This seemed to indicate consensus within the organizing group that the queen needed to have a foundation in Japanese culture.

These types of claims to culture as fake or authentic set off a debate among the many groups within the community about which group made better queens: monoracial cultural imposters or mixed-race women with culture. Most Japanese nationals and older Japanese Americans stuck tight to their racial understandings of Japanese Americanness, whereas younger Japanese Americans argued for a more ethnic and less racial understanding of group membership.

The first group(s) wanted "bananas," yellow on the outside and white on the inside, or women who had race but not necessarily culture. The younger, second group was willing to accept "eggs," white on the outside and yellow on the inside, with culture but not race. One candidate admitted, "If I was to judge an Asian contest and someone came in who was Asian, but totally whitewashed . . . I would probably not watch them as much or whatever. I guess it does in part have to do with the culture. But you can take the culture and learn it in the pageant." The implication here was that one can learn culture through cultural events like the pageant. A participant explained:

> A cultural impostor is just showing that you are only going to believe in your culture for the advantage of something. That is like abusing your background. That is disrespecting your family and everything. I don't know if impostor is the right word. A cultural abuser maybe because you are using your culture for an advantage.

Another said:

> When I hear "cultural impostor," I think of someone who thinks they know everything there is to know about their culture and purports to be the best representative of it, but are out of touch with what is really going on. She tries to portray that she is *the* Japanese American woman. That she is very cultured in a Japanese way but she is not! She is very whitewashed.

One woman who many felt was a cultural impostor was accused of doing the pageant as a dare or a bet with her friends to see if she could win. Many of the other candidates did not approve and interpreted this as the wrong reason to do the pageant. They argued that she used the pageant to promote herself and her film, which was about being Japanese American. They thought that in order to sell more films she had to have credibility in the community and that she was using the pageant to illustrate her ethnic credibility.

The interesting issue in this case was that the monoracial cultural impostors were also being held to ethnic standards. They also had to prove their ability and ethnic authenticity in order to be a legitimate queen. The above examples show how the women do race work through (a) learning and performing racial culture, most clearly in the culture classes, talent, and kimono sections in the pageants, and (b) building racial social ties, illustrated in their essays, in the speeches, and in the interviews. Both of these were also reasons women said motivated them to participate in the pageant in the first place.

The Mixed-Race Queen: Culture without Race?

The mixed-race queen disrupts the racial understanding of what is Japanese American. She is a collective symbol and the culmination of a production of collective identity. As such she is also a moral symbol of what the community is striving for and deems morally good.

The disruption of racial understandings because they are bodily disrupts other ideas as well. The mixed-race queen disrupts the link between morality and the body, which is assumed for Japanese American women to be linked to racial purity, sexual purity, and gender appropriate behavior (e.g., covering one's mouth when laughing). Because racial authenticity is questioned, other aspects of her "self" (gender and sexuality) are also questioned. Mixed-race women have to prove their Japanese Americanness to pass, but they also have to do the work of proving they are women and morally good women at that. This means that while the women need to "do gender" (West and Zimmerman 1991), they do it in the context of also doing "race work." The efforts of racial claims are inextricably linked to womanhood and femininity. It is not just any womanhood, but Japanese American womanhood on display. Race work must be done in order to make claims about gender

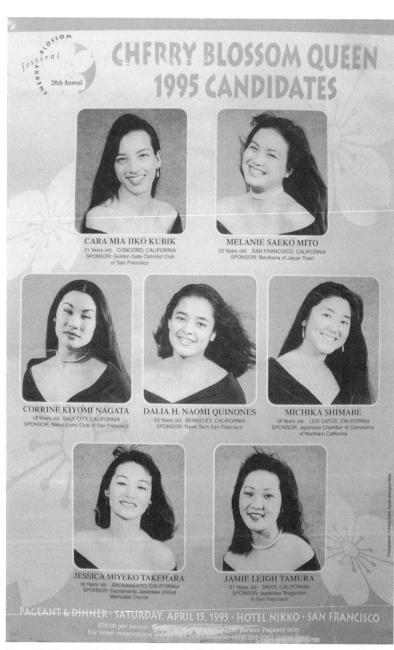

Figure 2. The 1995 Northern California (San Francisco) Cherry Blossom Queen candidates—more multiethnic than monoracial. Poster courtesy of the Northern California Cherry Blossom Festival (Sakura Matsuri, Inc.).

through race. Table 7 illustrates some of the ideal types of race working that are discussed in this chapter. They illustrate the racialized ideal types and enactments of hierarchies of authenticity and their affirmation or rejection.

The "Hapa Girl with Tattoos" is an illustration of a woman who did not have the racial appearance or embodiment to be considered Japanese American and used her body as a way to illustrate what was considered a non–Japanese American cultural practice such as tattooing.[3] Hapa girls were seen as white both in racial appearance and in their lack of Japanese American culture and were treated with disregard in the context of the pageant. The multiracial counterpart in terms of culture was the "Hapa Girl Speaking Japanese." She was seen not to have the racial embodiment that is identifiable as Japanese American but did have the cultural knowledge to back up claims to Japanese Americanness—usually through language. Several of the candidates fit into this category as mixed-race women often with mothers who were born in Japan and spoke Japanese fluently. They were not masquerading as Japanese as they felt they were more Japanese than many Japanese Americans because they had the "real" culture straight from the homeland.

The "cultural impostor" was the monoracial Japanese American woman who claimed to have Japanese American cultural values as well, but didn't. These women were more disdained than the hapa girl with

Table 7. Ideal types of race work

Racial claims	Ethnicity/Culture	
Low racial claims	Hapa girl with tattoos	Hapa girl speaking Japanese
	She has neither the racial embodiment nor the cultural practices.	She does not have the racial embodiment, but does have the cultural practices.
High racial claims	Cultural impostor	Super Japanese American
	She has the racial embodiment, but does not have the supposedly corresponding cultural practices.	She has both the racial embodiment and supposedly corresponding cultural practices.

tattoos because they were considered fake and just pretending to have more culture or community connections than they really had in order to further their candidacy in the pageant. Every candidate emphasized Japanese Americanness to some extent, which created a double standard, but there was added pressure as the women in this category, full-blooded Japanese Americans, were supposed to know something about their culture. Finally, the "Super Japanese American" had it all—racial embodiment (seen as 100 percent Japanese American ancestry) with a strong cultural awareness and knowledge. The winners were most often in this category, able to combine culture and race with acceptable gender practices and middle-class values.

Mixed-race women, in the top row of Table 7, disrupt the notion of what is supposedly the link between Japanese American bodies and the assumed corresponding cultural practices. As the quintessential Japanese American symbolic body, the queen is racialized. Many of the mixed-race interviewees themselves felt that mixed-race candidates wouldn't win even if they were qualified because they were racially mixed. One mixed-race queen's mother was quoted as saying that her chances were 50/50 because she is 50/50 (Japanese American/white). Her mother didn't think she could win because she didn't have full Japanese ancestry even though she wanted her to win. There also may be a sense of potential *hazukashii* (embarrassment)—her mother was being modest so as not to be too confident that her daughter would win. For many multiracial women their bodies become an important measure of their culture.

In an era of fear of dilution of the community through intermarriage and assimilation, mixed candidates serve to reaffirm that the community may be racially half but won't let the culture die. The preservationists' hopes may get pinned to mixed-race women. The queens may or may not see themselves that way. They participate on the same cultural terms and seek to reify the same cultural meanings through practices, such as wearing the kimono, to assure others that the culture and community won't die but will continue via multiracial participation. In fact, the women in the "Hapa Girl Speaking Japanese" category may feel that they are more Japanese American than their monoracial competitors, particularly the "cultural impostors," participating in a kind of one up-womanship in terms of culture and community participation. In fact, some of the judges seemed taken aback that a mixed-race woman could possibly have more culture than the more racially pure.

Mixed-race Japanese Americans and some younger Japanese Americans recognized that race does not necessarily determine ethnicity. They argued instead that there isn't always a correlation between how a woman looks (race) and how she feels about the criteria that determines the content of the category Japanese American (ethnicity). They recognized that race and ethnicity were not binary, but that each existed along a continuum. They had different understandings of Japanese Americanness than Japanese nationals (who used both national and racial definitions) and older Japanese Americans (who used primarily racial definitions). This view of race and ethnicity differs from the existing literature on Japanese Americans, which has thought of Japanese Americans as strictly a racial group (Kikumura and Kitano 1973) or an ethnic group (Spickard 1996). In the context of the pageants, many candidates argued for various reasons that mixed-race Japanese American women were actually more Japanese American or more Japanese than monoracial women.

> They are probably more Japanese than pure Japanese are. When I say "more Japanese," I think of mannerisms, I think of the way people approach things in their thinking, maybe things like being involved in [traditional] dancing, or stuff like that or the language.

A monoracial candidate noted:

> I've met women who are half Japanese who are more Japanese than me, a lot more culturally. I'm fourth generation. I'm probably more American than most of my friends. My family has been here longer. Does that mean I am not a good representative of the Japanese community? I don't know.

The question becomes whether the mixed-race women are more culturally Japanese American because they have to be. Is it because they have to prove their ethnic/racial identity to others? The mixed-race candidates seemed to understand that they had to interact with Japanese Americans who would have racial expectations about the queen. One mixed-race princess explained:

> I [a mixed woman] was teased a lot by the committee that I was the most Japanese out of all of them [the candidates]. During the festival when everyone wanted a snowcone I wanted *onigiri, mochi, or ume boshi* [Japanese food]. They would always tease and say that "you are more Japanese than the rest of them." I was thinking, Why wouldn't I be?

They didn't expect her to be the most Japanese, questioning even superficial food practices such as her taste in food. They thought that she shouldn't be the most Japanese and that it was ironic that she was. They were reminded in her actions that she is Japanese American culturally, but it jarred because she looks more white than Japanese. Or is it that she is more Japanese culturally because she looks white? One queen explained:

> Sometimes a hapa person is the one who speaks Japanese and is the most Japanese. Reiko was very Japanese. She may look hapa, but her mannerisms. She was raised by her mother. Her mom is from Japan. She's fluent [in Japanese] and is much more Japanese than I am even though I look more Japanese than she does.

The influence that her mother, who is from Japan, has on her creates her familiarity with Japanese culture. This queen is drawing on the idea that mothers, rather than fathers, are the culture carriers and transporters of cultures of resistance (particularly in minority cultures) to their children (Dill 1988). Others might consider that in a patriarchal society fathers and the passing on of their surnames to their children would be more influential in terms of cultural transmission. This woman is also assuming that because Reiko's mother is from Japan, that is, not Japanese American, that she has a closer connection to Japan, which is assumed to be the more authentic source of culture. The lack of race that Reiko has may, in fact, heighten the perception of her ethnicity because it is so unexpected.

The relationship between how someone looks and how she is culturally is a direct reflection of the relationship between race and ethnicity in a larger sense. We can see from this example that a mixed-race woman who looks more white than Japanese may have to learn to compensate for her racial deficiencies by using an ethnic strategy to convince others of her racial authenticity.

This race work then was often highlighted through a series of comparisons. Susan, a monoracial candidate, often compared herself to Diane, a mixed-race candidate:

> We have had some girls that are half Japanese . . . some have been more trained to the Japanese culture, exposed to the culture more than some of the girls who are biologically all Japanese. Diane is bilingual but she is half Caucasian. Is she more Japanese than me because she speaks Japanese or are they less because both of my parents are Japanese?

Clearly there is confusion about what criteria should be used to decide who is Japanese American. Is the criteria based on nationality and language (like some assumed Japanese nationals think)? Or race (as some assumed older Japanese Americans think)? The relationship between race and language is assumed to be a strong one. Race, at times, seems to be more powerful than language in determining what other people might think someone is. What are the relationships, then, between race, culture, ethnicity, and language? While language and culture appear more malleable/changeable, race remains an important constraint on how far ethnic or cultural strategies can be pursued.

This monoracial candidate denied that looks (race) determined one's culture, but said that it was the inside feeling:

> Somebody who's hapa is just as much Sansei as I am. It's completely based upon how they act and how knowledgeable they are. And what experiences they have had. Even though someone looks hapa doesn't mean that they haven't faced the same hardships. . . . They haven't come from the same background. Obviously if they're hapa they have some Japanese in them from somebody. In their lineage they've had to deal with the same problems that someone of full ancestry had to deal with. That is the most important thing. Whether that person is in touch with that side of their life . . . that is what matters.

But being in touch with that side of their life, that is, the Japanese American side, implies the influence of contextual factors such as family, extended family, geographic location, gender, neighborhood, and so on. This is consistent with studies of ethnicity that argue that ethnicity can be an option or choice (Waters 1990), but only when it is not constrained by race (Song 2003). One mixed woman put it this way:

> According to this thing [debate in the newspaper] if you are half racially you are half culturally. My argument was that just because I am half Japanese that it doesn't mean that I have 50 percent of pride about that. I grew up going to Cherry Blossom, Japanese school, eating Japanese food, speaking Japanese, why am I not Japanese American? I would say that I have found that with the half Japanese they have been more Japanese than the full-blooded Japanese because most have a parent from Japan. My friends on the court they used to call me an egg . . . white on the outside yellow on the inside. They would make me read the Japanese names. *So who is to say that what you look like is what you are.* (Emphasis added)

I noticed that in their speeches many of the candidates focused on how they were involved in Japanese American festivals, Japanese American community organizations, or Japanese cultural arts. They emphasized things like taking Taiko, tea ceremony, or Japanese dance lessons. This emphasis on how connected they were to the community or the culture gave some people a bad impression. They felt that the pageant should not be about culture, but about a candidate accepting who she is racially. Many people thought that if a woman was involved in the pageant then it was readily obvious that she was Japanese or half Japanese. They therefore felt that when candidates emphasized culture they didn't need to "shove it in my face." So although the pageant was about culture, to parade it too obviously was not in good taste.

How Much Race? How Much Culture?

The mixed-race queen candidates prompted new discussions about race and ethnicity within the Japanese American community. Japanese nationals, for the most part businessmen involved in the festival, had a race- and nation-based understanding of the queen; older Japanese Americans thought the queen should be racially 100 percent Japanese, but that she should be born in the United States and should not necessarily speak Japanese; and younger Japanese Americans understood that the queen could be mixed-race, but felt that she should still be ethnically Japanese even though she was not expected to speak Japanese or be from Japan.

Japanese nationals used a blood-quantum argument and did not consider mixed-race Japanese Americans to be "really" Japanese. One candidate talked about not being acknowledged by the community as a legitimate representative:

> A lot of time the mixed-race girls are not acknowledged at all. I have been called (by Japanese nationals) during the festival *hakujin* (white person). . . . I have heard them, Japanese nationals, say in Japanese, "Although you are the queen, you are not really Japanese. I like real Japanese women so don't think you are really Japanese just because you are the queen."

Clearly there is conflict here between the Japanese national who does not recognize the queen as his and the queen who is desperately trying to represent everyone. Many of the queens handled these situations in different ways. Some who spoke Japanese responded in Japanese that they understood what was being said about them. Others just ignored the remark and continued to be polite.

Not just Japanese nationals challenged the queen's racial and cultural legitimacy. Sometimes older Japanese Americans or even people from outside the community considered mixed-race women to not be Japanese American enough. One woman described the question she received on stage during the question-and-answer segment of the pageant:

> People laughed when I got it [my question] because, of all the girls, I was the half-Japanese one, and it was something like "What does it feel like to be a Japanese American?" Something stronger than that . . . and I happened to get that one and the audience laughed when I got it. It had something to do with the essence of being Japanese. It was obvious that it was funny that of all the people I would get that one.

Is it funny for the audience because she of all people is supposed to know less about what it means to be a Japanese American? They think, "How would she know? She is only half." Her presence as a mixed-race person makes the situation ironic because she turns the assumed race/ ethnicity/culture nexus on its head.

Many people assumed that mixed-race women were somehow less Japanese American and that they therefore would not make good representatives of the community. One candidate recounted, "People who say that they [mixed-race women] should not participate say that it is supposed to be Japanese; representative of the Japanese community and they should be pure Japanese." So there are limits to how far culture can get someone if she wants to be queen. Race at some point constrains who can be queen. Culture matters especially to the Japanese nationals as they are trying to maintain what they recognize as culture—often more updated cultural forms than more antiquated forms used by Japanese Americans—within the community. For others, though, this relationship between culture and race is about reconstituting Japanese Americanness. The public nature of the pageant and the fact that the queen is meant to represent the entire community gives Japanese American community members the right to comment on the queen candidates and presents, as in politics, an almost unattainable goal to make everyone happy.

There were clear racial limits on who could comment about the queen from inside the community. This right did not extend fully to the white parents of mixed-race Japanese American women. One white mother confided to me her opinion of the other candidates and criticisms of the pageant, but then asked me not to repeat her complaint to anyone. She commented to me that she needed to keep her voice down because "how would it look to have a white woman telling them how to run a Japanese American pageant?" Even so, the visibility of the women who participate and their openness to criticism is apparent. Even some of the mixed-race candidates understand that people will gaze upon them as somehow "less Japanese" and therefore think they are not worthy of being a good queen based on their racial composition.

Others consider themselves legitimately Japanese American and were surprised by the challenge to them from older monoracial Japanese Americans during the pageant. One mixed candidate recalled her interview with the judging panel.

> They didn't ask me a whole lot of questions about being Japanese American. They kept asking me questions about being mixed. That was their target. Like "I know it is difficult to be mixed; what are your most difficult situations?" I was, like, it wasn't difficult. I was, like, why are they asking me this? They asked, "Well, why would someone who is half Japanese want to do this?" I said that because the part of me that is Japanese is the part of me that participates . . . and me being American I qualify. I am half. It is a challenge. They kept referring to me as Eurasian . . . they wouldn't even say Japanese. I felt at that point that there was already prejudice because they labeled me as Eurasian, not Japanese or Japanese American. I told them before I left, "Although I may not be what you call Japanese here [indicating her face] . . . I am Japanese here [indicating her heart]." That took them by surprise.

Some people assume that being mixed-race (in this case the label *Eurasian*) and being Japanese American are two different things. This separation of Eurasians or mixed-race Japanese Americans from other Japanese Americans started to have a collective impact. The presence of not one, but many mixed candidates has sparked controversy in all four of the communities I studied. More and more mixed-race women showing up in pageants and other places like the Japanese American basketball leagues has provoked a debate about the impact of interracial marriage on the community. This may also be evidence of a generational gap in racial understandings as younger Japanese Americans, more familiar with racial mixing and more accepting of it, see little problem with multiracial queens.

In chapter 3, it was clear that this debate has, at times, been a very public one, as in the early 1980s in Los Angeles over the mixed queens.

Before the 1940s, there was no need to have blood-quantum rules about "how much Japanese" someone needed to be racially in order to represent the community as the queen. The first mixed-race queen in 1974 in Los Angeles was Elsa Cuthbert and she signified that the number of mixed-race people and therefore candidates was on the increase. One candidate remembered:

> You could see when half Japanese started running. In the late '60s maybe. Probably not too many ran, because they probably still thought that there was no way. I remember there was a mixed girl who ran three years before me [in the 1980s]. She helped to judge my local pageant and she warned me that it would be tough because I am half Japanese and she had it tough. A lot of Japanese people weren't accepting. Your die-hard Nisei who don't feel that half Japanese are really Japanese. So she said that it was hard and it was hard for me, but it wasn't hard for my friend, but that was ten years later [1990s].

The acceptance of more and more mixed-race queens as legitimate Japanese American representatives clearly signifies a shift in racial ideology for many Japanese Americans. The racism the queen above talks about in the 1980s was within the Japanese American community. It was not racism by whites from the outside, dominant society, but instead a debate within the Japanese American community about whiteness and relationships with whites. This is a different way of thinking about race, because it is not defined from without and based on discrimination (Bobo and Hutchings 1996; Wilson 1978), but instead it is based on how racial communities internally create their own definitions of race. This, in turn, shapes the experience of whiteness as a negative thing and makes some Japanese Americans in this time period suspicious of mixed-race Japanese Americans. Therefore, Japanese Americans don't necessarily want to be white or be with white people all the time (Shinagawa 1994). One mixed-race queen put it this way,

> I honestly thought that I didn't have a chance to win. I thought that it was a fluke that a half Japanese had won before. I was probably more relaxed because I thought there was no way . . . half Japanese don't win these things. My mom couldn't believe it. She thought I couldn't win either.

Even though the mother is a monoracial Japanese American she understands that her daughter may not have the best chances of winning. The daughter, who is half, also knows the she is marked as different in the context of the pageant. She explained:

> Being involved in Nisei Week I always felt I stuck out. I always felt different. I grew up in a very Japanese neighborhood, but I always felt different.

> I went to Brazil [as the queen] and I was surrounded by people like me. It was bizarre. For once I felt that I was in a majority of people.

Even though she speaks Japanese and has gained public respect in the local Japanese American community, that is, by being named by the original critic of mixed-race queens as one of the best queens, she still felt that she was different somehow and less acceptable to others as "their" representative.

The Queen as a Touchstone for Collective Japanese American Anxieties

On a larger level, how and when do ideas about Japanese Americanness as blood quantum (race) and ideas about cultural identity (ethnicity) get negotiated within the Japanese American communities? How do people explain that a mixed-race person can be more Japanese than a monoracial one? How does this relate to the above ideas about Japaneseness taken from and modeled on Japan? How do racial meanings embed themselves in social institutions and status?

I interviewed several Japanese American queens who used me, as a mixed-race woman, as an example or a touchstone for what they were saying about culture and race. Some responded that many mixed-race candidates were quite Japanese culturally even if they didn't look it. Others explained how they thought being mixed might be different from their own monoracial experience. A candidate I interviewed said:

> Maybe when you are mixed you are a little more aggressive. In your [the interviewer's] case it is different because your mom is totally American [monoracial Japanese American]. If you do something like that [run in the pageant], you are Japanese and you are part of the community, a lot of that goes both ways. A lot of Japanese girls would be wary of somebody coming out like that—it is immodest, too showy. It's the Japanese way . . . shut up and don't do it. If a Japanese girl was in there and she lost then the mother would be so ashamed after that.

This candidate clearly thinks that mixed-race Japanese Americans don't have the same familial ties and community ties that would make them embarrassed about their participation and potentially embarrassed by losing. She is making not only a distinction between monoracial and mixed race, but also between monoracial Japanese and Japanese American. This is particularly interesting given that her own father is a Sansei and her mother is from Japan. She is asserting a superiority of blood—

that she is full-blooded, that she won, that being mixed makes a person less Japanese and therefore more aggressive. Implicit here is an assumption of a link between blood quantum (percentage of ancestry) and cultural style: someone who is half Japanese ancestry and half Caucasian will be more aggressive culturally. Blood determines behavior and attitudes. But she also recognizes the role of socialization, mentioning the interviewer's "totally American" mother. There is a gendered assumption here that culture and values come from the mother. But she still doesn't seem to understand that a monoracial Japanese American mother of a mixed-race woman could be just as embarrassed as the mother of a full-blooded candidate because they are both equally Japanese American themselves. Even the assertion about the power of race ends up bringing ethnic considerations into its understanding of race.

Another former queen described a scene in which she felt that her culture was not readily obvious to the people she was interacting with.

> I used to work at a Japanese restaurant and one of the Caucasian ladies said to me, "Oh, what is a California roll?" And she looked at me and she said, "I'm sorry this is not a Mexican restaurant!" She kept calling *señora* and she asked for *agua*. It angered me because she wouldn't stop. She kept doing it. Even if I was Mexican and I worked at a Japanese restaurant, don't you think I would know? Later, I saw she had a chopstick sticking up in her rice. I wanted to go over there and just choke her, but I politely went over there and I said, "Excuse me, but in our culture it is bad luck and the symbol of a funeral," and she just looked confused. She was, like, "our culture." The lady sitting across from her said, "Oh, I forgot to tell you that I learned that living in Japan. I lived there for five years." Her friend says to me, "Oh, you must be half Japanese," 'cause I said "our culture." She started to speak to me in Japanese, very simple conversation in Japanese. The other lady who was calling me "señora" had her mouth on the table. She was speechless. There are polite ways to let people know that they are ignorant and patronizing, but I tend to not walk away without saying anything.

In the context of the pageant, people thought that race, meaning physical appearance, was even more important.

> A few people have brought it up to me that they [the pageant judges] are still biased towards full-blooded Japanese and I don't want to think about that . . . because I am half Japanese. . . . Thinking about it, then, I think there is no hope, you know? I don't know. I can see how it is sad that most of the girls are mixed. The fact that there are still people our age, in their 20s, who are full-blooded Japanese, so it's not like the Japanese American community is dying out or something. There are full-blooded Japanese Americans but they don't chose to participate in the community or they are alienated or estranged for some reason or another or don't know what

it is about. In a way, it is sad that it has to be half Japanese people participating, but if you look at it from the more politically correct point of view,
then it is really good because it is more diversity. Maybe it is like, internalized racism . . . on my part to agree with that and say that full-blooded
Japanese should run rather than half Japanese people . . . but in a way it is
true, but half of the girls [monoracial and mixed] wouldn't know anything
about Japanese culture. I mean, Tara has been doing cultural school, but
she didn't really know all that much.

There seems to be an internalized assumption here that if a person
is mixed, then by default she is less Japanese culturally or that she
wouldn't make a good representative. They think that because someone looks less Japanese, she is less culturally Japanese American. This
assumes that one needs a certain kind of Japaneseness in order to
be a good queen and that race is the determining factor. This idea
that race determines culture is reinforced at an interpersonal level (as
seen in the first quote) and at an internalized individual level (in the
second quote).

Negotiating Japanese American Race and Ethnicity

Because of this incongruity between how mixed-race candidates saw
themselves and how others, such as Japanese nationals and older Japanese Americans, saw them in the context of the pageant, candidates
felt they had to compensate to alleviate tension. In a sense, they had to
overcome their racial situation with ethnic tools in order to illustrate
their identity as Japanese Americans. They were not really changing
the definition of what it means to be Japanese American ethnically. In
fact, they seemed to agree with and reinforce the existing meaning of
Japanese America ethnicity, but what they challenged was the racial
meaning of what it is to look Japanese American. For example, they
asserted that while they may not look Japanese American, they were
more Japanese American culturally than most monoracial Japanese
Americans. They argued that those who looked Japanese American
(monoracial) may not know anything about the culture and are therefore "cultural impostors." The mixed-race women used their mastery
of Japanese culture and language to challenge the racial criteria being
imposed on them.

When the community was primarily monoracial, race was taken for
granted and the discussion was about retaining culture or not. Today,
however, the debate is still about culture, but it is also about race.

Because race is changing, it is now a discussion of race and its relationship to ethnicity.

> I feel like I've learned more Japanese things, but because I don't look it, it is automatically assumed that I'm not or that I don't know anything about it. I sometimes feel I have to prove it. Some Japanese Americans expect mixed-race women to be less Japanese culturally because they are less Japanese racially. They trust that what you look like, is what you are.

Another said:

> I think we [mixed-race women] had a disadvantage having white blood . . . it was like a disease. I know most people I meet don't think I am Japanese. I don't look Japanese. The more white you look, the more culturally Japanese you have to be to prove yourself. I think . . . like the girl who won last year plays *koto* [Japanese string instrument] and speaks Japanese. It is almost like you need that to make up for your white half.

While some see whiteness as an asset and as an automatic advantage in this society of white dominant images of beauty, others see it as a disadvantage, particularly in this, a Japanese American context. Whiteness, for those who don't think it is an advantage, is something to overcome and to compensate for. It ends up working against you.

> Maybe for me it is more important because I don't really look Japanese so I have to make up for it . . . in ways that are visible or audible to people so that the Japanese part of me comes out. So I think that a lot of people really trust if you look something then you will know more about it necessarily.

Whiteness, for this mixed-race candidate, is a liability. In this Japanese American–dominated context, if a person is not Japanese looking, racially she has to make up for it. Culture can be used as a commodity to increase their chances in running for queen. Race or phenotype (physical appearance) is so important in terms of the embodiment of race that the queen as both the body/symbol and racial/symbol has to use culture to resurrect the body, and she does so by using language and other ethnic cues to convince people that her racial body is sufficient to be the symbol of the queen. She has to prove she has culture in order to convince others that she will be a good queen. One mixed candidate explains that this is part of what made her want to run in the pageant.

> I did it because I wanted to be able to publicly express my Japanese pride. Most people, who look at you to get an ethnic . . . to categorize you, never ever think any type of Asian. I get Puerto Rican, I get Brazilian . . . I get Caribbean types because my skin is darker. Depending on how I do my hair . . . sometimes I get Mexican. It is hard . . . not that I feel a color or

not, but I feel an ethnicity that in my heart I feel Japanese because that is the way I was raised. I don't get a lot of opportunity to express it in my everyday life. I express it in my home and in my food, but to actually go out and express it is a rare opportunity.

The public nature of the pageant allows her to show the world "I may not look Japanese, but I am really inside." She does not feel a color (race), but does feel ethnic. She continued,

I wanted to make a statement that I was Japanese and very proud of it and no matter what people think physically . . . or I may not fulfill the stereotypical characteristics of a Japanese person . . . I am. I am proud to accept whether or not you will accept me or whether you believe me it is who I am. I am what I am.

She recognizes that some people will not accept her, will not legitimate her as a true Japanese American. She knows that she needs this acceptance of her authenticity to confirm her identity as Japanese American. The public nature of the pageant will allow her to declare publicly that she is indeed Japanese American. In order to fit into stricter definitions, more mixed-race women used cultural tools to prove to the audience and the judges that they were worthy of being named queen and were true and authentic Japanese Americans.

I always felt like the outcast [in her mostly Japanese neighborhood] so doing Nisei Week was like redeeming myself in a weird way. It was this sense of not being accepted which made many of the mixed women feel that they had more to prove than the monoracial women. The people who are involved that are mixed really get into it. Maybe trying to prove something, trying to make up for your other half, but they really get involved. And eventually it will have to be different . . . look at the population.

Yuri Ann Arthur, a mixed queen candidate in San Francisco, illustrates this in an article about the candidates:

"However, because of my predominantly Caucasian features, I've also felt as though I needed to prove myself to be Japanese," said Arthur, 19, who is the vice chair of the Milpitas Sister City Commission. "Therefore, I decided to immerse myself in the Japanese culture." Arthur reached an epiphany when on a visit to the Hiroshima memorial museum last year. "There, inside the atomic bomb memorial museum, I battled with a barrage of feelings and realized something important about myself," said Arthur, who was sponsored by the Golden Gate Optimist Club of San Francisco. "I did not need to prove myself to be Japanese any more than I needed to prove myself as being American. If I knew who I was on the inside, that was the most important thing. As both cultures met in reconciliation within me, I realized that I wanted to work hard to bring those two cultures . . . closer together." (Taguma 2001, 2)

Hierarchies of Authenticity

These internal community-driven hierarchies of authenticity are linked historically to the treatment of Japanese Americans and in turn their treatment of each other in terms of race. While mixed-race queens can be just as Japanese as monoracial queens, they do have a different racial position from which to make claims to cultural authenticity. These claims were deeply racialized as one pageant participant from Los Angeles in the 1950s explains,

> This was a big controversy in the 1980s. She [the queen] didn't look Japanese and she didn't have a Japanese last name. At that time, I thought, "Gosh, one of our daughters doesn't look very Oriental and the other is very Oriental looking. She is always assumed to be Oriental." And my other daughter—they always say, "What are you?" She says to them, "I'm a human being." The Japanese are so small-minded. They gossip a lot. They are really prejudiced. They had to accept interracial marriages because it was so rampant. When the Nisei Week Queen became half and half, people were not happy with that. There was a backlash. You know, they sent us to the internment camps. If you were one-sixteenth Japanese, you would go there. If that was the criteria, why should the Nisei Week Queen be any different?

The invocation of the blood-quantum rules during internment in World War II clearly draws this historical parallel using blood-quantum rules imposed from outside the community, that is, the U.S. government during relocation. She cleverly reappropriates them in the 1980s to define who should/could be Nisei Week Queen. But those blood-quantum rules don't stand up to intracommunity racial definitions of who is Japanese American. The Japanese American community asserts the right or political power to accept or reject various levels of claim to Japanese American authenticity. The political ideology of accepting these multiracial claims to community membership (more progressive racial politics perhaps) struggle with a strong purist (racially pure) vision of who makes up the Japanese American community and who can be considered an authentic representative or symbol of it. These claims and their acceptance are strongly linked to cultural (and even gendered) standards. One past Nisei Week Queen put it this way:

> It depends who is thinking about it because a lot of people feel as long
> as the person is part Japanese and is willing to represent the community
> and can do it well, that's all they ask. We've had some girls that are half
> Japanese and half various other things. . . . Some of them have been more
> trained to the Japanese culture—more exposed to the culture than some
> of the girls who are biologically all Japanese. Susan is bilingual and half
> Caucasian. Are they more Japanese than me because they speak Japanese?
> Or are they less because both my parents are Japanese? The current queen
> is only half Japanese but she does taiko and works in the Japanese hotel, she
> is part of the Little Tokyo community. I think she is an ideal representative
> because she knows the community. She is a part of the community.

In the end, it is the ties to the local Japanese American community,
and not the racial background, that makes this queen an authentic and
acceptable queen in her mind. However, all of this happens within the
constraints of racial eligibility rules so the conversation is not about
someone who is not at all racially Japanese representing the community, but instead about multiracial representatives.

Ethnic Strategies for Making Racial Claims

In order to be accepted as the queen, the mixed-race candidates had to
convince others that they were insiders and a part of the community.
Their strategies then shed light on the processes by which individuals
are deemed to be inside or outside the racial and ethnic boundaries of
a group (Barth 1969). It seemed to be hardwired into some Japanese
Americans that race determines ethnicity and that race is determined
primarily by one's physical appearance. They tried to convince others of
their authenticity and so legitimate themselves in many ways: by using
Japanese names to highlight their Japanese heritage; through spoken
language, speaking in Japanese to aurally tell people who they are; by
altering their physical appearance, such as hair, eyelashes, eye color;
and through interaction in their speeches and "talent" performances.

Names

Our names tell people about us. They say who we are and ethnic/racial
names tell people what group we may be a part of. But names are de-
ceiving. Some people can be named Lopez and not be Puerto Rican,
but instead Italian or have the last name Woo (through marriage) and
be Caucasian. This change in name, particularly to a name that is

clearly ethnic, may move one from being perceived as white to being perceived as a person of color or vice versa. Depending on one's name then, expectations would be different in terms of language and culture (Waters 1990).

The mixed women in the pageant used names to signal to the audience, community and the judges that they really were Japanese American. They used Japanese names to authenticate themselves and to help, they seemed to think, their chances of becoming queen. Japanese names, then, were badges, outward reminders to people of their Japanese Americanness.

In this context, having a Caucasian-attributed name, like "Sarah Smith," may be a disadvantage because people can't tell if a person is Japanese American or not. Having a Japanese last name, which might be bad in other situations, here becomes an advantage. People on the phone would immediately know that she was ethnic and Japanese. They would be surprised to meet her if she was mixed and say, "Are you Japanese?" With women it might be more confusing and they might ask "Is your husband Japanese?" The name in this case would not fit the face. Within the Japanese community people might think right off the bat, "Oh, she is Japanese American." When they met her, they might still think she was Japanese American because with this name she would have been treated by others as Japanese American and may also have faced racism and the experience of people mispronouncing and misspelling her Japanese name. The label that is a person's name signals to others how to treat that person and in the case of the pageant signals that the person represents an ethnic/racial group.

> Sarah Smith [mixed queen] is held up to everyone as having been one of the best queens ever, just because she is such a wonderful person. She happens to not be 100 percent Japanese, but I never heard anybody ever say anything negative about it. She was a good queen. Obviously people must have looked beyond her name.

Even though this past queen never heard anyone say anything negative about Sarah, the name was something clearly to be overcome. Her name worked against her. So how can a name work for a candidate in the queen pageants? "I think maybe the people of the community take offense to that, that they have a representative that doesn't have a Japanese last name. Usually I use my middle name, Kiyoko. It tells people that I am part Japanese."

One candidate's given name was Monica Midori Fishburn.[4] When she entered the pageant she went by Midori Fishburn. This caused untold confusion when her friends, who knew her from before the pageant, came to the backstage door and asked to speak with Monica. No one knew who Monica was. Monica's friends, getting impatient, shouted her name into the dressing room. When she jumped up and started out, everyone turned, surprised at the name change. This same candidate often didn't respond to the name Midori and it was clear to many that she had just started to use this name during the pageant and therefore didn't respond to it most of the time.

The importance of a Japanese name may also be tied to Japanese nationals' understandings of heritage and bloodline that they bring to Japanese Americans in the United States. In Japan, until recently, in order to be a citizen of the country one had to have a Japanese last name. This causes many problems, for example, for European Americans who marry Japanese women. They could be citizens legally, but must take their wives' Japanese last name to officially register themselves as citizens. Even if they didn't, their children must have Japanese last names to enroll in public school in Japan.

Language

Speaking Japanese was another way that mixed-race candidates convinced the audience, community, and committee members (particularly the Japanese nationals) that they were more Japanese than they looked. It is important to note that many Japanese Americans speak little or no Japanese at all. I found queens from the 1950s, primarily monoracial women, who didn't speak a word of Japanese. One queen from the 1970s stated:

> From what I've heard from other people who have gone to Japan, it's a negative thing to be full Japanese American and not be able to speak Japanese. Because of racial ideology, mixed-race women were assumed to be unable to speak Japanese. Even if others know that the mixed-race woman speaks and understands Japanese, they are not able to understand or always remember that someone can be mixed and speak Japanese as well. Because I don't look Japanese, even Japanese people who know that I speak Japanese, and know that I understand still refuse to speak to me. A lot of it is visual. So that even if they have the knowledge that she can speak Japanese, they forget because she doesn't "look" Japanese. This seemed to change over time, though. The more Japanese American you are getting, the more you don't speak Japanese. The younger generation aren't speaking Japanese. In

my era [1950s] we really didn't speak Japanese because it was right after the war. You didn't bring those things out. You just tried to be as American as you could.

In my research in the mid-1990s, it seemed valuable to be able to speak Japanese. Many people talked about how it might help them get a job or improve their chances in business. Also many people didn't speak Japanese anymore and they were envious of those that could. For example, they cursed themselves for not being able to speak and talked of sending their children to Japanese school to learn. They seemed to think if one speaks Japanese, one understands the culture. This was a significant change from the period after World War II, when most people knew Japanese, but they wouldn't dare speak it as they wanted to blend into the dominant society. This illustrates the changing role of the language according to social context. One queen from the 1940s told me, "In those days the counsel general spoke Japanese. They still wanted a Japanese representative of the community. I think they wanted someone who could speak both [Japanese and English]." Now, even though most people don't speak Japanese, many of the candidates did try to speak Japanese during the pageant. Even if they couldn't speak a word, many tried to use it in their speeches.

> I didn't speak Japanese at all, but I tried to learn some for the speech. I did it to show that I admired the Japanese heritage. Sometimes I put my foot in my mouth because I didn't know the language well enough. It was kind of a hindrance, not knowing how to speak Japanese well.

This candidate spoke in Japanese because she thought that it would help her win. Another candidate told me about others trying to speak in Japanese only for the pageant.

> She changed her speech after she heard me practicing mine in Japanese. She practiced it and had someone write out the Japanese for her. . . . It was almost as if she knew Japanese. I thought that was really sneaky. It must have helped her . . . not that the judges can understand. The day after the pageant, reporters were coming up to her and they were speaking in Japanese. They assumed since she spoke in her speech that she understood and she pulled me aside and said, "You had better help me!"

In the Nisei Week Queen pageant in Los Angeles, the pageant director and the committee decided that being able to speak Japanese might influence the judges and in order to keep the judging fair, they would not allow the candidates to speak Japanese on stage. They claimed that those who could speak Japanese were at an unfair advantage.

This was ironic given that most of the judges don't understand or speak Japanese so the language is more symbolic than functional. Clearly, just hearing someone speak Japanese they felt might convince the judges that they are more Japanese and therefore a better candidate for being queen.

No Eyelid Glue, Nasal Inserts, or Whitening Cream Here

Some mixed-race candidates actually tried to alter their physical "racial" appearance to appear more Japanese. Some of the women dyed their hair dark black instead of their natural brown. Others used eyeliner to make their eyes appear more almond-shaped or used colored contacts to make their eyes brown instead of blue. However, most mixed-race candidates did not try to alter their appearance in any way and far more of them tried to manipulate their ethnic selves instead through their names, speaking Japanese, or trying to appear to be culturally very Japanese.[5] Racial tactics and strategies, then, were by far out numbered by ethnic strategies in trying to gain acceptance and legitimation as a Japanese American queen. The success of these strategies shows us how racial thinking can cause ethnic strategies to be used. However, these strategies themselves may come to undermine the domination of race as the only criteria for determining racial/ethnic community membership. By playing with their racial selves and working to present themselves in this context as appearing more Japanese, these women were actually going against a larger trend that seems to encourage Asian women more generally to aspire to a predominantly white model of beauty.

Describing the increased interest in mixed beauty in Asia, Hannah Beech writes, "Diverse backgrounds and multicultural heritages are making Eurasians the poster children for twenty-first-century globalization. Why are they the right mix?" She explains that the increased use of mixed models from Indonesia to Japan in Asia has been "to promote a more cosmopolitan image . . . an international look that can be still be accepted as Indonesian." "When you look at Maggie [a mixed-race Vietnamese American from Hawaii], you see the whole world in her face. . . . She sells because she appeals to everyone. They are exotic, but not threatening" (2003, 1–2). These images of mixed-race, half white women, have encouraged Asian women to idealize white beauty, but not go all the way to white. The impact on Asian women in Asia and Asian Americans in America has been to increase the need to manipulate their bodies to be more white. For those who can't afford nose jobs, "Cleopatra nasal implants," which are pieces of plastic inserted in the nose to make the bridge of the nose more prominent, can be purchased in the Philippines (Hyena 2000, 1). Eye glue can be used to prop up eyelids for that "more Caucasian" open-eye look by Chinese Americans (Valhouli 2000, 1). Skin-whitening cream can be used in Thailand, including Luk Kreung (mixed-race) Snow White Skin cream (Beech 2003, 3). All of these examples link racial beauty and the idealization of whiteness very clearly to bodily practices which happen mainly though consumption of beauty products.

The perpetuation of the white or mixed image of beauty in Asia and for Asian Americans seems to serve the Western cosmetic companies well. In fact, the same dynamics faced beauty queens in Asia as Japanese American beauty queens. Cindy Burbridge, the first mixed-race blue-eyed Miss Thailand in 1995, commented, "They couldn't believe that I could be representing Miss Thailand. A lot of media were saying, prove you are Thai. How can you prove you're Thai? That is a tough question. How do you prove you are anything?"(Mydans 2002). In Japanese American beauty pageants, there was far less manipulation of the body in what were considered racial ways. In fact, while efforts were made to appear slimmer (such as slimming pants or girdles) and more busty (the Wonderbra included), very few actually attempted to look more Japanese. Like Miss Thailand, their mixedness made them different and "other" but also made them unique and set them apart.

These examples illustrate the power of race as an unchangeable idea in participants' minds. They felt that race was almost immutable, so they turned their efforts to cultural and ethnic changes. These micro strategies for making racial claims (using names, language, and the like) took place within the social context of the pageant, which brought with it larger meso-levels of racial/ethnic meaning and therefore work—particularly highlighted in the speech and talent sections of the pageant.

Speeches

One of the prime contexts that combined racial appearance, cultural knowledge, and that ephemeral characteristic "poise" was the speech section of the pageant. This was usually done in kimono. As the women took to the stage in the first part of the pageant, they dressed in kimonos and shuffled onto the stage to give a three-minute speech, which they had been practicing for weeks. Some had memorized the speech. Others had note cards to help remind them what they wanted to say. The speeches varied, but the themes within them were similar. Themes that impressed the committee, and were assumed to influence the judges positively, included commitment to family (filial piety), shown by thanking their family and illustrating strong and positive relationships with their parents and siblings. Thanking their sponsor was also constructed as paying necessary recognition to those who supported them. This all served to highlight the collective nature of the candidates' campaigns to be queen. It was constructed as a Japanese American cultural value to recognize obligation to others. In a sense, the failure or success of the woman's candidacy for queen was a collective one, including the hopes of parents, sponsors, friends, those who sold tickets and raffle tickets for her, and friends at her job/workplace, school, or church.

The content of the speech was a way to illustrate one's cultural and racial commitment and suitability or authenticability to be the queen. As one past queen put it,

> I think the content of the speech does matter. I think it shows whether you are a thinking person, whether you can articulate your thoughts. Whether there are any gaps. I've heard some speeches where candidates try to connect with being Japanese, but they really aren't a part of much that is Japanese. They haven't tied into their culture before they ran in the pageant. You sense it.

In this case, the hollowness of cultural claims rang through in the speech while others stuck to cultural topics they thought would win them points.

Even the weaker candidates tried to pay homage to a certain sense of cultural practice. One candidate listed her activities and said that she felt she would be a leader in preserving Japanese American culture. She assumed that her audience knew what that culture is, that it is being lost and needs to be preserved, and that they knew how to preserve it. She didn't say how she would do that though. She picked up the rhetoric, or the superficial layer of what she thought the judges and audience wanted to hear, but couldn't follow through with details, which made the judges think that she didn't really know what she was talking about.

There needs to be some evidence of connection or truth running through the speech for the candidate to be believable as queen. One past participant described it in the following way:

> If someone gave a speech where they didn't talk about being Japanese American . . . I noticed some of them talked about their activities and their participation in activities, but didn't specifically mention the Japanese American community. My impression is that they wouldn't fare very well because they need to be a representative of the Japanese American community.

Christie spoke about her work with Japanese American children and about how the pageant had been such a good experience. She then thanked the committee. She was smart to invoke the experience with children because it conveyed two themes. First, she had volunteered within the community and could be seen as committed to the community. It also conveniently led into the debate or anxiety about the future of the community (Fugita and O'Brien 1994; Spickard 1996). She had clearly invested in the future of the Japanese American community because she worked with Japanese American children. She was also more group minded and had thought of others beyond herself.

Many thanked the committee and discussed the pageant experience itself. In San Francisco in 2000, one queen candidate conveyed two aspects of collective identity recognition in offering these thanks. First, she argued that the pageant experience itself taught her a lot about herself. This is a common theme invoked to illustrate that the pageant brings a participant closer to the Japanese American community and culturally closer to the Japanese American ideal—often phrased as self development. She claimed, "The Cherry Blossom Pageant demonstrates that as young Japanese Americans we can participate in leadership roles, in the development of our community, and in the preservation of our culture" (Amy Kimura crowned 2000, 1). She was shaped by the pageant experience and considered herself more Japanese American because of it. Win or lose, she had the social capital (social ties) and cultural capital (knowledge of Japanese American culture) that came from the pageant experience. This viewpoint also helps to rationalize the perpetuation of the pageant itself. If women are still participating and still getting something out of it, even if they don't win, and it is teaching cultural values and practices, then it is seen as a reason to continue the pageant. Practically, she was also savvy because she knew that, win or lose, she would have to work with the committee in the future.

The Talent Section

The talent portion of the pageant varies from city to city and only San Francisco and Seattle have actual judged talent portions. Both Los Angeles and Honolulu provide entertainment during the pageant either in the form of professional dancers and entertainers doing a themed dancing and singing number (Los Angeles) or the queen candidates themselves dancing and singing to give the audience something more to look at and allow the women a chance to do something on stage that isn't judged (Honolulu). The judged talent portions in Seattle and San Francisco are not weighted heavily in the final judging, but they do help to create images of the women that can help or hurt them.

During the talent portion many candidates try to show how they can be conversant in Japanese American culture. Some clearly try to do something culturally Japanese to show their prowess at mastering Japanese culture. This can include hula, although it is a Native Hawaiian tradition, one that has been strongly associated with Japanese Americans in Hawaii, Japanese language poetry, koto, Japanese arts (such as *I-ai*, sword handling) or karate. Many candidates think a Japanese cultural art will lead them to the title. They assume the embodiment of cultural practices is linked to race and that this is one of the unspoken criteria. Some actually don't do a Japanese talent, but those who do hula and Japanese poetry clearly please the audience and receive the most applause. There were mixed gender and racial feelings about the karate presentation as the woman who did it was considered to be too masculine but, thankfully, culturally Japanese.

In other cities, like Honolulu, pageant organizers feel that there is no need for a talent competition. They argue that the winners never need to do hula as a part of their reign, public appearances and speeches, so why do it in the pageant. Honolulu prides itself on not having talent because it is superfluous to the queen's duties. However, Honolulu does have intensive cultural training classes such as ikebana and taiko lessons to teach the women about their culture. Seattle and San Francisco focus the most on the talent section. However, it is only worth 1.5 out of 10 points in San Francisco (15 percent). In Seattle, it is described as "contestants are asked to put together some form of creative expression lasting no more than two minutes. Talent, creativity, amount of effort put into the act, originality and ease of presentation are scored for 20 percent of the overall score."[6] Talent is also a racial performance and many candidates try, if they can, to do something culturally Japanese American to make clear that want to "appear" Japanese American.

In San Francisco, the talent portion was a way to entertain the audience, but it also promoted the sense of choosing a well-rounded queen. One past candidate said,

> They want someone of substance—someone well rounded, not just someone who can get up there and say a few words, walk in kimono and you are out of there. Even though talent isn't weighted heavily in the score, I wanted to do my best because you want to say, I've done karate or ballet or whatever for so many years. I want to showcase that. I remember one of the girls played piano but only on an elementary level. It was basic and that was what she did and I thought it was great. She was brave and not everyone is going to have a wonderful talent.

When asked if she thought the talent portion inhibits people from participating in the pageant, she replied:

> Yes, but then again, you get someone that is more well rounded with a talent requirement. We get someone who has done more than just ride on her looks.

Somehow the talent segment, even if not a significant portion of the score, works to ensure that the candidates in San Francisco, so they think, will be more substantive and a more talented or well-rounded queen than one who is just attractive. The talent display, no doubt, weeds out women who feel they have no talent and provides a screening device to capture the "right" type of woman for the queen pageant. The talent judging also subtly incorporates the opinions of the audience as it takes place in the presence of the audience reaction to each talent display. In this way, the role of the audience receiving the talent reflects the collective appeal of certain especially ethnic artistic and talent displays.

Conclusion

In this chapter, I have shown how collective definitions of Japanese Americanness are being determined in the context of Japanese American beauty pageants. In the past a nation-based paradigm of race had been used to judge who is Japanese American enough to represent the community as the queen. Now, racially based criteria are being applied to mixed-race candidates and the candidates are using ethnic strategies to prove their Japaneseness to those around them, particularly to the judges. In general, mixed-race women were made to feel inferior and thus on the defensive about their ethnicity, primarily because of their racial background. They understood this and accepted that the way they could prove themselves was via ethnic strategies such as speaking Japanese, using Japanese names, and trying to embody their Japanese culture through the cultural display of speech and talent. However, when they do this, they also draw attention to many monoracial candidates' lack of culture. This turns the race/ethnicity/culture nexus on its head and makes all of the participants see that race does not always determine ethnicity culture.

On a collective level, the embodiment of race and its correspondence with culture are disrupted by multiracial women in the pageant setting when they are placed in a racialized context where they must compensate for having less race by having more culture. This is clear in the ideal embodied types of the racial and ethnic intersections discussed in the first part of this chapter. Race is encased in bodies, and while some responses were bodily or physical (like changing eye or hair color), most were not. The beauty pageant participants compensated, regardless of racial background—mixed or monoracial—with ethnic and cultural cues to sway the judges (and others) into believing they were culturally authentic enough to be queen. Culture and race were so tied together in this particular social context (and more so than in most day-to-day racial practices) that cultural claims to acceptance and Japanese Americanness were used to try to influence racial meanings. The use of Japanese language or names, in combination with a correct appearance in kimono (as we will see in the next chapter), were worked upon in racial terms to achieve a bodily appearance in kimono backed up by a cultural knowledge demonstrated through speeches, talents, and language to make racial claims. The ideal types of the "hapa girl speaking Japanese" and the "cultural impostor" represent just a few of the different permutations that these racial claims could take. On different social levels of interaction, they show that the hierarchies of authenticity were often shaped most by which claims were accepted and authenticated and which were not.

The data in this chapter show how the definition of who is authentically Japanese American enough to represent the community has shifted over time and from context to context, but has remained strongly racialized. The racial component to Japanese Americanness has shifted, but is not totally erased. It is certainly not erased by the racial claims made by multiracial women who still want to represent the Japanese American community on a tried and tested terrain, one bound by racial eligibility rules and understandings. Erin Toki Barbaree wrote an essay after attending a Cherry Blossom Queen Pageant in San Francisco in which she writes about what her speech would be if she ran in the pageant:

> I did ponder what I would say if I had to give a speech about myself in the Cherry Blossom Queen Pageant. I thought about the position I would take, as a representative of San Francisco's Japanese American community on trips to Japan, where I had never been. I knew in an instant what my platform would be. I would address the changing face of the Japanese American community and that I am a representative of this new dimension. Proudly, I would stand before the judges and the audience in my kimono and tell them of the Hapas among them. I would go on and on, as an activist for the Hapa Community, speaking of the way that we cannot be ignored. We Hapas are a part of the Japanese American community, just as the Japanese American community is a part of us. As I realized, however, that I would never win with this platform. The judges would never allow someone who identified strongly as a person of mixed Japanese heritage to represent them. I believe that all but one of this year's candidates for queen were not fully Japanese. None of the multiethnic contestants, however, emphasized this aspect of themselves. They longer I sat there, the angrier this made me. It was as if in order to be queen, they had to pretend that they are something they are not. But what infuriated me the most was feeling that in competing to be the royalty of the community, declaring one's mixed would be suicide. (Barbaree 1995)

Some of the mixed-race queens challenge racial meanings by ethnically proving and working through race to make racial claims, but in the end they have to racially repackage themselves to fit in. In the next chapter, the analysis moves up a level of social interaction to examine how race work is done, not just in the pageant, but during and after it, and not just to control only racial meanings, but gendered meanings as well.

5 Patrolling Bodies: The Social Control of Race through Gender

The audience chatter dies down to a low hum. The crowd hushes and the noise recedes as the chair of the San Francisco Cherry Blossom Queen Pageant Committee takes center stage. He is met with excited and anxious applause. With a cordless microphone in his right hand, he raises his left hand in a welcome and says, "Welcome, ladies and gentlemen, to the Cherry Blossom Queen Pageant. Tonight you will see these young ladies and you will see beyond their superficial surfaces to see the women, really see them and the beauty found within each of them. Each of them embodies the grace and cultural pride of Japanese American women today."
—From the author's fieldnotes

Having looked at how race and ethnicity are constructed through individual racial claims being "done" in the pageant, this chapter looks more closely at the process of race work (how race and ethnicity are produced) and their link to social control. This racial production process is also a process of turning women into queens through the training and practicing to be queen.

Producing the Queen

Like race, gender and class were also performed in the different cities and regions on the stages of Japanese American beauty pageants. The moral link between gender and racial appearance and particularly the adornment (or lack thereof) of bodies took on a subtle class meaning that was all cast in a racialized normative gaze (Foucault 1979). Race and the process of racialization provided a way for committee members to rationalize their social control over candidates' bodies through repetition of gender norms constructed to back up claims to represent the local Japanese American (racial and cultural) community.

The morally "good" portrait of the queen, and corresponding class mobility that it takes to achieve being queen, is clear in the rules of the pageants. The rules state that: one must be eighteen to twenty-five or twenty-six (in Honolulu) and must not have been married or had a child, implying a good/nice girl image, which Christine Yano describes as banal and profound simultaneously. She writes,

> Are all beauty pageants banal? Perhaps, if they all only focus on the most superficial aspects of a woman. However, if in the process of crowning a Queen a beauty pageant galvanizes an ethnic group's sense of itself, if the Queen becomes a rallying point of group pride, if having a Queen proves a group's worthiness to themselves and to others, then I suggest that a beauty pageant under these particular historical circumstances rises above its own inherent banality and approaches profundity. (2006, 396)

The eligibility rules in the pageants serve as a screening device to shape the queen from the onset of the pageant training. When I asked organizers about these rules, they said that the women needed to be mature (in age) and, in the case of Seattle, which is a scholarship pageant, needed to be enrolled in higher education. They explained the rules by claiming that if a woman was married or had a family, she wouldn't have the time needed to dedicate to carrying out her duties as the queen. However, it is clear that the rules were also about projecting a certain image of a good, young, virginal, virtuous Japanese American woman. These characteristics seemed to be best judged through the practice of racially correct, middle-class (or aspiring to middle-class) values. However, the formal rules did not necessarily fit with the practices recognized or reinforced. For example, one of the chaperones and organizers in Honolulu told me that although they have those rules, they can't enforce them without prying too much into people's lives.

He told me, "Look, we know that we have girls living with their boy-friends, but what can we do? It is their life, but we tell them, 'Just don't get pregnant or you will have to go.'" In other words there should be no outward sign of premarital sex and if the transgression of the rule is so great that they can't ignore it, they will have to ask a participant to leave.

Ironically, the outside appearance of propriety is so important that in Honolulu they also guard the chaperones' and drivers' relationships with the contestants very carefully. The Japanese Junior Chamber of Commerce (Jaycees) of Honolulu, a predominantly male organization made up of business-oriented members, produces the pageant. The Jaycees who serve as supports during the pageant are not allowed to fraternize with the women in the pageant. The women are in close contact with these men throughout the year as they are driven to and from all appearances and chaperoned by them. As one chaperone ex-plained to me, "We tell them it is to protect yourself and ourselves for insurance purposes, but we are also trying to keep away the weirdoes from you. Put a girl in a crown and all types of weirdoes come out of the woodwork." Increased connections between Japanese American women and men is one of the stated goals of the pageant in the form of ties between the women and business people in the larger Japanese American community, but again only the "right" social relations can be pursued. In addition, the rules, phrased in terms of protection, also enable the chaperone to have tight control of the women's behavior and the image the organization and pageant are trying to promote. The women's deportment and behavior are controlled through the use of the potential to shame the community by their actions. In Honolulu, the Forty-fourth Cherry Blossom Festival Queen contestants' hand-book (1995) stated:

> During any public appearance, your behavior is a direct reflection upon yourself, your family, and the Cherry Blossom Festival. We therefore ex-pect you to act appropriately. . . . Please remember that as a queen contes-tant, many people will be watching and judging both you and the festival by how you act. (2)

By invoking cultural norms, the good behavior they want the queens to exhibit becomes oddly racialized. One chaperone explained to me that no smoking was allowed while dressed in kimono because it may burn the expensive fabric (silk) of the kimono (usually borrowed or donated for the occasion and very costly), but mainly because "it

looks bad to see a woman in traditional Japanese kimono with a ciga-
rette hanging out of her mouth."

Another used the pressure of community representation to control
behavior. In the instruction packet given to the queen and her court
before their visitation to Los Angeles' Nisei Week Festival, the San
Francisco Pageant Committee wrote:

> The Los Angeles visitation was established over many years and has been
> one of the ways that the Cherry Blossom Festival and the Nisei Week
> Festival have been able to renew its ties with one another. Many lifelong
> friendships have been established and the goodwill and understanding
> between the two groups has grown stronger.
>
> The trip to Los Angeles is an official visitation by the Cherry Blossom
> Queen and Court to the Nisei Week Festival. It should, therefore, not be
> construed as a personal vacation or holiday. Anyone choosing to attend this
> trip does so with the understanding that one will follow the program as
> prescribed. You are responsible and accountable to Cherry Blossom regard-
> ing your conduct and behavior while guests of the Nisei Week Festival.
> Your actions and activities reflect upon the Cherry Blossom Festival and
> are therefore to be carefully considered. This is not meant to put a damper
> on your activities, but is a reminder that you are in Los Angeles as guests
> of the Union Bank (Queen and First Princess) and the Nisei Week Festival
> (Everyone) and are representing Cherry Blossom Festival. Each person
> who goes on the Nisei Week Visitation should act as a goodwill ambassa-
> dress for the Cherry Blossom Festival with the purpose of cementing rela-
> tions between our two festivals. Oh yes, about boyfriends. No boyfriends!
> No family members or close friends not approved by the committee can be
> included in the group. (Goals and Purpose, Visitation packet)

In this passage, committee members invoked the community as an
extension of the family, thus separating a queen from her biological or
immediate family. The community becomes an extended family defined in racial/cultural terms, which the queen reflects and represents.
This uses the concept of *enryo* (obligation) and expands it beyond the
borders of the family to the Japanese American local community and
beyond. Bodily behavior on Japanese American women is enforced
through shame and social pressure to do race and gender in very particular ways. This is all couched in terms that draw attention to the
queen's role as a symbol and her corresponding work as an ambassadress. The politic, tiara-wearing, community tie builder takes on a
responsibility of being used by the committee and local community as
a representative of all local Japanese Americans to others through her
closely monitored appearance and behavior.

The attempts at socially controlling the queen have not always been successful, however, as several women didn't comply with the demands of the job of queen, either during or after their reigns. One female chaperone from Los Angeles explained,

> We have rules about curfews, abusive language, bad behavior, you know. I sent one home from Hawaii one time because her boyfriend was there, too, and she would be off with him and then come to things with us and she was saying swear words and we got complaints from several people, so I sent her home, but I got permission from the chairperson and from her sponsoring organization and they were supporting me.

Behavior wasn't the only reason for disqualification. Appearance also mattered. She continues,

> She broke the no-tanning rule twice. We told the girls that you can't get tan with straps because in your gown it looks lousy. Can you imagine being on the stage and having these big ol' strap marks? We told everybody—but she said, "Oh, but they'll fade by next time," and then she came next week with these even darker tan lines and we said, "You are just not ready to run if you can't abide by the rules."

Interestingly, in 1954 there was no need to spell out these behavioral issues. The main concern of the committee in the 1954 Nisei Week Queen Pageant in Los Angeles for bringing "disqualification for misconduct" as being "unethical" was stuffing the ballot box to try to cheat to win the pageant, which at the time was based on ticket sales. The definition of behavior and expectations has changed drastically over the years, responding to the changing social context in which it takes place. All of this draws attention to the way that gender is constructed, acted, and worked upon as a form of social control during and after the pageant experience.

Training and Practicing to Be Queen

The Kimono Segment and the Wearing of Race

Bodies, too, have to be trained to be royal. For example, the queen production process is racialized as many of the queen candidates, like contemporary women in Japan, wouldn't have ever had a reason to wear a kimono, much less own one. The cost alone (between $10,000 and $15,000) prohibits most women in Japan from owning one, and they would rent if they did have cause to wear one. Similarly, most of the queen candidates borrow or rent the kimono or the committee rents it on their behalf. The cultural meaning of the kimono is transient, borrowed or rented for the day and then returned. One of the big draws of winning the pageant in all of these cities is winning a kimono donated by a kimono company in Japan.

The women need the cultural connection to the community in the speech to complete the picture of the ideal Japanese American woman in kimono. Their appearance, including their racial uniform, is highlighted when in the kimono. Mixed-race skin against the kimono "looks different." One mixed-race queen in San Francisco said,

> But there again, when you don't look Japanese, it looks funny wearing a kimono. There are some pictures where to me I look funny, it doesn't match—culturally it doesn't match. The face doesn't match the clothes and I didn't really feel that way until I saw the pictures because at the time I felt wonderful when I was wearing the kimono. My mom said that she didn't realize, until she saw me in kimono, she told me, "Although you look the least Japanese out of all the candidates, my body structure is what back in her day a Japanese woman wished to have because of how you look in kimono." Because I have a long neck and that is important. She acknowledged it, it made her aware. It was like, "Wow, you may not look it, but there are other parts of you that are very Japanese."

Her physical and racial appearance looked funny or incongruous to her and possibly others because the assumption is that race equals culture. When these two concepts are disrupted by the mixed-race queen who is really very culturally Japanese, she disconnects, for only a moment, the idea of race from ethnicity. In the above quote, though, the mixed-race queen reinscribes race and physical appearance with power because it is the wearing of the kimono that makes her more authentic precisely because it is a physical experience and embodiment of culture.

In Honolulu, the kimono section of the pageant was given more credence and time in the pageant schedule. Each woman was introduced slowly in both Japanese and English (the only section of the pageant that was bilingually translated) by an interracial couple (he, who was Caucasian, spoke English, but apparently had very good grasp of the Japanese language, and she, who was Japan Japanese, spoke in Japanese). Each woman, clad in kimono, glided from one corner of the stage, bowed, and took a Japanese parasol from a man clad in traditional Japanese garb (usually a Jaycee who had to be strong-armed into doing it). Then, walking slowly, she turned, put the parasol down, and bowed to the audience before she left the stage from the opposite side. This was accompanied by the English and Japanese explanation of the kimono she was wearing, the color and why it suited her, what the pattern on the kimono meant, and why it was important.

The kimono section also provides practical training for all of the appearances the queen will make in the upcoming year. The queen will need knowledge of the community or appearance of some knowledge in order to make comments about how they will represent the Japanese American community. All of the women use race work to do this. Familiarity with Japanese American culture (through displays like those discussed below in the talent section of the pageant) combine with discussion of community ties to highlight their appearance as the typical Japanese American woman.

The kimono also symbolizes the racialization of the body in Japanese terms. One pageant organizer in San Francisco explained:

> I think the kimono is important. I think the queen would feel privileged to wear a kimono. She would be proud. It is just another pageant without it. The kimono presentation and the formal kimono segment, that is the only real Japanese thing they are doing, culturally and that is why I want to incorporate the real Japanesey stuff at the beginning to get that across.

Traditional beauty in kimono in Japan is assumed to follow different standards. The shape of the body in kimono is padded to have a straight waist. The hourglass figure is out, replaced by the flattened chest and widened waist of the kimono. In order for the *obi* (belt) of the kimono to be tied appropriately, the waist must be flat and wide and extra padding is added if a woman doesn't have enough natural padding herself. The bodily transformation of the women often brought the Japanese and Western beauty ideals in contrast with each other as the women verbally complained or sighed when their trim waists were padded for a rounder H-like figure rather than an hourglass figure. The hair, too, was changed. Even if they didn't have long hair, hair extensions were added to give them big hair with cotton batting. Then it was tied up on top of their heads, loosely interspersed with flowers and trinkets. The big hair took getting used to and the weight of the hair made their necks ache. The most sexy part of the body in kimono was meant to be the nape of the neck, which had to be shaved in some cases and exposed with hair up and kimono collar pulled down and back a bit to reveal some, but not all of the nape of the neck. Most of the candidates again had to be told this and shown how to best wear their kimonos to be beautiful "the Japanese way."

The women said they felt racially inauthentic at having to be taught not only how to wear the kimono, but also the symbolism behind each of the layers that they put on and how to move in it. They felt that women in contemporary Japan would have this tacit knowledge and wouldn't have to be taught how to do this part of culture, but in reality they probably would be. The kimono teacher in San Francisco explained why Japanese American women need guidance to learn how to wear the kimono properly.

> It is really hard to teach them. I guess it is just easier to show them what we mean and I don't mean to be picking on them, nitpicking them, but we just want them to be able to do it properly, especially when they are on stage because we do hear comments, "Oh, God, those girls don't know how to walk in kimonos, do you see them in their zori?!" So we want to try to teach them so they look a little bit . . . better, more natural.

However, Japanese women in contemporary Japan would also need help getting dressed in the kimono and, like the women in San Francisco, would need to pay a dresser to help them achieve the desired effect. They also have had no experience wearing a kimono or walking in one. In fact, all the women, regardless of racial background, talked about the wearing of the kimono as a real treat and how they learned about their Japanese culture through the pageant specifically because of the chance to wear a kimono. One past Nisei Week Queen describes the experience this way,

> The kimono represents our heritage. We've all got part Japanese in us. It is a great way for us to learn some of the traditional garbs. How our great-great-grandparents had to wear these clothes and how they had to care for them. A lot of it is not so much having to wear it or walk around in it, but learning the culture of Japan. By wearing kimono you learn a lot of the etiquette and how to respect what you are wearing. You learn how to respect other people who are wearing it. It is a good way to bring a physical part of your culture alive.

It is the bodily experience of wearing the kimono that makes them feel more Japanese and enact what they deem as culture in a physical realm.

From backstage training, I know that most if not all of the women in the pageant had never worn a kimono before and needed to be taught or trained how to wear it. They needed to be told what each layer symbolizes and what the parts of it are called. Once it was on their bodies, they had to learn to walk in it. One entire practice session was spent learning how to bow and "walk Japanese" with toes pointed slightly inwards, knees slightly bent, and thighs stuck together like glue. Some women walked so American, parting their thighs, that the instructors tied their legs together with pantyhose at the thighs so that they literally could not get their legs apart. Others tried to accomplish this by wearing a *ukata* (light summer wrap style of kimono) for practice, which they could get easily, instead of the expensive furisode kimono. This then, was a racialization of bodily movements writ large, as they had to learn and be trained to embody Japanese womanhood in the cultural practice of wearing the kimono.

They also learned Japanese deportment, with flirtatious movements using the sleeves of their kimono in the opening musical number to display both themselves and the kimono to the best of their ability. This is a highly choreographed performance where traditional Japanese dancing moves are used to highlight the Japaneseness of the bodies involved. They learned to bend their knees slightly, turn 90 degrees to the right with their upper body, while planting their feet firmly on the ground and lifting the long sleeves of the kimono with both hands to show the pattern of the sleeve to the audience. They also had to learn to tip their heads slightly to the right and look fetchingly over their shoulder—flirting in kimono, Japanese style. The effect was one of total and complete feminine wiles and emphasized coquettishness while not revealing cleavage or leg. The contrast to Western bathing-suit competitions was clear. Less was definitely more in Western terms, but in Japanese terms these women had to retrain themselves to think of covering up as sexy. Moving slowly and flirting with body language and not body parts was part of the performance of Japanese femininity.

The kimono section of the pageant was also the gendered cultural pinnacle of the pageant. It symbolized the ties with Japan in the material good of the kimono as a symbol not just of Japanese culture, but also of Japanese womanhood. Kimono wearing was also a symbol of the social ties between Japan, where the kimonos come from, and the local Japanese American community. However, it focuses on particularly antiquated forms of Japanese femininity that are not present even in modern-day Japan. Again, the correct deportment was important because of larger community views. One past Nisei Week Queen said,

> The queen does appear in kimono a number of times in public. I think when you hear the public ask the Nisei Week Queen to appear, a lot of

people want you to be in kimono. It is that whole flavor of the Japanese American community. You can look very awkward in a kimono if you don't walk correctly, if you don't handle yourself nicely. I think they [the committee] are just worried. The person who donates the kimono—that is a very large gift. He would just cringe if he saw people crossing their legs in it or waving their arms around or wiping their mouths on their sleeves. I think it is just a traditional look.

In Hawaii, they claim that their pageant is more culturally authentic than others through their kimono competition. The kimono segment of the Honolulu pageant is a very somber affair with bilingual Japanese and English presentation of the women and the kimonos. Unlike Los Angeles and San Francisco, where they wear similar or identical kimonos, each woman in Hawaii wears a different kimono, which is chosen for her by the Kimono Company and dresser to suit her body and personality. They then read the story of the design of the kimono, usually focused on the natural symbols printed on the silk itself, such as leaves, flowers, water, mountains, and the colors or mood that the kimono creates on its wearer. In this sense, the woman's body is truly a field on which the artwork of the kimono's design and color are exhibited. She is just the model of the kimono and it defines her, not she it. The women in Hawaii also do much training to be able to walk in the zori, display the kimono properly (without the long sleeves, which signify the unmarried status of the women, touching the ground), bending carefully to show how well they have learned to move within the Japanese cultural art of kimono wearing.

The Hawaii committee also trained the women in the cultural arts, requiring them to take classes. Believing that the women do not have the cultural knowledge they should as the queen and future court, the committee decided to train them in taiko, ikebana, tea ceremony, and, of course, kimono. This cultural training was just what some of the women wanted; they joined the pageant ranks to learn more about their culture. One queen wrote,

I believe that I have become much more knowledgeable about my Japanese culture by attending these cultural classes as a Cherry Blossom contestant. Also, by participating in these cultural classes I learned about the discipline and patience needed to perfect the Japanese art forms. Now, when I think of my Japanese culture, I no longer imagine only mochi-pounding and rice. Instead, I also consider the artistic and ritual aspects of the Japanese culture and I reflect upon my Japanese identity with greater appreciation. Becoming more familiar with my cultural heritage has made me prouder to be Japanese because by learning more about the Japanese culture, I gained a new sense of ownership of it. Now, I see myself as truly being Japanese rather than just being of Japanese descent.

Now she is no longer a cultural impostor with race but no culture to back it up. She has learned the culture that fits with her Japanese ancestry—the queen and court are not natural expressions of race and ethnicity, but are produced as symbols of the tie between ancestry and culture. But to what version of Japanese culture is she referring? There is a tendency, illustrated in this instance in Hawaii, to associate authenticity with antiquated Japanese values supposedly apparent in the cultural arts. Somehow, Japan and its corresponding arts were thrown back into time, a time when the queen's grandparents or great-grandparents came over from Japan. These antiquated versions of Japanese culture are no less or more authentic than Japanese modern art or jazz or Japanese American adaptations of Japanese cultural forms, for example, Spam *musubi* (a traditional Japanese rice ball with the American addition of Spam, a popular food in Hawaii after World War II). In fact, one Cherry Blossom Queen in Hawaii was shocked to learn that they don't have kimono segments in pageants in Japan. She told me,

> I was so surprised because when we went to Oda Wada on our trip, we met up with the court members. There were three of them that represented their community and we were asking them about their pageant in all broken Japanese and we said, "Oh, what about your kimono phase?" and they said, "Oh, no we don't have a kimono phase because it is way too expensive!"

The conditioning of deportment is racialized as the women are taught how to bow, to hand business cards to people with two hands, and to move their bodies in distinctly Japanese ways. The kimono segments in all the cities studied reveal almost a preoccupation with the bodily and racial deportment of the queen, but it is not just bodily practices that get learned, taught, and worked upon in the pageant. The "voice," too, of the women is racialized and made more culturally appropriate through training and practice.

Judging the Interview: Racializing Voice

My fieldwork in the mid-1990s with the Cherry Blossom Queen Pageant Committee in San Francisco brought me back into the field as a judge for the Northern California Cherry Blossom Queen pageant a few years later. I was sworn to secrecy about my impending judgeship because if no one knew that I was judging, no one would try to influence me. When we arrived, the judges were sequestered away into a back conference room and I learned that I was to be made head judge because, the chair explained, they trusted me to guide the other judges. I interpreted this to mean that they thought I knew the cultural norms of what they expected of these women and they trusted me to pick whom they wanted us to choose. However, I was not so sure that it would be easy as the process was explained and the other judges made their visions about who would be good very clear. We had received the essays in advance, and I was struck that all of them mentioned the pageant as community service and all of them invoked cultural betterment for themselves or others in their essays. There were certain racialized discourses that ran through the essays and the interviews that I examine here.

The judges introduced themselves and talked about what they were looking for. We learned that scores for each section ranged from 1 to 10, with 10 being the highest. We were then coached to start at 5 and then work up or down as we saw fit. The highest and lowest scores in each category would be thrown out, so since there were seven of us, only five scores counted. I thought, do I give 9s to ensure that my 10 won't get thrown out? Is it a race to the middle with a mediocre 5 or 6 across all the categories winning it all?

The judges were a past queen, two academics (including me), a modern dance teacher who was multiracial, a Japanese American businessman, and a well-known younger community leader who headed a Japanese American youth organization and has in the past been extremely critical of the pageant. He wondered aloud what qualifications he had to judge. This was a good point, but the committee soon assured him that he had the cultural knowledge and the social connections to know what a good queen is. As soon as the women came into the room, though, it was clear why he had been asked. All the women talked about community service and the links to being Japanese American. The young man ran a community service organization and seemed well able to detect genuine interest in community service from the pageant lingo of "saving the world." The community service that they purported to do in the pageant took on a much more visible nature (i.e., others could see them doing it) than much of the work he had done in the past. The judges seemed to be looking for leadership ability, artistic ability, political awareness, and thoughts about the future of the Japanese American community and youth involvement.

Next the candidates came in one by one. They were dressed either in kimono or a business suit with big kimono hair piled up on top of their heads. It was almost farcical with the big swoops of hair pinned tightly onto their heads and their pale-faced makeup with lined eyes and small, pert, red mouths outlined. They were geishas in powersuits, dressed this way because directly after the interview they must be dressed in kimono for the pageant. They were nervous. We tried to make them relax with jokes and smiles, but ultimately this might have been the hardest part of the pageant for them. I knew from rehearsals that the women had been coached to "be yourself" and "imagine the judges in their underwear, they are people, too." I hoped that mine were clean and in respectable condition.

The judges all asked different questions about how the younger generation sees the changes in the local Japanese American community. The dance teacher asked one candidate about the importance of hula, her talent, and how it helped her express herself. Others asked about her best characteristic and what she felt should be done to increase youth involvement. Questions took on a consistent pattern. Where have you traveled? What do you think the future leadership of the community will look like? If selected as queen, how do you see yourself in the mainstream community? The first candidate did well discussing Japanese American traditional culture and heritage as a source of strength. I thought, It sounds good, but what does it mean? Finally she was asked the real question: "Why do you want to be queen?"

She explained that being queen for her was about contributing individually to the community and representing the community. She appeared egalitarian because she was willing to settle for being a princess, but this might reflect not being able to make up her mind and be a good leader. Judges may see it as a weakness to not want the title of queen enough, but all the women are caught in the dilemma that if they want it too much they violate the Japanese American cultural value of modesty. This is a difficult situation where community service is linked to competition *and* self-recognition.

In other cities, the interview is handled differently. In Seattle, for example, the interview happens before the pageant proper and is a one-on-one interview with each of the judges, not a panel interview as in San Francisco. The speech in kimono is where the Seattle candidates are asked, according to the Pageant Judging Criteria (1996), to "prepare a one-minute biographical sketch about herself which should include her reasons for seeking the title of Japanese Community Queen."

One of the strongest themes that emerged from the interviews in all the cities as well as in essays in Seattle and San Francisco was that the pageant was a way to contribute to "community service." This is a nice way to cast their participation because it is not, supposedly, motivated by self-aggrandizement, but giving back to the community. The participants in the pageant I judged claimed that Cherry Blossom is different from mainstream pageants because they are not pyramid pageants and do not have big money or recognition tied to them. The Cherry Blossom pageant has mostly local recognition but all of the women become princesses and will be in the Japanese American public eye. Women also feared their family would be shamed by their loss because the pageant was so public and so local. Pageant participation was seen by some as a feminist move to still put themselves out there and to risk losing and shaming family and friends to serve the community better (Wu 1997).

Another candidate explained that she was a student at a local university. She was asked for clarification about why she chose to read poetry as her talent. She wanted to be queen in order to mentor young people and make them aware of their Japanese American cultural history. The committee liked the answer. She said that she thought that as queen her age worked for her in reaching out to young Japanese Americans in their formative preteen and teen years to get them to be more involved. The committee loved this as they knew that the future of the community depends upon the involvement of the "nosei" generation (who are so named because they feel that the old Issei, Nisei, Sansei, Yonsei classification doesn't fit them and/or they feel they have "no say" in what goes on). She capitalized on the increasing anxiety around the youth in the Japanese American community and the future of the community. She also invoked the community service narrative, but she made it clear that she wanted to do service to the Japanese American community because of obligation to the community, illustrating a desire to have strong ties to community. This social capital can also be parlayed later into jobs and political connections within the Japanese American community. In a place like Honolulu, where much political and economic control rests in Japanese American hands, this is a meaningful link to future ethnic opportunities.

When asked why she wanted specifically to be queen, she gave an ideal answer: "It is important to be involved, not just to be queen." Somehow when she said it, it didn't sound wimpy or too egalitarian. It was modest without seeming weak and we were on the way to finding a winner. She did the best of the group because she was serious, direct, and well spoken, but she had a sense of humor, too, and had paid her dues, working locally in her grandparents' shop. She also had the all-important commitment to a social cause (youth), a particular worry for many aging Japanese Americans and their organizations, and she sprinkled in Japanese American cultural values, such as commitment to participating in the group and community and making sure young people know their Japanese American culture and history. As she spoke, it was clear that she was linking Japanese American youth (defined racially) to not knowing about their cultural history. By linking race to culture through community she accomplished the goal of tying the future of the community to racial and ethnic members. The only way to save the community is through the cultural education of racially Japanese American youth—a claim that judges are unlikely to question.

As the interviews wore on, we, the judges, tired of asking the same questions and some of the questions started to change. "How would you represent our [the Japanese American] community inside the community to Japanese Americans and outside to the mainstream community?" One woman answered, "I would do community service and receive from others and I would give young Japanese Americans leadership roles." In addition, her community service was missionary work in her church-related activities in Japan and that made some of the judges uncomfortable. When asked, "What opportunities are there for Japanese American women?" she claimed that Japanese American women can have any position.

The women didn't always follow directions; they spoke about explicitly political issues, and were too loud and brash, against the wishes of the committee members and various handlers, who saw this behavior as distinctly non–Japanese American. The tie between behavior and culture gets racialized because the link between bodily behavior and cultural practice implies certain gendered codes of behavior. The committee members again have coached them to try to control what they say and the image of Japanese Americanness that they portray. They monitor the women in order to depict them as the representatives of the Japanese American community and they need community connections and authentic cultural resources to do so.

In the interviews in San Francisco, a mixed-race candidate was immediately asked about her multiracial background even though none of the others were asked about their monoracial ones. She talked about traveling to Tokyo and attending bilingual (Japanese/English) language school and visiting her family in Japan (all ways to prove her cultural competence and social ties). The others didn't do this, possibly because they didn't need to do this to prove their Japanese Americanness.

One judge asked how mixed-race kids could feel more connected to the Japanese American community. The question assumes that they aren't or that they are rejected and an effort should be made to incorporate them. She didn't pick up on this but used the multiracial case as a way to argue for more Japanese American community participation. She said that if they see other mixed-race Japanese Americans of their age involved, they will become more involved and feel more welcome. She felt that she could be a representative to the younger generation with her Japanese American side and bring Japanese American culture to them. There was no discussion of white culture or her white side. She was clearly sending messages through her facial and bodily appearance to others who didn't consider her to be fully Japanese American. She then had to do cultural work such as using a Japanese name, speaking in Japanese, or proving her Japanese American cultural connections to be seen as Japanese American (King 1997).

The next candidate was not from San Francisco. She felt her strength came from having immigrant parents and going to a Japanese school with kids from Japan. She felt that she needed to give back and say thank you, despite the fact that it wasn't to this community that she owed thanks.

She was a social worker and said she saw how the stigma of mental illness is handled in the Japanese American community via shame; she saw being queen as an opportunity to give back and do community service and also, as queen, she recognized that her opinion might get more attention and people might listen to her more. Either way she wanted to represent the community well both inside and outside the community. She was also asked about the role of young people. She said that she felt the queen needs to advocate for the younger generation through modeling service to community and encouraging more young Japanese Americans to go into social service jobs. For her talent she wrote poetry in Japanese, which many of the judges felt was the first real artistic (and authentic?) contribution. As the judges we couldn't judge because we don't know what is authentic and what is not. In fact, we might or might not have any idea what is good talent or not and are not sure what that has to do with being queen other than trying to ensure that she was well rounded.

The mixed-race queen disrupts the racial and gender understanding of what is Japanese American. She disrupts the link between morality and the body, which is assumed for Japanese American women. Because racial authenticity is questioned, other aspects of her self (gender, sexuality) are also questioned. Mixed-race women have to prove their Japanese Americanness to pass, but they also have to do the work of proving they are women. This type of work is constructed as race work that must be done in order to make claims not just about race but also about gender and class. That is not to say that "gender work" and "class work" do not get done, but "race work" seems to underpin many of these other claims and is often the basis of whether gender or class can be claimed after and below race.

In an era of the "fear of the dilution" of the community through intermarriage and assimilation, mixed women seek to reaffirm that they may be racially half but that they won't let the culture die. Preservationists' hopes may get pinned to mixed-race women's bodies. Their candidacy for queen is a platform to discuss the anxiety about the dissolution of the community that they represent. The queens may or may not see themselves that way. They participate on the same cultural terms and seek to reify the same cultural meanings as before—such as through the kimono wearing—and they assure others that the culture and community won't die but will continue via multiracial participation. Throughout this process the emphasis is solely on Japanese Americanness and Japanese American parents, as their non–Japanese American parents are written out of the community's script almost completely.

Question and Answer

The question-and-answer section of the pageant brings together the themes of the community and Japanese American cultural preservation. This is often the "make or break" point of the pageant as it comes at the very end of the pageant and is the last section to be judged before the tallies are done and the winner announced. In rehearsals, the candidates were given preparation questions to think about, but on the night of the pageant, not knowing the question made them anxious. The year that I did research, there was such secrecy around what the question would be that the committee chairman didn't want to write it down and we came to the question-and-answer phase of the pageant without a question in the envelope to hand to the emcee. With the emcee stalling on stage and the first candidate nervously tugging at the hem of her dress, the chairman came running from the audience and quickly scribbled the question onto a napkin. He wrote, "Being a Japanese American woman, how do you think that Japanese American women can work to change the stereotype of Asian American women today?" There are assumptions in this question that Japanese (and by default all other Asian) American women have an undesirable image. In addition, there is embedded in this question a question about feminism—an often unspoken concept in the context of the pageants. Other practice questions have been:

What is your reply to people who criticize pageants?
What is it going to take for this country to elect a woman president?
What is the biggest challenge facing women of today?
If you were embarking on a grand adventure, what would it be?
What have you learned most from this pageant experience?
Only 20 percent of eligible voters under 25 years of age vote—in your opinion, why?
Is there too much violence and sex on TV today? Why?

The questions are general social- and political-interest questions mixed with questions about the candidates themselves. Their purpose, we were told, was to see how the candidates each think on their feet and articulate their thinking in front of a crowd. The chairman explained to me that this is one of the most important skills that the queen will need when she goes out into the world to represent the "us" that is Japanese Americans. The irony is that the stereotype of beauty queens does not really include someone who is intelligent or politically aware. However, she is expected to be able to speak on all areas of life on behalf of the Japanese American community she represents. She will be interviewed by many local and international press sources and will need to show she is smart, thoughtful, well educated, well informed, compassionate, well spoken, and in touch with the local Japanese American community. The chairman explained that this is the section of the pageant where "winners are made." Although the candidates appear in very sleek evening gowns and high heels, he feels that the appearance in this section really takes a sideline to the content and style of the answer.

When I was a pageant judge, each candidate was asked in turn, "If given the opportunity to ask any question of any generation of Japanese American what question would you ask and why?" All are asked the same question and the others can't hear the question being asked or answered.

The impromptu answers reflected knowledge of the history of Japanese Americans and recalled and illustrated respect for the Issei through responses like "I would ask the Issei, why did you come to the U.S.?" Others looked to the future, saying that they would ask the Yonsei, "Why are you apathetic?" playing on the existing anxiety about the future of the community and its dependence upon the youth. The ultimate winner asserted that she wanted to prove to the community and ourselves (meaning the candidates) that we (youth) can help and that we can make or break the community. She identified the youth as crucial in the changing demographics of the Japanese American community. She claimed, in California slang, that she wanted to "pump it up one level." Her knowledge, enthusiasm, and commitment got her a high score.

Others illustrated cultural and historical knowledge by discussing the Nisei and the internment experience and responded that they would ask, "What was it like being a citizen in camp?" or "How did internment affect the Issei and Nisei emotionally and physically?'

There was strictly no conferring among judges and I began to wonder whether we were looking for the same things. There was no prior discussion of, or agreement on, the criteria upon which we were basing our judgments.

Judging and the Judges

The pageant judges play a crucial role in perpetuating or changing racial, gender, and bodily norms in the process of choosing the queen each year. After being a judge, which included much internal arm-

twisting and personal anguish, I realized that judging itself is not systematic within each city and certainly not consistent across cities. The
same bodily racial requirements are not played out in the same ways.

Judges are carefully chosen by the committee and screened. Usually
there is an attempt to have some Japanese American or Japanese business leaders and some local community Japanese American leaders.
In Los Angeles they draw from the entertainment (primarily movie
and television) industry but try to limit the number of non–Japanese
American judges for fear that too many mainstream criteria will seep
in. Many times judges are local Japanese dance teachers, local youth
organizers, community leaders, lawyers, businesspeople and political
office-holders, professors, and past queens. Recently in San Francisco
an effort has been made to include women's issues (read: feminist) leaders in the Japanese American and mainstream communities in order
to dispel antiwomen and antifeminist critiques of the pageant. They
have also recently tried to include Japanese American academics, reporters, and businesswomen who are known feminists. One reporter
who was asked to be a judge broke the call for silence about being
asked and called me to ask my opinion on the matter. As a feminist,
she was concerned; her knee-jerk reaction was to say, "No, absolutely
not." However, after coaxing from her husband and daughter, she was
reconsidering and wondering if she could help change the process to
make it better by being a judge. This type of situation was symbolic of
the anxiety around the pageant and its relationship to feminism.

The issue of feminism and its impact on judging is clear in the
questions asked by judges in the conversations that I had with several
of them in the years since 2000. Our conversations focused on our
commitment to feminist ideals and trying to work from within the
system to undo culturally specific patriarchal structures. When inside
the pageant, though, neither I nor the other feminist judges were rude
enough to be a total rebel. We didn't choose an inappropriate queen
or question or refuse to participate in the process. I think we tried
to make sure that we brought our ideals of a politicized outspoken
woman into the pageant judging criteria, but in the end we were com-
plicit with the pageant form. The other judges asked me if it is possible
to be a feminist and a judge. In both my case and the case above, we
two decided to participate, much to our discomfort, because we were
asked by people whom we knew and felt obligated to people such as
former students who were now involved or fellow church members.

We found the judging criteria to be difficult to fault because it was primarily about speaking, thinking critically on one's feet, writing well, and being committed to social change or cultural preservation within the Japanese American community.

Once the judging categories are laid out, it is up to the individual judges to interpret the criteria. This process is both arbitrary (it can go any way on a given night) and carefully calculated (minute details are scrutinized in the scoring). In San Francisco, each section is weighted; for example, talent is worth less than Q&A, and each section is marked on a 1–10 scale with 10 being the highest. The points are very exact and the high and low scores are thrown out. The scores are then calculated by professional accounting-firm employees gratis. There is a numerical scale and the weights are very carefully calculated. In San Francisco the pageant organizers are trying hard to distance themselves from the mainstream (and, they think, sexist and vacuous) pageants to emphasize community service and culture. This echoes other discourses in more mainstream pageants like the Miss America contest that integrate service as part of the judging criteria. The difference here is that there is a direct, not a vague and general, service to a clearly defined racial/ethnic community.

The criteria officially judged are essay, interview, speech in kimono, talent, and question-and-answer in evening gown in San Francisco. All of the criteria above require spoken or oral communication skills, quick wit, and thinking. The kimono and evening gown are really just accoutrement to the mainstay of the judging, which is speech and Q&A. That said, appearances clearly matter. They don't just give the speech in a t-shirt and jeans, and the questions are not asked with the candidates behind a screen as they could be. Clearly, the appearance, particularly the racialized bodily appearance of the women, matters. In fact, the choice of dresses they wear in the evening-gown part of the competition is almost always shaped by the committee/organizers. They suggest a long (full-length), not-too-revealing gown. The color and style are up to the candidate. In Los Angeles, the gowns are the same and designed and donated by a local Japanese American fashion designer.

Attempts are made to draw attention away from the beauty and embodiment issues, but can women who are too large to squeeze into spaghetti-strap dresses and too "butch" in terms of talent win? It seems that having a big bust or being tall is not necessarily as important as being well spoken and neatly pulled together. Class is embodied and the need to have money to get all the right tasteful outfits, either through borrowing or buying them, is subtly judged.

Certain middle-class cultural capital is needed to be well read, politically aware, articulate, and a quick thinker on one's feet. Caren, a past queen, was asked in the question-and-answer section, "If you could cure any disease, what would it be and why?" Her answer was "If I could cure any disease it would have to be ignorance." This was immediately deemed a clever answer and was a way to work in a politically correct agenda about teaching tolerance for difference. It also showed her intelligence and political savvy.

Judges may have subjective perceptions of what is beautiful, which may vary greatly. Despite there being no official place to put "beauty" on the voting ballot, it finds its way into the judging criteria through noncategorical qualities like "poise" and "grace."

Participants' height and weight vary and there are no rules about who can enter based on bodily characteristics. In fact, in San Francisco, they ask for the height of the women privately with a long explanation about how this helps them to assign the right length kimono and will determine how they stand. But all this happens under racial rules. Typically they are arranged by height, with the tallest in the middle and the two shortest on either end. Many people told me that age certainly helps with older, more mature, better spoken, less flighty or superficial candidates doing better. However, the candidates deemed too serious didn't do as well either. There needs to be a balance. The queen needs to be well versed in Japanese American issues. When asked in Q&A about claims that the community is struggling, one candidate didn't know what the emcee was talking about. She said that she had worked in her grandparents' store locally and that she and her family go to a Japanese American church and that everything is just fine. There was stunned silence in the judging pit as her answer clearly indicated her ignorance of Japanese American community issues and a lack of recognition of the larger political and cultural sphere.

Preparation of the judges beforehand included attempts to standardize and condition the voting and to remind the judges of the goals of the pageant. The judges were also trained and monitored by the committee members and organizers. For example, one of the long-standing pageant organizers, Cedrick, sat in the judging room. The committee told us that he was there to protect the girls from unnecessary or inappropriate questions, but I know from my time on the committee that he was also there to subtly shape the judging process and hopefully to shape the outcome so that the committee would get someone they can work with in the year to come.

Who Is the Audience?

Those who attend the pageant and constitute the audience receive and shape the pageantry being produced and presented. The literal bodies in the audience at the pageant represent the imagined larger audience of the Japanese American community to which the pageant orients itself and aids in the enforcement of the image of the good Japanese American girl through the pageant. Many studies of pageants analyze the role that audiences play in pageants in terms of the public and often vocal support or disapproval of the way the candidates are chosen, the criteria for judging, the support for the judges themselves, and ultimately the choice of queen (Callahan 1998). These studies examine pageants as cultural texts that reflect larger social and cultural issues and debates. Here I try to go beyond the textual analysis of pageants to analyze the process of the pageant itself. Who is shaping the text that is witnessed as the performance on the pageant night, and how are race and, particularly, real bodies construed in this process?

Differences in class, gender, politics, and culture, as well as racial and ethnic meanings, all have to be managed within the pageant. The pageant serves as a platform for people to cast their vote for the version of Japanese Americanness that they want to celebrate. It is a chance to debate cultural and community issues in a socially acceptable, not too serious way, without disrupting the harmony of the community too much.

The audience, then, is as telling as the queen herself about the nature of the "we" that is being culturally constructed in the pageant. The judges particularly, but the audience more generally, tell us who is invested enough in the pageant and what it stands for to pay to attend or participate in it. For the most part, the pageant is quite small and attended by mostly family and friends of each of the candidates and committee members and visiting royalty from the other cities such as Los Angeles, San Francisco, Seattle, and Honolulu. Also in attendance, and highly catered to, are the sponsors and the local ethnic press. Very rarely are mainstream press present or people who just drop in to see the pageant. The emcees are almost always known in the community, have some connection, that is, are Japanese American, and are public figures such as newscasters, actors, past queens, or radio personalities.

This audience spins outwards, getting larger and more complex, as the pageant year wears on. In San Francisco the queen and court initially appear only at the pageant. However, the next morning they are brought out in the public eye having only been seen publicly in the newspaper and on the posters up to that point. On the first day of her reign, the queen and her court appear in kimono walking through the Cherry Blossom Festival, sampling the food, greeting children, posing for photos, and ultimately appearing on one of the open air stages in the Peace Plaza, centrally located in the center of San Francisco's Japantown, to draw the winning raffle tickets. The excitement builds as each princess and finally the queen is introduced and the emcee chats with them, strategically drawing out the process of awarding the grand prize, a new car, through raffle-ticket selection.

The following weekend they will ride, clad in their kimonos, with the queen in her kimono, on the final float of the parade. The highlight of their performance will be when their float stops in front of the viewing stand filled with the major (Japanese business) sponsors and the queen and her court bow to the sponsors and dignitaries. The committee members trot alongside the float trying to make sure that no one falls off and to facilitate their relationship with the audience of the parade watchers by drawing their attention to people they should wave and smile at.

In addition, the queen and her court make local courtesy calls in the lead up to the pageant itself, both advertising themselves and the pageant in general. These appearances are used to boost interest in the competition, introduce the women to the community, and sell raffle tickets. They visit the Japanese Tea Garden (one of the candidate sponsors) for a photo shoot under the very fragile and hopefully blooming cherry blossom trees, a golf tournament, and, of course, endless press conferences. Then they visit Seattle in late May, Los Angeles in August for Nisei Week, and Honolulu in March for the Cherry Blossom Festival. Each of these appearances is for a slightly different audience, moving from the local Japanese American community in the Bay Area, for example, to the larger community and then to other Japanese American communities.

Who Me? The Winner? Gee . . .
Learning to Manage Emotions in the Pageant

The cultural and racial expectations in front of the audience, whether on stage or during an appearance, also extend to the behavior and even the emotions of the participants. Part of being a good Japanese American girl was also not to appear too needy to win the pageant nor to want to win it too badly. The mantra of "we are all here to better ourselves and have a new cultural experience," though, did not hide the raw competition that exists just behind this motto. Competition was masked also by the discourse of community involvement and cultural learning. It did, however, still deliver social ties (competitive and negative ones included) to those who participate. In fact, in the pageant, many of the committee members in San Francisco who were the most involved year after year, long after their court had been retired, were women who did not win the pageant and were particularly disappointed. They saw their role now, as organizers of the pageant, to console women who did not win. After all, they knew how it felt to lose. They also justified their participation as due to the fact that they hadn't quite gotten a fair chance in the pageant and wanted to make it better for others so this was a way to stay involved with the pageant without being queen.

Often female committee members performed bodily and beauty advising and fixed the looks of the participants before photos and similar occasions. Immediately after the queen was crowned, the former queen and committee members would flood onto the stage, as if they were invisible, and perform what would usually be a backstage behavior such as primping, fixing makeup and hair, straightening sashes and crowns so that when the formal photos were taken by the press and others they all looked their best. The female past queens turned committee members also subtly spoke gently to the losers, encouraging them to *gambatte* (persevere) and to above all keep smiling and try to be happy for the queen and hide their own personal disappointment. In reality of course, in addition to the discourse of "doing it for the community" or to "learn more about the culture," the women did clearly want to win and were often disappointed when they didn't. Thus, the committee members attempted to control the women by managing them through their emotions to create the desired effect and emotional atmosphere—one that is calm, without tears of loss (only tears of happiness cried by the queen are allowed or expected) and one that is not openly crassly competitive. This was all possible because the committee managed the places where the community impinged on the queen and all of her public appearances. Queens in general were supportive, but never served on the committee for very long as they had usually had their fill of the public eye and service to the community. After coming into the pageant with the rhetoric of community service, one year of service was usually plenty. However, some family members of past queens stayed involved. They felt they were there to ensure a good experience for the other girls and wanted to make sure that the bad experiences (disorganized visitations or no visitations) that they or their daughters had were not the same for the other women. They also had the intracommunity ties to make the visits successful. Often they were the only ones who had been to visit these cities with queens during the festivals in the past and this institutional knowledge of how things worked, what the gifts should be, and what to wear and how to behave were crucial knowledge in making the right impression.

Gift exchange was a particularly important part of these visits. Often it was the sole responsibility of the committee members to bring the proper omiage for each host from the group. T-shirts, pins, and food items from local merchants were often desirable. For example, from Hawaii we received chocolate-covered macadamia nuts, Hawaiian nut cookies, fruit squares, t-shirts picturing Spam musubi, and other Hawaii-specific goods. This symbolized the ties that were being made, but also incurred obligations of reciprocal gifts and hospitality.

The committee members and past queens who organize the pageant have inordinate control of the bodies of the women in the pageant. One of the committee members who works closely with the candidates backstage admitted to me that she was concerned because five of the six candidates that year had tattoos. "What will the sponsors think when they spend good money to support these girls and they are up there looking like Harley Davidson riders? What are we going to do?" A hunt ensued for cover-up makeup, flesh-colored band-aids, or anything that could be used to hide the tattoos. The ankle tattoos weren't going to be too much of a problem, but the one on the back of her shoulder blade? Suffice it to say that the image of the beauty queen was changing fast.

For Japanese American women a tension remains between assimilation (which Japanese American women have been accused of doing particularly well through interracial marriage to white men) and the exoticization of difference (to which they are consistently still subjected). These women crave both true acceptance and cultural empowerment through these racialized bodily performances in the pageant, but there are bodily limits on how far their agency can go.

Why do the women comply? For the most part, they see the pageant as a way to learn about Japanese American culture and they have to place their trust and themselves in the hands of the committee members to train them how to do it right. This gives the control to the committee members to determine what these Japanese American women will symbolize, look like, act like, and even feel like as symbols of the community. For example, during the visits to the other cities, there was intense pressure to be on time so as not to be disrespectful to the local organizers who often provided transportation to and from appearances. Managing the itinerary of a large crowd of beauty queens meant a lot of hurry up and wait. We were often told, "Don't keep the group waiting—think of others first. Let's all be the first ones down so as not to hold up the group."

Finally, in this instance, race was gender and class specific—therefore a change in racial meaning questioned the meaning of gender and class, too. This can be seen when those around her invoked the queen as a goodwill ambassador. As such, the queen was a point of cultural exchange where she herself was the token of exchange. This increased the objectification of the queen's body and increased her symbolic capital. She is meant to symbolize the bridge between Japanese American communities, but also the ties, both politically and culturally, with Japan. But this objectification of the queen can be complicated because this symbol can talk back.

This symbolic capital is often paramount when the queen visits Japan or Hawaii. The activity that demands the most time is the photo shoot. Having photos taken of the queen with various business leaders, community leaders, and politicians is often the sole goal of the visit. Often these visits were described as "walk-throughs" where, one chaperone explained to me, "Very little would be said—just walk in, wave, smile for the cameras and walk out." In terms of skill, anyone could do it, but what makes it meaningful is that the person has a crown on her head and is the titleholder for that year. It is not about the personality or even the personal ties that they may or may not have with that person. In a bureaucratic sense, it just matters that she is who is in that title or office at the moment. In the "walk-through" what matters is that she shakes hands, looks good, and behaves appropriately, makes contact symbolically, and that it is publicly recorded. The fact that many times the queen cannot communicate—she can't speak Japanese to the Japanese businessmen—or may not truly understand or spend time with the people whom she is conducting the cultural exchange doesn't matter.

The queen does spend a lot of time with the other courts and mentoring goes on of most newly crowned courts. This is encouraged and often seen as a chance for the girls to say, "This is how it is in our Japanese American community. What about yours?" This perpetuates the motivation that most women have entering into the pageant—developing greater social networks and contact with other Japanese Americans. These visitations symbolize and solidify the networks that make up the Japanese American community, which has become more geographically dispersed.

The ways that these visits were recounted also strengthen this notion of the queen as a symbol. One queen, Gail Ideno, wrote in her farewell speech, which appeared in a Cherry Blossom Festival program booklet in 1993:

> My unforgettable trip to Japan occurred in October, travelling with my parents and grandmother for three weeks. My parents and I had never been to Japan before, so we were very excited. In Tokyo, we stayed at the beautiful New Takenawa Prince Hotel. We met with executives from the Bank of Tokyo, and were hosted by Union Bank to an evening of Kabuki Theatre. We also visited Mr. Seishichi Ato, president of the Fujiyasu Company Ltd., who generously donated the Queen's beautiful furisode kimono each year . . . although it would help immensely if I could speak Japanese to understand signs and directions, my grandmother was a wonderful translator . . . I have learned so much this past year—about different cultures, different people, and also, about myself. What I appreciate in learning about my ancestors from Japan, as well as reflecting upon my life here in the United States—makes me feel proud to be a Japanese American, most of all.

In sum, the pageants perform the relationship that Japanese Americans have within themselves, with other Japanese Americans in other cities, and with other mainstream communities.

Nonetheless, it is clear that the bodily and social control of the women as representatives of the culture, community, and as future mothers of the race was strictly controlled. Women also had emotional labor imposed on them, and they were often handled and shaped by the committee members in the name of not letting the community down. Through this the women are trained to be racialized symbols.

"What Would the Community Think?!"
Widening the Frame of Social Control after the Pageant

Given the pressure to represent the community, the occasions when discontent was expressed by the candidates against the committee and chaperones are particularly interesting. For example, Amanda, who was known for being too outspoken, explained to me that she didn't use the "f-word" (feminism) in public. She didn't feel it right to bring up the f-word because then people would just tune her out and would not listen to the other parts of her message. She felt it best to lead by example and show how much Japanese American women are doing today. Amanda also tried to exercise control over some money that the court (queen and princesses) had earned volunteering at a Japanese American–run bingo operation. She felt they should have the money to use at their discretion to defray the costs associated with being the queen and court and became frustrated that the committee wanted to control how they spent the money. From the committee members' point of view, the court had raised the money under the name of the "Cherry Blossom Queen Pageant," a nonprofit organization. Therefore, they could not have the court just spending the money on whatever they deemed necessary. This is not to imply that the court was running off spending the money frivolously. However, the committee was keenly aware of how it would look in the community if anyone audited their budget or got wind of this type of spending. The image of propriety, primarily to other Japanese American community members, was at stake.

Angela, a mixed-race princess in San Francisco who spoke Japanese, kept speaking Japanese publicly at events. This in itself didn't seem that important until I learned that the queen, who was monoracial, didn't speak Japanese and felt completely undermined. In this case, the committee intervened (without the queen asking them to) and asked Angela to please not speak Japanese because it undermined the queen. At the next event, where almost all of the attendees were Japanese nationals who had very little English, the queen asked Angela to help her be understood by the party guests. Angela, in revenge against the committee and the queen, refused to speak Japanese because "the committee said I couldn't."

The committee's efforts to control the participants and their rebellion partly represent a power struggle over gender roles. However, the chaperones and committee members used the apparently gender-neutral mantra "think what the community will think" in order to gain and legitimize their control over the women. They realize the power of the collective racial and ethnic identity and that this is accentuated in the queen pageant and they use the concept of the community (without ever really indicating who they mean) to control the participants. Even female committee members tried to assert control over the candidates, legitimizing this by arguing that they had more experience dealing with the community. Jane, a former queen, remarked that there was little difference in age between Lisa, a committee member, and herself. She told Lisa, "Look, don't mother me. I *am* your age!" Jane didn't like being infantilized by the committee and tried to strike back when she got totally fed up. One committee member ironically put it this way, "We treat them as adults and give them responsibilities. Naturally, if they don't carry out their responsibilities, then they are going to get a scolding, but that is not being treated like a child." In this statement he claimed that the women are respected and treated like the adults that they are, but then goes on to talk of "scolding" them as if they were children. This is illustrative of how both of these processes seemed to be going on at the same time in the name of being a collective racialized symbol.

The committee also tried to control what the queen said in public. For example, they didn't want the queen to be too political. One pageant organizer said:

> We tell them to stay away from controversial subjects. We are not looking for their views on abortion or apartheid or anything like that. If you talk about controversial subjects, the tendency is it is going to get too intense. We don't want a really intense person because then people shy away from her.

They want a person who is kind and approachable, and being political is seen as taking away from that.

Again, the social control exercised in the name of the community is used to censor what the candidates and queens might say if it was political. This fits with the fact that she is representing the community in that it would be very difficult for her to represent all the diverse political views of all Japanese Americans.

However, there were limits as to how much the committee could shape the outcome of the pageant. They have much less control over the judges who can, on the night, do what they feel is right. The judges are very transient in nature. They come, judge, and don't really have to live with their decision. The committee is not supposed to give any sign of coaching or befriending any of the girls before the queen is chosen. However, subtle individual coaching is going on as committee members recruit some candidates. In these ways, the committee members do coach the candidates, but they can't be seen to be doing it outwardly because they gain legitimation from others by purporting that the pageant is totally objective and without bias. Even with coaching, though, on the night of the pageant the judges are free to do what they want and are sometimes fooled by a good performance on stage that night. This has led some to challenge the judges, push for scores to be publicly available, and complain that the pageant is fixed. In the 1981 Los Angeles Nisei Week Queen Pageant, two disgruntled candidates and their families went public with their complaint and held a press conference calling for a recall of the scores, citing unfair judging. However, in this, as in most cases, the pageant results remained unchallenged and most people seemed to accept the winner as their queen. The queens likewise felt a continuing responsibility to the public, regardless of the result.

In reality, by the time the pageant takes place, the training sessions run by the committee have already subtly exercised control over the outcome through the cultural coaching that the women have received. This training, more so than the managing of the scoring or even individual coaching, shapes the selection of the winner. They also managed the judges very carefully—screening and discussing the "reliability" of judges at length in the committee meetings before the pageant training. Often the committee members from one city were well able to "handicap" other pageants, because they could tell who culturally fit the bill and was to become queen. They were rarely wrong.

Conclusion

This chapter illustrated how the queen is produced each year through the Japanese American beauty pageants as a form of not just bodily, but social, cultural, and moral control as well. The pageant participants learn to manage and control not just their racialized bodies, but also their management of their ethnic self-presentation and emotions in the context of the pageant. They wear the kimono in a particular context with a specific goal of winning, and persuading the audience of their cultural and racial authenticity. Ultimately, the community and the audience formulate a version of social control over these women, as they feel free to pass judgment on them as their future representatives.

This chapter shows that race work is not just interactional between individuals, but is also a collective social action, which draws on communal understandings of race and ethnicity to gain meaning. It takes community cultural institutions like pageants to produce and reproduce those meanings across individuals each year in the queen pageant. In the last two chapters we have seen how race work is produced in the pageant by individual and collective social actors. In the next chapters, we see how race work is done between racial and ethnic states in the United States and Japan.

6 The "Ambassadress" Queen: Moving Authentically between Racial Communities in the United States and Japan

Being the queen changed my life. I could never go out now, go out, you know, to a community activity, and not be properly dressed. It was, still is just too much of an image to uphold. I really felt the pressure. I mean how is it really possible to make all Japanese Americans happy as their representative, their queen? Especially Japanese Americans—you can't keep them happy! [Laughter.] Someone is always going to criticize!
—Nisei Week queen

Motivation for Participation and Community Connections

How did the racialized meanings factor into the candidates' motivations to participate in the first place? While their motivations varied, certain trends appeared in their expressed reasons for participating in this grueling exercise, the Japanese American beauty pageant. As we saw in the last chapter, there were many acceptable ways of framing participation in the pageant, and the most prevalent way of rationalizing participation was by claiming participation as an extension of community service, cultural preservation, or cultural learning.

Framing their participation in the pageant as community service allowed candidates to emphasize the Japanese American cultural values of giving back to the community and thinking of the larger whole before oneself. In their speeches or in the answers to their questions many women emphasized their community activities and how they viewed being queen as yet another opportunity to volunteer. It was clearly an acceptable way to rationalize dedicating so much time and effort to being queen and drew attention away from the self-motivated and, perhaps, material gain and fame they might enjoy as queen. Instead the rhetoric of volunteerism was reinforced by the audience who would clap loudly, or by sponsors, who liked to hear about young people willing to pay their community dues. Instead of having to pay them by sweeping up after the Cherry Blossom Festival for years on end before being allowed to have a voice, being queen was an instant, much cleaner, and more publicly viewed way of volunteering. It also was seen to win points with the audience and hence the judges. This is an interesting claim since the rhetoric of volunteerism and the reality seem to be splitting further apart with Sansei less likely to volunteer than either their parents or grandparents and more likely to feel the need for cultural preservation (Osaki, Omori, Shiraki, and King 2000).

The second motivation cited was to learn about Japanese American culture. Again, this plays on the anxiety about young Japanese Americans not picking up the leadership torch from older Japanese Americans. By far the most often mentioned reason for participating was because they didn't know very many Japanese Americans and didn't have a chance to wear a kimono or participate in Japanese cultural activities. Many women joined the pageant, then, to learn about their culture. Surprisingly, very few mixed-race candidates invoked this reason for their participation, perhaps because they felt that they couldn't admit they weren't familiar with the culture for fear of seeming to have either race or culture on their side (King 1997). While many admitted that they didn't know much about Japanese American culture, they didn't say they didn't know anything. They all claimed to have some culture, but just wanted to learn more. In reality, it was the networks of Japanese Americans, not just in their local communities but also in other cities and beyond, that taught them about their culture and community. Cultural activities were less important as they contained little cultural knowledge, according to the candidates themselves.

The third reason many of the participants gave for their motivation to participate in the pageant was wanting to participate in preserving the Japanese American culture and community. Recognizing community anxiety around the dilution of culture and the dying nature of community organizations, many of the participants had worked out ways to bring this issue into their speeches or answers to the Q&A section of the judging. Many of them talked about youth involvement, emphasizing that clearly the future belongs to the youth and that it is very important to pass on history or information (through informed Japanese Americans like the queen) to other young people. By invoking the history and the impact of the internment experience, the women paid respect to the older Nisei who lived through the camp experience and thus hoped to score acceptability points with the judges for doing so. This fit well with the rhetoric of the pageants themselves. Prospective Nisei Week Queens are told,

> Being a part of the Nisei Week Queen and court is a once-in-a-lifetime experience. Not only are young women able to learn more about their Japanese American heritage and meet other young women interested in their heritage, they are given the opportunity to represent their community as ambassadors to the Southern California community as well as Japan, Seattle, and San Francisco. (Nisei Week Queen Rules and Regulations 2004)

Using community service as a rationale for participation reveals that the women felt that they didn't know much about their culture and in fact, might have felt quite unconnected or even false about being a representative of the community without culture. If they felt they knew Japanese American culture well, they might not need to come to the pageant to learn about their culture. Participants therefore may represent more assimilated, but not completely assimilated, Japanese Americans. In making this claim, these women also link knowing about culture with traditional arts and cultural festivals. In Hawaii, the fifteen semifinalists are required to take a small number of Japanese arts lessons. The rationale is that it exposes the girls to their culture. I argue that it is also used to make claims of authenticity to Japanese culture (i.e., the other cities don't do this) and to make sure that all the candidates have some grounding in culture so they can't be seen as "hollow bamboo."

The queen also attends cultural events like Japanese New Year in San Francisco. The pageant committee and the queens frame this cultural learning as part of being in touch with and meeting other Japanese Americans locally and nationally. This may mean that they don't have any very many Japanese American friends, or few, and need to meet/find other Japanese Americans. Finally, the pageant was a way to join the community in a more glamorous and prominent way and participants enjoy the public attention they receive.

Some reasons for participating in the pageant were deemed unacceptable. Only women who have some of the characteristics discussed above volunteer to do the pageant. They are also initially screened by the committee to ensure that they are not doing it for the "wrong reasons" or are not appropriate for the pageant. In the end, I know of no one who came forward to participate in San Francisco who was rejected. There was discussion, though, about the fact that other cities had to reject candidates and that, in retrospect, they themselves should probably not have allowed some women to run because they just wanted to win the prizes. For example, one year in San Francisco, a woman who was very competitive did not win and never participated in any of the appearances or in the following year's parade. It was very unusual to disassociate completely from the other women and the pageant committee in this way. In addition, she left owing the committee for the cost of a table from the pageant night and the organizers and committee members were sure that many Japanese Americans would not welcome her and her family again. This was an extreme case where she was deemed to not have the sufficient understanding of obligation, even in the face of disappointment, and was socially stigmatized. It was also unacceptable to do the pageant to promote oneself or one's book, find a job (explicitly), find a boyfriend, or to make political connections. Of course, most of these happened implicitly, but they were not recognized by the organizers as being legitimate reasons to participate.

The pageant also allowed very practical connections to be made within Japanese American communities. One participant said, "It is a bridging of the generations. It's a vehicle in that it's a way for parents to teach their kids. It's not like we can all afford to send our kids to Japan and show them what Japan is like. We can at least show them what the traditional music and dance is."

The intergenerational nature of the participants, committee members, and community members can be seen on various levels. There were many participants in the pageant/festival, and the queen was supposed to represent a diverse set of community ideas and interests. Some of the groups involved were Japanese businessmen from Japan who didn't see the queen as representing them, Japanese American business owners who saw the queen as a local girl, parents of pageant participants who saw the queen as a status to aspire to, committee members who saw the queen as a true representation of the community, sponsors (community organizations/individuals) who saw the queen as a way to attract business, and other attendees who saw the queen as the archetype of Japanese Americans. The types of participation ranged from ads from Japanese American businesses in the program, invitations throughout the year from various community organizations to do appearances, and donations of prizes, floats, and so on from Japanese-owned banks/companies. All of this activity connected the queen to many people in the Japanese American community. Many of these different interest groups also had very different agendas and the conflicts over the pageant reflected some of the positions of the people involved.

Some people argue that the benefits of this connection to the community entice some women to become involved in the pageant in the first place. Many women did it to get to know the Japanese American community better, but others did it to make connections with those outside the Japanese American community. Many tell of meeting famous actors, politicians, and even the emperor and empress of Japan as well as several local and national officials and businessmen. More than one job has come from these outside connections. Each city, though, has its own unique twist. In Los Angeles, with the entertainment industry nearby, many of the Nisei Week queens have used their title and the connections that followed as a stepping-stone into modeling and acting careers. Others, like in Honolulu where the Cherry Blossom Queen is perhaps most prominent in the public eye due to the large Japanese population, used their positions to find jobs or get into politics or newscasting. But learning about Japanese American culture and making connections through the pageant still happened under a racialized gaze and in connection with meanings of race. In fact, making connections across Japanese American communities highlighted the notion and role of race in determining the type and degree of community connections.

The Queen and "the Community"

Although many queens have been able to use this social network between Japan and the United States to further their individual careers and obtain access to power, it does not mean that they are free to do as they please. For the most part they are still carefully under the social control of the Japanese American community in an abstract sense and the committee in a specific sense. Examining who has control over the queen and how they exercise this control illustrates the collective nature of the queen's position and what is at stake racially. Chaperones and the committee constantly remind the women that people in the community are scrutinizing their behavior and appearance although "the community" never gets specifically defined beyond the sponsors. This sense of responsibility was the most often mentioned theme in the interviews with the participants. One queen said, "When you run in Nisei Week you are representing your area [region] which is a big deal, but then if you win, you are representing the Los Angeles community which is a bigger deal." This sense of "bigger deal" and responsibility is usually a direct reference to the fact that being queen is not just about the individual woman, but something bigger—the community. One participant said, "They [the queens] are not representing themselves. They are representing something larger. They need somebody who has a better understanding of the Japanese American community and why the festival is important." The ability to represent the community is tied to understanding the community in order to be legitimate. One of the criteria seems being able to know and understand how the community, as if it was homogenous, would want the queen to respond. The queen must have some understanding of the community, and this understanding is sometimes debated.

This collective responsibility is very much in the minds of the committee organizing the pageant, the chaperones, and the judges. A committee member told me that the goal was "to choose the perfect public speaker, a representative of the community. A person who is well rounded enough to represent each and every person in the Japanese American community." This implies that there is diversity in the Japanese American community and that the queen should become a compilation of all of those, sometimes very different, interests. This committee member is not saying that all Japanese Americans are like her or even that all Japanese Americans support the idea of the pageant. They don't. But the queen does represent more than just herself and this puts her in a different category: much like a politician, her life is open to scrutiny. She has to have better values, and live a clean life. In the Nisei Week rules, the queen is instructed as follows:

As a representative of your sponsoring organization and the Nisei Week Foundation, it is your responsibility to conduct yourself properly at all times. Your role as the Goodwill ambassador for the Nisei Week Japanese Festival is very important, therefore, appropriate behavior and conduct is required at all times, including, but not limited to: be mature, courteous and respectful at all times to everyone you meet, smile when meeting people, especially during official visitations and events, do not smoke or drink alcoholic beverages, chew gum or use profanity at official events or during Nisei Week while in Little Tokyo, avoid the sun and tanning until after the coronation ball.

Again, it is the collective and symbolic pressure of representing others that also made the queen more open to criticism and scandal than others. The queen's chaperones recognized that the queen often had opinions about pageants, but she was also the person who must be subjected to the control of the Japanese American community. One woman put it this way:

> In the speech the candidates really thought about what's important for them. They seem to understand that the Japanese American community [here] is very much a family. The way you represent them and participate in the community is very much the way you participate in a family. The people who have won understand that.

Here there is a clear delineation that the queen must be part of the family and, like a family member, must be sure to show loyalty to the family and not air the family's dirty laundry in public. The queen is of the community and she has obligations to the community like a family member. One of the judges told me, "We interviewed the candidates. We figured this person represents us. We don't need the fire chief or the local butcher to choose our candidate."

Since the queen is a representative of the community, she also must think not only of herself but also what image she portrays as she is speaking for the community both racially and culturally. Therefore, community members may express their discontent if they feel an inappropriate person has been chosen or if their interests are not being met. One queen explained the responsibility of this collective voice being on one person, namely herself:

> They don't want you to embarrass them in public. You don't know who you are going to meet. You may meet the mayor of Los Angeles. You will meet the mayor of Nagoya, Japan. Someone may choose to speak to you. I met the Grand Prince of Japan.

This pressure on a queen who has to represent not only herself, but the entire community as well, even if she isn't sure what the standards are, pervades most proceedings involving the queen and her court. Everything from how they walk in kimono, to what they say in their brief speeches on stage, to how they put on their makeup are all cast in terms of "what will the community think?" The chaperones and committee members spend much of their time helping the candidates to put their best foot forward and not incur the criticism of community members who will criticize the fact that they look sloppy, don't know how to walk in kimono, and so on.[1]

This concern about what others will think also pertains to appearance. One candidate who felt she was underdressed at a press conference described it this way,

> I was not the image they are trying to project on us . . . they were wearing all these power suits and stuff. They were all dressed up and they were just very proper. It is kind of a Japanese thing anyhow to be very proper . . . very, very proper. In a way, being proper protects you because if you aren't you leave yourself open to a lot more attacks and criticisms from a larger Japanese American audience.

Throughout my research, I heard comments that candidates were not feminine enough, not pretty enough, not racially Japanese enough, and not culturally Japanese enough. In addition to appearance, what the queen says in public was also controlled in part by a larger social collective identity. One candidate describes a notoriously outspoken queen:

> She [the queen] has always been . . . there were times where I know he [the chaperone] had to say, "Now look, this is the situation we are in. Hold your tongue." It is hard because when you are in the Japanese setting, there are only so many things you can say that's representative of the community. I found myself biting my tongue until I got home.

They were thinking, I don't really want to talk to this person; he is boring, but instead had to put on a happy face because they represent the community.

Even with the threat of the community hanging over them, several of the queens managed to be quite outspoken and some argued that they should be good speakers for certain causes such as feminism, but they just couldn't be too political.

> Because you represent an organization you have to know . . . you can't be too political. I think you can be outspoken in terms of your own beliefs as

long as you keep them separate from Nisei Week. As long as you don't say, I'm speaking as the Nisei Week queen and I think . . . x, y, z. For example, there was one queen who was a vegetarian and when she went to Japan they kept serving her meals and she wouldn't eat them. That was something that she didn't need to compromise.

Or did she? This event might be remembered precisely because she actually did do something she wanted regardless of the circumstances for others. Thinking of herself over the community's reputation when she refused the food, she risks being accused of making the Japanese in Japan (Nagoya) think that the Japanese Americans in Los Angeles are rude because she refused their hospitality, that is, food. This can get translated by some community members into "Don't you know to be polite?" or "They will think we, as Japanese Americans from San Francisco, are impolite because of your [the queen's] actions."

One queen learned the hard way that what she did say would be taken very seriously, especially by the Japanese American press (Japanese/ English regional newspapers). She explained how embarrassed she was when an article came out in her college paper, which was entitled "[Her name] Ran in Cherry Blossom Queen Pageant as a Joke." "I was really upset with that headline. When I interviewed with this young reporter, I told her I did it for fun. There is a big difference between doing something for fun and doing it for a joke. The headline was totally wrong and I felt so badly. It was on the front page." The reason she felt bad, she explained to me, was that she was afraid that the committee or the Japanese American community would think that she didn't take the pageant or her concomitant duties as queen seriously, which she did.

The essay question, on which the candidates were judged in San Francisco, asked what their motivation for running in the pageant was. There seemed to be more respect given to the candidates who said they didn't want to win, and in fact acted surprised when they did, than those who just wanted to win. In reality many of the candidates took the pageant very seriously and tried very hard to win or least tried to convince others that they did. To not take it seriously and to run as a joke would mean they disrespected what the pageant was about and, by association, disrespected the community. Ironically, then, to win a participant had to say she didn't want to win and if she did say she wanted to win, she couldn't because that was not part of the credo of being queen. It wasn't the image the judges or the committee wanted to portray.

One candidate I spoke with did say that she had entered on a dare from her friends. When she made this known to the other candidates and the committee members, she was castigated as being too self-interested or making fun of the whole enterprise. She was named first princess and her lack of commitment to the idea started to show when she was unavailable for many appearances throughout the year because she had moved out of state (a direct violation of the CBQ contract). The embarrassment of being named princess as well as trying to show how easy it was to win put her in the awkward position of being a part of something that she didn't respect. But her imputed selfish motives got her into trouble and people never fully trusted her motives because of her cultural inauthenticity. Her friends teased her because they said she actually was superficial enough to do well in the pageant, and the pageant participants were angry with her for doing it as a joke and disrespecting the pageant and the Japanese American community. Even though her participation was never questioned, most people felt that she had just used the pageant to get what she wanted, which was considered "not very Japanese American of her."

Even long after their reign is over, many of the queens talked about always making sure that they looked nice when they went out in public for fear that they would be recognized as a former queen and embarrassed. One former queen said that it never failed if she was just in sweats with no makeup running to the grocery store for milk she would bump into an older Japanese American woman who would remark, "Weren't you a Cherry Blossom Queen?" Another queen describes it like this,

> For years after that I felt I had to keep that image up. I felt like I was still representing the Japanese American community and I didn't want to get caught partying somewhere because I was an ex–Nisei Week Queen. It never failed that if I went to the bank to drop off a check with no makeup on someone would say, "Hey, weren't you Nisei Week Queen?" It is like once a Nisei Week Queen, always a Nisei Week Queen, at least in the Japanese community anyway. One time I was calling about this lemon of a car I had and I am screaming at this guy and then he says, "Weren't you Nisei Week Queen?" and then I am, like, I am mad at the company, not you personally. And all of a sudden it was like I can't be mean to this person because I am an ex–Nisei Week Queen. I did feel that stigma for a long time that I represent the community.

By using the word *stigma*, she implies that one advantage for a queen is that "community" feeling, but the disadvantage is that the same community feeling is a responsibility. The outward appearance is important and marks her as Nisei Week Queen and therefore community property. In addition rules set forth in the contract that each candidate signs in every city guide the queen's characteristics, behavior, and speech. Most formal rules, such as the queen can't drink or smoke at official functions or can't get pregnant during her reign, like the informal codes discussed above are put in terms of a larger sense of self. This transforms that "self" of the queen into something more—a reflection of the collective community.

The generalized other of the Japanese American community guides much of the queen's life. While some women were able to leave that sense of responsibility to the community behind, by moving away, shirking the duties, or ignoring the criticisms, most tried hard to live up to their title. Many, like the woman above, could not shake that sense of responsibility even long after their term as queen had ended. However, the specific expectations of this generalized other were a matter of contested racial and gender politics.

Exiting the Pageant Stage into Dealing with the Community

Sponsors and Community Politics

The pageant is a nonprofit civic and cultural ritual but it is also strongly commercialized. There is a constant battle to get financial sponsors, and when the pageant committee of the festival secures a sponsor for itself, the general committee tries to steal them away since they need big financial sponsors. Many sponsors are Japanese or Japanese American businesses or are businesses where a Japanese American person has connections within a company and has asked them to sponsor a candidate.

The pageant and the festival started out as a way to bring business into Japanese ethnic enclaves, but soon the pageant became the signature event of all the festivals. However, as with many Japanese American events (e.g., basketball leagues), it is completely run by volunteers and is officially nonprofit. Therefore the pageant and festival need people to buy into it and volunteer time. Typically, the Cherry Blossom Festival in San Francisco has over one hundred volunteers. Many of them are people with a steady income and free time, mostly

Nisei and some Sansei with a business or organization or who have children who can benefit from their participation. The business leaders and community players in Japantown in San Francisco are heavily involved in organizing the festival each year. In the pageant, these interests are seen to use the queen for business and festival openings. Like a hired clown, the queen is an attraction to look at and to bring attention to an event including the possibility of media coverage to entertain. She appears for free or for a small token gift, and usually doesn't speak very much, but if she does she gives a very small, usually uplifting, and socially aware speech about the Japanese American community. These motivations for using the queen link selling and monetary gain to cultural and gendered values. In this sense, she is a symbol and a valuable racial and ethnic commodity.

There are important commodification issues here (Lan 2001). Shiseido cosmetics provides free makeup consulting to advertise their products and to sell to the women themselves and to people who like their look. The marketing of the sponsors happens at the beginning and ending of every speech. For $1,200 it is a good investment for Japanese American companies or organizations to get advertising. The names of the businesses or organizations appear on the sashes of the candidates and are worn publicly for several months before the pageant until the titleholders are crowned, when the sponsors' names are replaced on the sashes by the women's titles.

Until then, during a large number of public appearances, queens literally wear the name of the business or organization on their body and thank the sponsor at the beginning of every word they speak. They must thank the sponsor and say the sponsor's name aloud publicly. This links the body of the woman and her mastery, or lack thereof, of cultural practices to the sponsors. In San Francisco many of the sponsoring organizations wanted a chance to choose the candidate they would sponsor, although this was discouraged by the organizing committee. Sponsors wanted to choose and back a winner.

In San Francisco, the vetting is done by the main queen pageant committee because the local organizations are not as strong at finding young women to represent them or be supported by them. Therefore the chair of the committee who has long-standing ties in Japantown and the local community, matches the candidates to the organizations.

The sponsorship of the candidates by organizations and businesses is used to show the civic nature of the Japanese American organizations that sponsor the women in the cities. In San Francisco, at times the organizations wanted a chance to meet the candidates in order to ensure the one they backed was a "winner." The committee and the chair largely discouraged this, as they didn't want any of the women to feel rejected by any of the organizations/companies. The committee also tried to downplay the competition element in the pageant, but the organizations still want their candidate to win.

The women in the pageant are used to sell raffle tickets, raise money, and appear at business ribbon-cutting ceremonies. In the past, they were used to advertise local wares (see Figure 3). For example, in San Francisco, the Japanese Tea Garden is used perennially as a photo site for local ethnic press and for the program booklet of the festival. Candidates spend hours getting adorned and wrapped into their kimonos, getting their hair done kimono style, and then being transported to the Tea Garden where they are posed under the softly falling petals of the cherry trees. The photos appear in the local papers, which in the end advertise the location, the Tea Garden, which also just happens to be one of the sponsors of the pageant and one of the candidates.

A prominent Japanese restaurant sponsors a dinner, but provides complementary meals only for the queen and her court, while all others are expected to pay, making money for the restaurant. They know that where the queen goes, others will follow. In the end they sell a lot of steak dinners. In hosting the queen and court they try to make the business look like they are doing it just as "good Japanese American community members." In reality, it brings business into Japantown and the sponsors get publicity.

Sometimes there is a connection between the candidate and the organization and sometimes the women arrive already having solicited a sponsor, but it is not a requirement. For example, one candidate served on the board of the local Japanese American Citizen's League (JACL) chapter. The JACL national headquarters was not sure how it felt about sponsoring candidates, and the Women's Concerns Committee had explicitly criticized JACL sponsorship and participation in pageants. However, the local chapter still decided to sponsor her because she had been on the board and worked hard for them. They felt obligated to do it and bought a table and sent people to support their candidate on the night. She symbolized her ties to local organizations,

Figure 3. 1965 Nisei Week Queen, Carol Kunitsugu, advertising automobile tires. Photograph courtesy of Carol Kunitsugu Itatani.

and the local JACL chapter probably wouldn't have attended otherwise, as they didn't the following year.

The women are used to sell goods, to sell the festival, to sell Japantown, and to sell Japanese American culture. The kimonos and the bodies they are wrapped around are needed to send visual cues to people.

Race, it seems, is the prime component of that embodied culture that people need to see. It sends meanings and assumptions of cultural knowledge to people who see the queen in her kimono. Certain types of gender are needed to sell Japanese American culture and Japantown businesses to Japanese Americans, and to those on the outside of the community. The tourists need to look at the queen riding on the float in the parade and be able to see Japanese American culture. The queen's body, then, is the field on which the issues get debated, but it is also the embodiment of cultural practice. The tourists need to feel that what they are getting is the exotic and Japanese cultural feel that they have come for. They attend the festival, and the queen's float is the last float in the parade as the culmination of the festival and parade. Like Santa Claus at the end of the Macy's Thanksgiving Day parade, her body, precariously balancing on the highest level of the float, is the ultimate Japanese American cultural icon.

Each pageant is local to the Japanese American community it claims to represent and each is sponsored differently. In Los Angeles, the local Japanese American organizations conduct their own screening processes in order to select their regional representatives. These usually mirror the dispersed geographic areas of Los Angeles. It is up to these local geographic (e.g., Gardena or West Los Angeles) organizations to enforce the rules of ancestry and eligibility. Any question about the eligibility or authenticity of any of the candidates is sent back to the local organizations and the main Nisei Week Queen Committee does not get involved in trying to legitimate or test claims to eligibility.

Therefore the vetting of candidates is done locally and no one can just sign up to run in the pageant. One must gain local organizational support first in Los Angeles before entering Nisei Week. The women in the Nisei Week pageant have strong local organizational support when they begin preparing for the pageant in earnest. They have completed their budget and various levels of "training." In some organizations in Los Angeles, the women are recruited, and some even have preselection pageants or competitions to see which woman they will chose to be their organizational representative.

In Honolulu, the Jaycees sponsor the women so the candidates don't have to find sponsors and there isn't the same pressure to thank sponsors all the time. The same group of corporations and organizations sponsors them all and all are used as advertisements for the Jaycees. In Honolulu, too, all the candidates are vetted and screened by the

Jaycees before they reach the rehearsals and the pageant. Sponsors could possibly put pressure on the Jaycees to take certain specific types of women in the pageant. In fact, in Honolulu, where the Japanese American community is the strongest politically, demographically (in size), and economically, there are rumors every year that only certain women with fathers in strong business positions or with money to donate via their business or organization get to participate and even win. The given rationale is to make business and political links between community organizations and businesses and to ostensibly provide training for Japanese American business people. However, the local social network connections made can link money back into the festival year after year, helping to make the Honolulu festival one of the best funded of all.

In Hawaii candidates are not sponsored by set groups, but the money is raised by the Jaycees from outside organizations and then distributed evenly among the candidates. The sponsorship is done by levels, with Diamond being the highest level of donations, and Gold and Silver sponsors donating slightly less money. This makes the money given more equal and in theory should weaken the tie between the sponsors and the women. However, there is still strong recognition of the sponsors even though the women don't actually wear and embody the names of the sponsors. The money is a chance for the Honolulu community to link into Japanese American and other business opportunities. Predominantly male, the Jaycees now recruit future members from the past queen and court members (Yano 2006).

The candidates also are not encouraged to ask the sponsor for more money (beyond the table and admission fee). If the candidate asks for more money it is thought to ruin the relationship with the sponsor for the future. The committee works hard to cultivate positive relationships with sponsors so that they can call on sponsors year after year. While the candidate may move on from a bad relationship with a sponsor, the committee is stuck with the sponsors from year to year. The committee then is very strict and clear with the women that their behavior can make life difficult for them and that they are dropped into ongoing relationships and obligations that are sometimes years in the making and maintaining. The women may rotate in and out of the pageant, but the sponsors stay (with some variation) from year to year.

There is also an emotional relationship with the sponsors in an abstract sense. The candidates are meant to feel very obligated to the organization that puts up the money for their candidacy, even if they don't know anyone personally in the organization. In some instances, there are deep personal connections between the woman and the organization, such as for women who are sponsored by their church or community organization. In this sense, the candidate may have deep personal obligation to win not just for herself, but also not to let the organization or church down. The festival and committee draw on these homegrown loyalties to boost their revenue and attendance at the pageant. The pageant audience, then, varies from year to year depending on who is running and who their supporters are. This can be seen in the queen's farewell speech, which often speaks of the emotional bond to the committee members, other girls on the court, their parents, and their sponsors. Kari Ann Hiraoka, a queen at the end of her reign, wrote in the Thirty-fifth Anniversary Seattle Japanese Community Queen Scholarship Program Booklet (1995):

> Within the past year, my court and I have actively participated in a variety of events that are also essential in helping to maintain a sense of community identity. To Michiko, Jennifer and Misa, together our lives have been enriched by this experience. It has given us the confidence to stand up for what we believe in so that we can make positive changes for the benefit of the community. Best wishes and thank you. Without the support of my family and friends, I could not have endured this past year. Each of them was there to provide assistance and advice that I value very much.

While the activities that the speech describes change from year to year, the formula of the speech itself is relatively unchanged. The themes of overviewing the year, thanking supporters, and furthering a platform all come across clearly in the "farewell speech" printed in the program booklets in all the cities each year. But the pressures to thank people are not just emotional. Many times they are financial as well and the thankfulness of the queen lays the groundwork for the selling of the queen image for the next year.

Selling the Queen

The pageant is sponsored in the most public sense by the organizations that agree to sponsor a candidate. In addition to buying a table and providing the sponsoring fee for the women, an organization may also give money and gifts to its candidate to make her dresses for appearances better. The ownership of the women is most apparent in Los Angeles where the local organizations will not only financially sponsor their candidate but may also help her choose her clothes for appearances and so on. Rules and practices were instituted in Los Angeles to attempt to even the playing field because some organizations were more supportive and outstripped others with less funding. They got a local but internationally known Japanese clothing designer to donate a set of outfits to the women to wear for their appearances. This suit was the same for each woman and custom made for her to wear so they all got the same clothes. Their gowns and kimonos were also all the same and given or loaned by the central pageant committee so as to make things as fair as possible. Still, differences in the level of financial support from parents and local sponsoring organizations affected how many people could afford to sit in the golden circle on the night of the pageant and cheer for certain candidates, and how many other bodily services, such as makeup, eyebrow tinting, manicures, and leg waxing the candidate could afford.

In many cities the sponsors who gave prizes were mostly Japanese, including Japan Airlines, Japanese-owned jewelry stores, clothing stores, and kimono companies. Ads in the program were mostly from local Japanese American businesses and organizations as well as a few mainstream organizations like local popular radio stations in San Francisco. While the Japanese business financial assistance for the festival pageant is necessary for the survival of the event, Japanese businessmen had less direct control of the cultural content or structuring of the pageant or festival. In fact, in San Francisco, they had to split the general chairmanship of the entire festival into cochairs (one Japanese and one Japanese American) to resolve conflicts in what each subcommunity wanted to see done. While these financial ties illustrate the diasporic nature of the Japanese community and clearly symbolize a link between differing Japanese cultural traditions, there are conflicting notions about culture. One of the reasons that kimonos are still part of the pageants (a very old-fashioned cultural practice that women in Japan don't really use or wear anymore) is that kimono companies are willing to donate the kimonos to be worn, which are very expensive.

Money was raised for the festival and pageant in many ways. In San Francisco, there was pressure to sell raffle tickets and tickets to the pageant itself. In Honolulu, candidates sold program booklets of the pageant contestants with big glossy photos of them with their families;

the candidate who sold the most programs (or tickets) was rewarded with the title of "Miss Popularity." The selling of the programs allowed people to see the candidates and cast their votes at the dinner table without attending the pageant. It also allowed physical and limited personality information about each of the women to enter the local public discourse on who would be queen.

Having "Miss Popularity" crowned based on who sells the most programs became problematic one year in Hawaii when the woman who sold the most programs was deemed to be inappropriate to be a part of the court. Not chosen by her colleagues as Miss Congeniality, and not a winner of any title via the pageant but only through program sales, she was looked down upon and considered not a true titleholder by some of the court and organizers. This was exacerbated when she didn't have the money to travel to many of the mainland festivals and appearances. Her class background, although not that different from some of the other participants in the pageant, was discussed openly as being a hindrance to her ability to fulfill the duties of her role. Some of the organizers seemed visibly relieved when she couldn't make appearances, arguing that because she was from a lower-class background and had a tough boyfriend, she didn't exude the desired image they were after. Clearly even working hard to sell one's way into a title doesn't buy the middle-class cultural capital required to be an authentic court member.

Financial Relations with Japan

Until 1997 the pageant in San Francisco was in both Japanese and English and simultaneously translated. However, in 1998 the committee stopped Japanese-language translation, recognizing that the audience, primarily English-speaking, didn't really need it. It also signaled that the number of Japanese business sponsors had decreased slightly and that many of the businessmen could now speak enough English to follow what was going on in the pageant.

Funding from Japan gives Japanese Americans money for their festivals and activities in the name of spreading Japanese culture. The recent Japanese economic downturn has had an interesting effect on this. With the closing of the Sanwa Bank in San Francisco, Japanese American community organizations realized that one of their major funding institutions was drying up. They founded the California Nikkei Leadership Council with money donated from the bank as a final financial obligation of gently letting down the Japanese American organizations that they used to sponsor. The dependency on Japanese money has meant that Japanese businesses have more say and are more highly catered to because their yen talks. This is clear in the leadership of the San Francisco Festival which typically has two general co-chairmen (almost always men)—one a Japanese businessman and one a local Japanese American community person—in order to represent the views of two increasingly different groups living in San Francisco. Taking money from Japan also reinforces ties with Japan as the mother country, which essentializes Japan and Japanese people as more authentically Japanese than Japanese Americans. This can be seen in the context of the pageant in the discussions of the visits to Japan, which are seen as foreign or strange by the Japanese American queens.

Even with strong financial support locally and from Japan, candidates and their families still feel tremendous pressure to contribute extra money. On an individual level, candidates have the sponsor money to help them pay for their gown(s), shoes, zori, and other similar items, but the cost of travel outfits and gowns as well as the hotel rooms, airfare, and other travel expenses are not covered by the sponsors. The queen's travel expenses in San Francisco are covered by the pageant committee through donations, but candidates have tremendous financial demands as well. The issue of social class is a significant factor, not only in terms of having articulate middle-class cultural capital (or higher education as in the case of Seattle), but also practically in terms of who can afford to travel and make appearances in other states or Brazil to attend the Miss Nikkei International pageant. The candidates with less money or with little funds to get the right clothes often needed a new dress for each appearance so as not to repeat. They creatively traded and exchanged dresses with other queens in other cities in order to get the best use out of each dress. They went to rack sales and bridal trunk sales to get good deals. In the end, some candidates couldn't afford to travel, couldn't take time off from work, or just didn't want to go on the trips with the other court members. Class ultimately created an in-group and an out-group of those who could take advantage of the title and travel to represent the local community and those who couldn't afford to. Money and financial backing then enabled racial claims to be made, by having authentic zori or having money to be dressed by a proper kimono dresser in order to be seen as more Japanese.

The debate around change of racial rule in Hawaii was centered for some on the way that the mixed-race queen, if she was chosen, would be received in Japan by many of the important Japanese financial backers. Many worried that if the queen didn't look Japanese, the Japanese in Japan would not accept her. This would threaten the sponsorship necessary to continue the pageant and that would mean a loss of the pageant and possibly the festival. They were highly sensitive to the fact that if she wasn't authentic enough, based on her phenotypic appearance and cultural behavior, she could threaten the future of the pageant, the community, and the festival. This may draw on the very real racial understandings in Japan about the pure race of Japanese (as opposed to, say, racially inferior Koreans in Japan) (Armstrong 1989). There remains an obsession with racial purity in Japan. Katsui Yoshinari, head of the Asian People's Friendship Society in Japan explains,

> Japanese society still has fantasies about our pure blood, and about the ability of Japanese people to understand each other better than others. Even if the government or the business community accepts more foreigners, without much more effort on our side, these feelings of rejection towards foreigners will remain strong. (French 2000, A11)

Pageant organizers were highly conscious of their connection, even if only through money, to these Japanese supporters and their corresponding understandings of Japaneseness. One organizer in Hawaii said, "I think with regards to sponsorships here in Hawaii, we have a lot of Japanese companies that sponsor us, and because Japan is so homogeneous, I guess we would be concerned if there was a hapa queen."

In Los Angeles, one past Nisei Week queen discussed with me the fact that there are more and more multiracial queens. "I think we are starting to get away from that [racial rules]. I don't know how the Japanese corporations are going to feel about this though." Money clearly gives the Japanese businesses and corporations some influence over the pageant and therefore the queen. What racial meanings, then, did the Japan Japanese bring with them to influence the selection and reign of the queen? Most of the past queens interviewed talked about Japanese culture and Japanese American culture, but some were not sure about the difference between the two until they traveled to Japan as a part of the reign, where many were surprised by how big the racial, cultural, and gender differences were. The queen in her duty as the ambassadress between the two countries, often emphasized by the sister-city relationships between two local areas/cities (e.g., Osaka/San Francisco, Nagoya/Los Angeles, Kobe/Seattle), relaying information or goodwill between the two, and her reception in Japan as a representative of the local Japanese American community at times highlighted the vast differences between the two.

Many of the queens described their surprise at how Japanese they felt they were (regardless of racial background) in the United States, and how when they went to Japan they realized how different they really were from people in Japan. This idealization of the culture in the homeland further served to perpetuate an antiquated sense of culture being sourced only from Japan. One Cherry Blossom queen from Hawaii told me about her trip to Japan,

> My strategy in Japan was that I can speak enough Japanese to survive there, but because I look Japanese, but then really, like, people would say, "There's something different about you, you don't really look Japanese," but if I tried to ask a question in Japanese, people would speak back to me and they would rattle off in Japanese, so my strategy from that point on [was] I would ask them, "Do you speak English?" in Japanese. Then they were clued into the fact that I wasn't a national, but for people, that was like when I went out in the town, but for people who knew, who were, they were very warm and accepting. . . . In Hawaii, we have things that are uniquely Hawaii customs, like folding cranes for weddings, and people in Japan ask, "Why do you do this?" and my home stay mom in Japan would say, "We don't do that. We fold cranes for when people get sick." It turned out to be [a] uniquely Hawaii thing so I guess people in Hawaii like the Japanese kind of modify things to fit them.

Both race (looking Japanese American, but perhaps not Japanese) and ethnic cultural traditions (folding origami cranes) highlight difference rather than cultural similarity. She felt that she should try to speak Japanese out of respect for her sponsors in Japan, but she wasn't proficient enough to have deep conversations in Japanese. Being monoracially Japanese, she assumed that people in Japan would confuse her with Japan Japanese and expect her to speak Japanese. A Nisei Week queen had a similar experience. She described,

> In Japan, they knew I was American, just as if I saw a tourist here I would know that they weren't American just because of mannerisms. I was surprised in that since they knew I was Sansei that they didn't think I would

eat right. They would offer me things that I already knew what they were. "Have you tried sushi?" I mean, come on . . .

She was slightly offended by their assumption that because she is American she knows nothing about Japanese food. She went on to explain though how when it came to speaking Japanese she felt out of her depth.

It was exciting, but a bit scary. I couldn't speak the language. It was the first time I'd been someplace where I couldn't read a thing. It was a learning experience for me. I always thought to myself, "I am so Japanese. . . . I am so Japanese American." I know about my culture and heritage. Then you throw yourself in the mix and you are like, "Oh my God! I feel stupid. I don't know a thing." You feel a bit out of touch. At the same time everybody is looking at you as a complete American. I wore a kimono for the parade and a lot of people though I was Nagoya [queen]. It was a compliment for me. I just remember the first time I was in Japan, it was a big shock. Some things are really familiar and other things are really strange.

She thought that she was Japanese culturally, but when she confronted Japanese culture in Japan and traditions that have continued to change and grow, she didn't recognize Japanese American culture as Japanese. She felt unprepared when in Japan because she didn't speak the language and didn't "feel" the connection to Japan, as it is both familiar and strange. This concept of familiarity and strangeness, the echoing or resonance of culture, can be a part of the same process, but it is made relevant and important because the queen feels obligated to prove her Japaneseness to appease the Japanese funders on her trip to Japan.

A Cherry Blossom queen from San Francisco was monoracially Japanese, but was put on a float with *haole* (white) students attending school in Japan. She described it to me this way,

In Japan, they assumed I was Japanese. The interesting thing was on the float they had students from Kobe on the float and they are all haole and I'm Japanese ethnicity-wise. Half of them could speak Japanese. They were all speaking English, assuming I couldn't understand English. I asked them to translate from Japanese to English for me and then they were like, "Oh! Okaaaay!" People I met in Japan though think I'm Japanese. They say, "You look Japanese. You look like a Japanese girl." That's more when I got the "You look Japanese, but you are really American."

I was writing my name in *kanji* and they would be like, "No, no" and they would rewrite it for us in *katakana* or *hiragana* [phonetic Japanese alphabet] and I'd tell them, "No, I am Japanese American. My great grandparents came from Japan." They would say, *"Americajin, americajin!"* [American person] and I would be like, "No! *Nikkei-jin* [Japanese descent person]."

She was trying to convince the people she met in Japan that she was authentically Japanese both racially and culturally, but by Japanese standards they did not see her as such because of her lack of language. They got into a heated and contested battle over what she is and what criteria should be used to decide what she is. Even though she was making racial claims to similarity and familiarity, she was cast as "Americajin" in Japan.

This was exacerbated by the antiquated and often static understanding of culture that many in the pageant had. The trip to modern Japan often highlighted just how antiquated the cultural traditions enshrined in the pageant, such as kimono wearing, had become. One Cherry Blossom queen from San Francisco said,

> I think there's two different cultures that need to be looked at, like the Japanese cultural system that came over with the Issei and Nisei and then the Japanese American one that we have now, and I think that Japanese American culture is not Japan. It is what's here so I think it's kind of awkward that they do that or that they say. . . . But people would say to me, "Gosh, don't people have a problem with you not being able to speak Japanese?" and I would say, "Well, I understand that some people and some of the older generation would have a problem with that or think that it is not the greatest thing that they have a queen who can't speak Japanese," but I always felt like, "Gosh, I was picked to represent the Japanese American community here in San Francisco and I do." I represent the Japanese American community today.

The Influence of Japan on Japanese Americanness

Language and cultural values were also dynamic though within Japanese America and this included understandings of race/ethnicity that were different from those in Japan. One queen argued that Japan Japanese and Japanese Americans weren't that far apart in terms of cultural values. She explained:

> Japanese culture is so based on your inner soul. It is nothing to do with the superficial stuff. Although you might do Japanese dancing, it's what you learn internally that matters. Certain morals and guidelines . . . you know? Not to disgrace my family and be true to myself. Don't put on a show. I think that goes along with part of the Japanese tradition.

An example of this is the language and vocabulary that people use in the Japanese language. For example, some noticed that the Japanese language that the Issei brought with them is now antiquated and unlike the Japanese language in contemporary Japan today. One past queen in Los Angeles talked about when her friends from Japan came to visit her and her family and commented about her father.

> They told me that he [her father] spoke beautiful Japanese, but it was almost overly formal. It's old fashioned and more formal than they are accustomed to. Japan has moved on and incorporated slang. He speaks in a much more formal style. It's arrested from the time his parents immigrated. In some ways even the Nisei are more rigid than Japanese. . . . They really want to hold on to the rigidity of what in their mind they remember as what being Japanese was about.
>
> You have heard that expression "the lost generation," I'm sure. The Issei are the lost generation. I think that is still true. They keep up more of the traditions than they do in Japan.

Others recognized that it is not the same culture that has persisted and therefore people today should not be expected to live up to those old-fashioned ideas of Japaneseness.

> We have respect for the culture that our ancestors have brought to America from Japan and we do try to carry on the traditions. It is not the same as what they have in Japan because we have been here for five generations and it has changed so much.

Even so, most recognized that Japan is a homogeneous country and in some ways has less of a need to hang on to their Japaneseness because they are the majority in their country unlike the minority position of Japanese Americans in the United States. They can accept and adapt Western ideas and styles without a feeling of loss because they are the majority. One queen explained,

> I think if we do this [pageant] in Japan . . . the kimono wouldn't be that important because it is already a part of the given history. Because we are in America and we do share society with Caucasians and blacks and people don't know that much about the Japanese community, let alone the Asian community . . . what the kimono segment does and the appearance in kimono in public does is draw more awareness and attention to the actual Japanese community without having to say long speeches. It is a more visual effect. Sometimes that lasts longer in people's minds. If we were to go around in business suits everywhere and speak then we would look like normal Americans. The kimono adds a highlight. The emphasis makes us stand out a bit so that people pay attention to the fact that "Oh, they are Japanese American or they have Japanese in them" that is because we are in America. If we were in Japan, it wouldn't be a big issue.

But part of being a minority community in a multicultural society means that this feeling that makes one Japanese American can only go so far.

The queen must still be distinctive culturally or racially in order to represent this racial/ethnic community. In addition, the garb of the queen (tiara and sash) becomes particularly important to identify her role. One queen commented that she pushed the committee to allow her to make appearances just as herself without the crown and sash. She explained the response to that request: "Without the crown, sash and kimono, they don't want you." Her racial distinctiveness had to be highlighted by her queenly apparel. Because Japanese Americans are still a minority in the United States, there is definitely a perceived need to keep a distinctive community and the culture alive (Fugita and O'Brien 1991). This distinctiveness seemed more accentuated in the United States than in Japan.

All of the queens in all four cities travel to Japan as a part of their duties during their reign and many of the participants talked about how they felt while visiting Japan. They expressed that in Japan they felt empowered by having so many people who look like them. They liked the feeling of being in the majority, not in the minority, which is the way many of them feel at home. In Japan,

> One of our girls was like "Wow! This is better than Nisei Week!" I was like . . . well yes, because this is a whole city. It is not a subcommunity or an ethnic enclave within a community. I started to think, then, How do we fit in here? What do they (the Japanese) want from us? You are never really sure.

The racial connection of looking the same was clearly a relief from being a minority face in places like Seattle. But as we saw above, Japanese culture is not the same as Japanese American culture and most Japanese Americans in Japan didn't feel Japanese. They felt American of Japanese descent. Even so, there were still strong connections between Japan and the various Japanese American communities in the United States, which were promoted by the queen pageants.

Many of the sponsors of the pageants are Japanese companies from Japan. One of the largest benefactors of the pageant in San Francisco, Mr. Ato, is a Japanese national who benefited from Japanese Americans who tried to help Japanese in Japan recover after World War II. He felt so indebted to Japanese Americans that he started donating the queens' kimonos for various cities' pageants since he owned the Fujiyasu kimono company. This donation of a full *furisode* kimono, valued at approximately $10,000, is considered by far the most generous gift to the pageant from Japan. Each year during the pageant one of the past court members reads the story of Mr. Ato and his generosity and asks the audience to recognize his donation and the ties it creates between the Japanese American community and Japan.

The links to Japan are not just in terms of what people think Japaneseness is, but also in terms of tangible benefits for both sides. The links are often financial and very real. A large number of visitors from Japan attend almost every pageant/festival. In San Francisco, almost half of the participants in the parade are from Japan and come to dance and sing or perform in the Cherry Blossom Festival. Debates about authenticity are evident not just in the queen and court's participation in the parade, but also in the other spheres of the festival. Discussing a long-standing debate about having non–Japanese American marching bands in the parade, one long-time organizer explained,

> The festival has evolved more and more and more to involve Japan and parts of Japan. Probably the largest components of the festival that really have increased ties to Japan are the parade and now there are lots of groups now coming from Japan and that always adds some excitement. And we are becoming more and more known so there are a lot of groups who offer to come. We can't pay for them, but they come. Taiko groups, singing groups, art and crafts groups, all kinds. It always adds. There is a standard. We have koto and singing. We have dancing and taiko when you bring in these other components especially from overseas, it kind of adds. As far as any festival in San Francisco is concerned or in the Bay Area is concerned, ours is probably one of the purer ones, in the sense that the people who do participate are for the most part all Japanese American or Japanese. It is the philosophy . . . to kind of keep it like that not that that it is restricted to keep out non-Japanese. We want to keep it as much as Japanese American or Japanese and so the comments from the public have always been yours is the most colorful. The most ethnically pure type of festival.

The purity of the festival, judged by who participates in it, becomes one mark of the cultural authenticity. The mixed-race queen rides along on this cultural wave and may possibly problematize the racial purity of not only her float, but the parade and festival as well. But was the San Francisco version of Japanese acceptable to those in Japan? People in Japan excluded Japanese Americans by emphasizing the level and authenticity of their Japaneseness. Japanese Americans, according to some of the Japanese nationals that I interviewed, are not, by Japanese standards, really Japanese. This is a highly sensitive issue even for monoracial Japanese nationals who have lived abroad for too long. Children of these businessmen are called *shikoku kyujo* and are considered to not be true Japanese anymore because they have become too westernized, too exposed to foreigners, or are not collectively minded enough to conform to society in Japan. This is particularly upsetting since one of the mainstays of Japanese society is the idea of fitting in. For example, while teaching and living in Japan, I was told that to stick out was one of the worst things that someone could do in Japan and that in fact "the protruding nail gets hammered down." One queen said,

> Japanese Americans are trying to prove to Japan that we are Japanese because you always hear that you are not "real Japanese" even if you are full-blooded because you are not born in Japan. There is a real struggle because people in Japan don't think that Japanese Americans are Japanese unless they speak [Japanese].

This Japanese American thinks that Japanese determine that "real" or authentic culture is defined by being born in Japan or by being able to speak Japanese. But in thinking this, she reinforces the idea that Japan is the source of the real Japanese culture and using it within the Japanese American community means one is more authentic. In this sense, notions from Japan are racial (ideas that Japanese nationals feel that one must be racially Japanese to be real) but more than that they must be ethnic too (must be culturally Japanese, i.e., speak Japanese).

In the time I spent studying the pageants, I saw this clash between the Japanese national businessmen involved in the festival and the queens, the committee, and other Japanese Americans. Many of the Japanese national businessmen did not think the queen was legitimate. They felt that she did not meet their criteria for the queen, that she should come from Japan or be born there, speak Japanese, and be monoracially Japanese. Their racial and ethnic perceptions of what she must be in order to be their legitimate queen clashed with other Japanese American versions. Japanese American festival organizers for the most part disagreed and saw the queen as a legitimate representative, but they also knew that they needed the money that Japanese nationals would donate for the festival and therefore tried to see that the Japanese national interests were honored.[2]

The main place that I observed this debate was between the general committee (made up of many Japanese nationals) and the queen pageant subcommittee (mostly Japanese Americans) in San Francisco. The general committee felt that the queen pageant was expensive and was too fancy and ended up being a possible financial burden on the general committee. They questioned the importance not only of the queen and her legitimacy, but the legitimacy of the pageant as well. The subcommittee planning the pageant was then constantly put on the defensive to not ask the general committee for too much money or support and was made to justify why the pageant was necessary. It was a very interesting argument given that the queen pageant without the fancy sit-down dinner could possibly lose money, since the guests paid the price of the ticket because it included a nice dinner at a hotel. Throughout the entire year, there was ongoing conflict between the general committee and the pageant committee. I found the general committee's attitude interesting since they often used the queen at the pageant committee's expense. For example, the general committee expected the queen to appear at certain events to advertise the Cherry Blossom Festival, but her actual expenses (i.e., kimono dressing, trans- portations, and so on) would be paid for by the subcommittee.

Ironically, the Cherry Blossom Queen was not just challenged by Japanese nationals for not being Japanese enough but she also faced a lack of acceptance as an American by non–Japanese Americans in the United States.

> If I stand there in kimono they will ask me. "You are from Japan?" I say "No, I'm not." They say, "Wow, you speak English," and I say, "Yes, I do." They don't understand. They think that just because we are Asian we don't fit the typical norm. No matter how many generations we are here we're considered not American.

The asker of the question, a white American with a racial definition of who is American that does not include Asians, does not see her as a legitimate American because of race. Japanese Americans, like the queen, find themselves in a liminal position, then, in terms of culture. They are not Americans and yet they are not Japanese by Japanese nationalist racial and cultural standards. Out of this has developed a delicate balance between race and ethnicity in the United States by the Japanese American community.

The U.S. racial state, constructed clearly on the premise of white- ness as access to Americanness (Haney-Lopez 1996; Goldberg 2002; Ignatiev 2004) is challenged by the mixed-race queen claiming American- ness. But equally the Japanese racial state (Armstrong 1989; Dower 1986) would not allow for even monoracial Japanese Americans admission to recognition as Japanese. Both the racial ideologies embedded in state regimes were played out in interpersonal interaction in and around the Japanese American queens and their visits to Japan, precisely because she was not just there as an individual, but represented a racially defined collective and was a transnational symbol of the relationship between Japan and the United States, as the ambassadress between the two.

Gendering Japanese Americanness

The queen is more than just the body of a woman—she is a symbol. It was difficult for the queen to represent all Japanese American women or all Japanese Americans or even claim to represent them. There were clearly other women and community members who didn't support the pageant or feel that the queen represented them as Japanese Americans.

This was evident in the local community's political debates. The emergence of the pageant in San Francisco coincided in 1968 with the renovation and redevelopment of Japantown. The city tore down many of the older buildings where elderly Japanese and Japanese Americans had lived. This raised the issue of housing for seniors who had lived much of their lives in Japantown and prompted a move to preserve housing for the Japanese elderly by Sansei activists. The building of the Kintetsu building and the Peace Pagoda in 1968 signaled a new time for Japanese American organizations. Some that had been crucial to Japanese Americans in the past, such as the Japanese American Citizens League, seemed less relevant now. Many Sansei started new organizations, which catered to new and different needs like the needs of the elderly, for example, Kimochi and Japanese American Services of the East Bay. Redevelopment and the new building of the Japan center and Kintetsu center were controversial.

The pageant started as a part of this redevelopment program in 1968 to boost buying in Japantown and center a community that was becoming more geographically dispersed by generation (most Sansei do not live in San Francisco or locally near Japantown). This also signified a significant shift in leadership. One of the first Sanseis to become the leader of the Cherry Blossom Festival, Steve Nakajo, tried to revamp the out-of-date nature of the festival by replacing the pageant with a scholarship contest. He was supported in 1988 by the Women's Concerns Committee, led by Mei Nakano, who tried to ban pageants and particularly community organizational sponsorship and participation in them. This resistance to the pageant again illustrates the power of the queen as a symbol of the community. Even those who don't support her, or the idea of her, still care enough to involve themselves in debates about her existence.

Others argued that the pageant was a solution to the threat of cultural dilution because it preserved culture and community. The symbolic ethnic practices of the festival and pageant are thought to bring Japanese Americans to a center to be in communion with each other and thus are good ways to recreate the community. Bill Watanabe of the Little Tokyo Service Center in Los Angeles argues for the establishment of a gym in Little Tokyo:

> We need a place for all generations of people. If we miss that, and we miss a whole generation of people who don't connect to Little Tokyo then we will lose them forever and Little Tokyo will just become a façade or a shell of what it used to be. (Chen 2001, 1)

Chris Aihara of the Japanese American Culture and Community Center, also in Los Angeles, said:

> I don't know if it promotes the continuation of Japanese American culture or Japanese American values, but if we can bring them in for basketball, we may be able to sell them on all the other parts. (Chen 2001, 1)

Similar hopes are tied to community beauty pageants to reinvigorate local economies, bring people together, and reinstate culture, but both basketball leagues and beauty pageants do this within racial restrictions (King 2002). Pageants are not just about choosing a queen, but are a touchstone for community debates about economic development, preservation of culture and continuance of community. We can see issues like the impact of multiculturalism and especially the anxiety about interracial marriage played out in the context of the pageant. Pageants have always been political even before this. The pageants were started because of the exclusion of Japanese American women from mainstream pageants and therefore the crowning of a monoracial Japanese American woman was a statement of positive self-esteem for the community, a way of saying "Look, we can be beautiful, too." The crowning of a monoracial Japanese American woman for all those years was a political act just as the politics of identity is disrupted by the bodily presence and then crowning of a mixed-race Japanese American woman as the queen and representative of the community. In this sense, the queen symbolizes the negotiation around this demographic shift.

But the pageants are not just about femininity. They are also a public reassertion of Japanese American masculinity and heterosexuality. We can see this in the overt and covert attention paid to the attractiveness of the candidates, which is assumed to be evaluated in a heterosexual context. The comments by the predominantly male emcees, and the public posing of the queen with the Caucasian or African American male mayor, illustrate the predominantly male social world in which the queen operates. On an interpersonal level, too, much of the social control of queen and court is done by the men who run the pageant and the festival. Yano (2006) explains how this played out in Hawaii where the women in the Cherry Blossom Pageant in Honolulu were racialized and feminized precisely so that the Honolulu Japanese Junior Chamber of Commerce men could make claims to deracialization and masculinity. This has been and continues to be reflected in debates about feminism and the beauty pageant.

Pageants have been much maligned for maintaining superficial notions of beauty and have been criticized as being just about dominant (i.e., white) models of beauty. Pageants have also not been studied because they are sexist, or because they are just for women and therefore not important. Feminism has clearly had an impact on the pageants as the most often repeated mantra was "It is not a beauty pageant!" This is important because the participants, well aware of the feminist critique of pageants, argued that Japanese American pageants are community pageants, not beauty pageants. They claim the Japanese American pageants are different and not degrading because they are not based on appearance, but instead are about culture and community service.

In 1988, arguments exploded around the Cherry Blossom Queen Pageant in San Francisco. Although ostensibly about the sexist nature of pageants, there were important undertones about race and ethnicity. These debates about race were apparent in discussions of beauty. In the 1980s the Women's Concerns Committee (WCC), based in San Francisco, formed to combat sexism in the Japanese American community. They targeted the Japanese American Citizens' League (JACL) for sponsoring pageant candidates. WCC chair Mei Nakano said, "We know that we are going out on a limb on this since beauty pageants have become almost a tradition. But we feel strongly that as a civil rights organization committed to the principles of fairness, equality, and dignity of all human beings, JACL has no business in the beauty contest business" (JACL women 1985, 2).

The WCC argued vigorously that the pageant was just based on looks and that it encouraged Japanese American women to feel bad about how they looked if they didn't approximate Anglo-European looks. Once again, we find the belief that Japanese Americans have internalized assimilationist white standards of beauty and would choose to look white and the candidate who most closely approximated that. Nakano said, "Too many of us are already into cosmetic surgery and heavy eye makeup to get away from the look that is natural to us and perfectly good" (ibid.).

The committee raised this issue and a workshop was held to debate the proposal to ban the JACL from sponsoring or participating in beauty contests. The committee in the workshop argued "that beauty contests reinforce a shallow concept that physical attributes are of paramount importance in women, relegating to secondary importance such features as intelligence, compassion and wit and they enforce negative stereotypes of Japanese American women" (Nakano 1985, 6). The WCC wanted the JACL instead to sponsor scholarship or debate contests to reward focusing on positive aspects of Japanese cultural heritage, leadership development, and interpersonal skills. The response to the critique of pageants claimed that:

1. Historically JACL became a vehicle for Japanese American women to participate in such beauty contests—since they were prohibited from entering non–Japanese American contests.

2. Contests afford the winner opportunities to expand her career horizons and cultivate her personality.

3. Winners can work to strengthen cultural ties within the community and to enhance the image of Japanese Americans vis-à-vis the outer society (Nakano 1985, 6)

Needless to say, the WCC faced resistance within the community about this issue and were misreported in several of the Japanese American newspapers. The committee went down to defeat, as they expected they might, but they still argued forcefully that beauty contests were an unnecessary evil. They admitted that they had anticipated that it would be difficult to change such hard-set institutions such as the queen pageants. Nonetheless, they felt that feminism should have an impact on the pageant and that Japanese American women should not be afraid to criticize the traditions of pageants. Both in the workshop sponsored by the committee and in the Japanese American press (primarily aimed at in group discussions), the committee remained concerned about the status of women and their continuing to be judged based on beauty alone. They also managed to tie it to civil rights. Nakano explained,

> The problem of the organization is involving itself in an activity (beauty contests) that prohibited some persons from participating because of race . . . a clause in the contest rules which specifically requires one parent of the contestant to be "100 percent Japanese" blatantly violates civil rights laws. (1985, 6)

In 1988 the pageant in San Francisco was canceled. One of the general cochairmen of the Cherry Blossom Festival that year, Steve Nakajo, said that he decided to do away with it for financial reasons. He substituted a scholarship contest in its place. There were mixed reactions to this. Many supported him, particularly the WCC, since they felt that he was taking their suggestion by doing away with a superficial sexist contest based on looks, and substituting something more substantive. The chair himself thought that the pageant was outdated and a waste of money. But many disagreed and there was public outrage including letters to the two Japanese English newspapers in San Francisco arguing that the pageant was a tradition of Japanese America and that "we" had no representative at important cultural events in other cities and Japan, if "we" had no queen.

There was a flurry of letters in response to the chairman's decision to eliminate the queen pageant and *Asian Week* newspaper ran a two-page spread with the banner headline, "The Queen Is Dead!" Those outraged by the elimination argued, taking their lead from the feminist challenge to the pageant made by the WCC, that the pageant was not sexist, not just about looks, but about intelligence and culture as well. Mei Nakano was not convinced,

> No matter what the other virtues of the queen the single most important factor of the contests is the physical image . . . the winner is most apt to be one who most resembles Miss America–slim, tall, round eyed, and light skinned, a look not exactly inherent in most Japanese American women.

> And about benefits—most of those go to the winner, not the community.
> Not all traditions are positive. All the more credit to the chairperson of the
> Cherry Blossom Festival for their courage. (Nakano 1988, 7)

Reiterating the concerns of the WCC, Nakano and other opponents of the pageant welcomed the chairpersons' decision. They based their disagreement with the pageant firmly on feminist grounds, echoing common themes found in larger, more mainstream feminism—that the pageant was superficial, that it perpetuated white models of beauty and benefited no one. Again, the argument was based, for the most part, on the idea that part of the evil of pageants was that they encouraged Japanese American women to try to approximate a "white," that is, Miss America, model of beauty. Nakano is very specific in her description of that white model when she reiterates that the winner will most likely have white features. Most of the participants in the pageants were aware of this "white is right" bias sneaking into the pageant. They agreed that Nakano and her supporters may have a point about standards of beauty.

But did the Japanese American community, in the process of the pageant, just adopt a white standard of beauty and practice without a critical examination of it or without altering at all? The pageants were never a direct and mindless acceptance of assimilationist white models of beauty, but instead the pageants had for a long time been a place to create alternative models of beauty specifically for Japanese American women. For example, many of the beautiful (read: white) models are quite tall and slim. In most of the pageants, height had very little to do with it and queens were both very tall (one was 5 feet 9 inches) and very short (one was 4 feet 10 inches). There then may be more than one model of beauty at work in the pageants. Much of the literature about beauty including feminist critiques of beauty is unable to analyze this issue because they focus solely on white women (Wolf 1991). They are weak at analyzing alternative models of beauty perpetuated in women and communities of color. But, in fact, there are multiple and sometimes conflicting models of beauty. So while this debate in San Francisco was supposedly about feminism, it actually revealed much about what people were thinking was beautiful in racial terms.

Others argued that because the pageant was only about "the community" that Japanese American standards of beauty were at stake, not white standards. Still others argued that actually looking white and approximating the white beauty standards worked against you in the pageant. One pageant candidate said,

> She did really well. The only reason I can think of that she didn't win is that she doesn't look full Japanese. She was too white looking. You can't have too fair of skin and obviously with the eyes you can have round eyes, but they have to have double eyelids.

Ironically, I found that most of the queens, both past and present, felt that looking light-skinned with round eyes actually made it more difficult to win, while Nakano and others seemed to be implying that this would have been an advantage for them.

The supporters of the pageant fought back on similar turf, taking the feminists at their word. They worked harder to disprove the idea that the pageant was just about beauty. They extolled the virtues of the pageant and pointed out that the criteria on which the queen is chosen does not have anything to do with how she looks. While moving away from the racial and physical markers of women in pageants, the supporters of the pageant oftentimes made ethnicity-based arguments. They believed the pageants to be not about looks, but about culture. But they still weren't willing to do away with the racial eligibility rules.

Still 1988 caused such a debate and complaints from community members that the pageant was reinstated the next year and certain changes were made, again in response to feminist critiques. The scoring criteria were made public and the committee stopped giving the measurements of the candidates. Ironically, the first real feminist challenge to the queen pageants had come from within the ranks of the participants themselves in Los Angeles in the 1970s. While most of the Japanese American pageants did not have a bathing-suit competition, Los Angeles was one of the only cities that did, until 1979. In 1979 the contestants themselves collectively refused to wear the bathing suits and said that it was degrading to women. The committee panicked at the embarrassment of it all, quickly canceled the bathing-suit component of the pageant, and there have not been bathing suits since.

Even though this debate seems to have died down, the effects are still traceable in the pageant itself. Most of the interviewees felt that women these days didn't want to participate in the pageants because they were stigmatized. In recruiting new candidates, the committee tried diligently to convince women that the pageant was not about beauty, but about culture and community service. Before the impact of feminism and the WCC, these protests weren't happening.

This debate over the pageants tells us much about the internal debates over feminism and its impact on the Japanese American community, but it also tells us about the outside forces which can and do impinge on the community. Interestingly, the WCC also based its criticism of the pageants on the idea that they were racist because some cities required one parent of the participant to be 100 percent Japanese. They argued clearly, but somewhat unsuccessfully, that the pageants discriminated against mixed-race Japanese Americans. So while they thought they should defend the mixed-race women, they also seemed to despise them for looking too white or maybe conforming too much to the white standard of beauty. However, there is some evidence that both white and Japanese standards of beauty are being constructed and reinforced in the context of the pageant. As we saw, the candidate best approximating ideals of whiteness didn't always win. While this debate was started by feminist critiques of pageants, it also had and continues to have racial components, which mirror debates that went on before in the 1980s about mixed-race queens. "Doing gender" within the pageants was deeply intertwined with race and racial meanings through racial control of gendered bodies in the queens.

Conclusion

The pageant is a stage that reflects the ongoing concerns in the local communities about a decline in community commitment and service, loss of culture, and racial dilution. Through the interview and Q&A sections of the pageant, we saw how the themes of community service (obligation) and cultural education and preservation serve to highlight the racial intent of the candidates aspiring to be queen. The judges were also seen to impact how conflated much of the judging criteria really are and how they are differently, but still fairly consistently interpreted.

As the queen moves outward from the pageant night to her larger audience of the community and other locales in her visitations as queen, she comes in contact with sponsors and larger community politics. The sponsorship of the pageant was examined in reference to the commodification of the women as "selling mechanisms" and the corresponding emotions that they must master in order to be successful symbols of not only the community, but also its economic interests. Finally, we saw how the queen as a symbol of the community struggled under the pressure of debates about her which put her in conflict with some of the "community" (feminists and antipageant groups) that she claimed to represent. The queens were positioned between the U.S. racial state, which wouldn't let them be American (you speak English so well!) and the Japanese racial state, which wouldn't allow them to be Japanese. The queen is a symbol of all of these as the ambassadress doing race work by networking between these racial states.

In the end, the queen is clearly a symbol not only of a racialized ethnic community, but she is measured against cultural and gendered criteria. Her negotiation of feminism in particular highlights how gender is racialized in the case of Japanese American beauty pageants. The larger process of racial and ethnic claims is narrowed as the queen moves from the relatively safe setting of the pageant proper to the world beyond in her visitations and public appearances. Many of the claims she makes, to racial authenticity and representativeness of local Japanese Americans, are challenged through control of gender, demands of sponsors, and the "community" in bodily (seen as racialized) ways. Race, though, in this instance is also used to limit certain types of gender and femininity allowed in the context of the pageant.

7   Percentages, Parts, and Power: Racial Eligibility Rules and Local Versions of Japanese Americanness in Context

The pageants reflect the communities from which they come and the specific local flavor of being Japanese American. One of the queen candidates in the 1990s explained to me, "Los Angeles is glitzy, Hollywood, you know, the girls are glamorous. San Francisco, well, they are politically aware. Seattle, they are smart. It is a scholarship contest, you know. In Hawaii, the girls are all full blooded and the pageant is a big deal."
—From the author's fieldnotes

This chapter extends the discussion of race in the local Japanese American communities to show how institutional forces and structural characteristics and pressures can shape racial projects. Specifically, it examines how Japanese Americanness is negotiated collectively in relation to other racial and ethnic communities through local beauty pageants. I examine how definitions of Japanese Americanness in racial terms are narrowed on more macrolevels of social interaction. Larger structural forces such as political and economic power and demographic size strongly shaped race, culture, ethnicity, and gender throughout the beauty pageants. This chapter illustrates how Japanese Americanness has been constructed and reconstructed in different ways in different Japanese American communities in Honolulu, Los Angeles, San Francisco, and Seattle. The critical factors in this process (demographic structure and size, relationships with the majority community, and economic and political power) are the focus of the analysis. The analysis illustrates how these larger structural forces shape the way that race work is done at more microlevels of social interaction.

We saw earlier how Japanese Americanness is negotiated via language, names, and how one looks or appears to others physically (often attributed to the social constructions known as race). These are illustrations of how larger group expectations about race and ethnicity affect individual behavior and how social actors can develop innovative claims for legitimating a hierarchy of racial and ethnic identities. Mixed-race candidates often feel deficient because they are mixed, and must compensate for this by trying to be "more" Japanese. Through race work, they are responding to larger understandings of race and ethnicity, which structure their social actions. The debate over mixed-race queens in Los Angeles, the racialized debate about feminism in San Francisco, and the conflicts between Japanese and Japanese American notions of racial and cultural authenticity illustrate the fact that the queen is herself a symbolic bodily representation of larger social groups and forces and an object of "race work." Therefore, debates about her are by definition about the community as well.

On a relational level, we also saw how different Japanese American communities relate to other outside communities, particularly whites, and challenge or recreate existing racial and ethnic hierarchies. Through the pageant we can see evidence of the Japanese American community's relationship with others and how it is structured by economic and political power, demographic size, and rates of intermarriage. These larger relationships, which impact the definition of who is Japanese American, trickle down into the collective and individual levels of racial and ethnic negotiation. In this chapter, I focus on how the respective Japanese American communities fit into the racial/ethnic hierarchies of their local communities and look at how these relations are reflected in and influence Japanese American self-definition. To understand this empirically, I focus on the negotiation of racial ancestry rules, which guide eligibility for participating in the pageants, and how this varies across the communities.

All of the pageants I studied had racial rules, and thus race was at the center of debates around eligibility. These rules were the mechanisms used to construct the boundary of who is within the group, and therefore qualified to represent it as queen, and who is not. Because the criteria are assumed to be linked to bodily traits, that is, one would look Japanese if one was 50 percent or more of Japanese ancestry, the focus on racial rules reveals the continuing importance of race as a way to organize Japanese American social life. It is a distillation of Japanese American cultural values and norms into a racial form.

This chapter uses the ancestry rules in each of the Japanese American pageants to illustrate how each community is different and has dealt with demographic change differently. The language of each rule is slightly different, but in three of the four cities the rules use the word *ancestry*, as in, "the candidate must be of 50 percent Japanese ancestry." Others, mostly scholars in the Native American community, have written about these types of rules as blood-quantum rules because it draws attention to the fact that major decisions, for example, federal reparations to Native American tribes, are based on "how much blood" one has of a certain tribe (Wilson 1992; Hamill 2003). The formula of blood quantum dictates that the amount of blood denotes ancestry and that ancestry is divided into biological parts. Likewise, the ancestry rules in the Japanese American pageants are dependent upon parts, usually percentages or fractions, for their meaning. For example, the rule in San Francisco states that a candidate must be "of at least 50 percent Japanese Ancestry," meaning she can have one natural parent who is of 100 percent Japanese ancestry and one who is not, or she can have two parents who are each of 50 percent Japanese ancestry and still meet the rule. The 1954 Nisei Week pageant rule number one was "The candidates for Nisei Week Queen Contest [must] be of Japanese ancestry at least one half."

There were three main purposes to the ancestry rules. First, from their founding the pageants had ancestry rules in order to preserve the beauty pageants sphere for Japanese American women. Excluded from mainstream pageants precisely because of racial attitudes that favored whites, Japanese Americans began their own pageants and tried to preserve them for Japanese American women representing the community. Second, racial rules were implemented to make sure that the women participating did indeed have connections to the local Japanese American community. By using ancestry rules, it was possible to check up on claims to Japaneseness by locating their family, usually within a fairly tight network of Japanese Americans. In Los Angeles in 2004 the Nisei Week Queen rules and regulations specified that an "[a]pplicant must be a minimum of 50 percent Japanese ancestry. Applicant will supply parents' names and birth certificate if requested." Other rules were aimed at compliance with being a "local girl," emphasizing place rather than race. For example, in San Francisco one must "have lived in the Northern California area for at least one year," meaning that a student from, say, New York, could compete as long as she was now residing in northern California. Seattle had a more complex residency rule; it claimed that in order to run in the pageant a woman "must have family residing in the greater Seattle area" and "must be attending school in the greater Seattle area." Being a scholarship pageant, the residency rule for school was a logistical one (which incidentally rules out women not pursuing higher education and narrows the class background of the candidates), but more important is the idea that the women running would be made local representatives through their familial (read: racial), blood-related kin. The importance of being local was particularly significant in Hawaii where the queen must be a resident of Hawaii and local nice girl (Yano 2006).

The third reason the racial eligibility rules were so uniform in all the pageants, even from an early stage, was that the appearance of the queen needed to reflect physically and bodily (and racially) the local Japanese American community that she represented. The residency and racial ancestry rules work both to create a pool of women who fit the criteria and to rule out a whole range of other women who could not become queen (women not in higher education in Seattle, women who were not local in San Francisco, women who were less than 50 percent Japanese, however defined, in Los Angeles and so on).

We can see how these debates about the pageant and the queen are shaped by the culture of the larger local community and its impact on Japanese Americans, the size and power of the Japanese American community in the local racial hierarchy and the beliefs that Japanese Americans have about their relationship to others (particularly whites).

Over time, demographic shifts have led to changes in the ancestry rules in each city. It is ultimately the relations that Japanese Americans have (or their perceived relations) with others that shaped how each Japanese American community came to define itself racially through these racial eligibility criteria in the pageants.

The Politics of Racial Eligibility Rules

While the Japanese American communities in Los Angeles, San Francisco, Seattle, and Honolulu are very different in many ways, they all have queen pageants and racialized rules about how much Japanese ancestry one must have to participate. In every city, the rules require that a potential candidate must have a percentage of Japanese ancestry in order to participate (ranging from 25 to 50 percent). By basing participation on ancestry requirements, there is an implicit assumption that blood is directly related to culture. In order to have an authentic Japanese American queen, it is assumed that the ancestry rules ensure that the candidates will have some culture. In addition, the rules also serve to ensure that the queen will physically (racially) look Japanese. The fact that the rules exist at all and are based upon the same criteria, that is, ancestry, signifies the dominance across various communities of the idea that in order to be a representative of the Japanese American community one must be racially Japanese. As we saw earlier, racial or blood-quantum rules had been used in the past to control the Japanese American community—from the outside in the internment camps and internally within the community in other areas, such as participation in community basketball leagues.

The racial eligibility rules also highlight women's bodies as the locus of debate about race and gender in the pageants. Elena Tajima Creef writes how the bodies of multiracial women problematize Japaneseness Americanness: "such a multiply-marked body problematically exists outside of simple visual categories of racial and national representation" (2004, 177). While the cultural, or ethnic, component of the queen is important, it is clearly not the only criteria for selection. If selection were dependent solely upon culture, a white or black person who had lived in Japan and who was sufficiently familiar with Japanese or Japanese American culture would be acceptable. But they are not even eligible to represent the community as queen because of racial rules.

While the presence of the racial rules is an important indicator of how Japanese Americanness is continuing to be defined in various communities, the difference in the racial rules in each city signify important differences in negotiating race and ethnicity in these different contexts. The variability of the racial rules in each community is directly related to their demographic size and political and economic power. This can be seen in the fact that Honolulu, the largest Japanese American community (and largest in relation to other ethnic/racial groups in Hawaii), maintained a racial rule for queen contestants of 100 percent Japanese ancestry until 1999. Other communities, such as Los Angeles and San Francisco, have racial rules that state that "at least one parent must be of 100 percent Japanese ancestry." The demographically smallest community with a pageant, Seattle, has very vague racial rules that seem to have disappeared from the criteria for the queen, but in the past have been thought to be as little as 25 percent Japanese ancestry.[1]

In order to participate, candidates are asked to prove that they are of Japanese ancestry and thus their racial authenticity is questioned. Some candidates showed their birth certificate upon which the race of each parent was written.[2] If there was no birth certificate, as in the case of Japanese nationals who have Japanese birth certificates upon which there is no race or if the race of the parents was not on the certificate, the candidates were asked to either bring their family in to be interviewed or to draw their family tree. Again, compliance with this rule has been regulated in different ways in different cities. In Los Angeles, the candidates are sponsored by local Japanese American community organizations and there are local pageants or competitions before they get to the finals of the Nisei Week Queen Pageant. According to the Nisei Week queen coordinator, it is up to the local organizations to ensure that each candidate is eligible and meets the racial rules. Therefore, the Nisei Week Queen committee trusts the word of the local organizations.

In Hawaii, potential candidates are interviewed in their home along with their parents by the pageant organizers to reassure the committee members that the racial rule is being maintained. The use of the birth certificate and family interview to prove and authenticate racial claims in biological terms essentializes and reinforces the ideal of biological race, even in mixed-race households. The interview and authenticity checks for mixed-race women are about proving that they are indeed 50 percent (one parent) of Japanese ancestry. Even though mixed, this does nothing to undo racially essential thinking in terms of the eligibility criteria. In Hawaii the women deemed authentic by the committee were then weeded down to fifteen semifinalists and were photographed and pictured with their parents in the pageant booklet. The racial line, it is clear, comes from the parents, and proof of race is accomplished by placing the candidates within a photo of familial relations. It also makes claims to being a good Japanese American girl who has filial piety to her parents and is clearly part of an intact family evident to public consumers of the pageant.

Many of the women also verbally thanked and recognized their family's contributions. Two goals are accomplished in this process: racial fact-checking and family investigation. Other cities don't do these family photos, although the parents' names are listed. Perhaps it is difficult to get the girls who live far from their family into a family photo (less so in Hawaii) or maybe the divorce rate or prevalence of split families doesn't fit with the image the committee is trying to transmit. It also saves the committees in San Francisco and Los Angeles from having to photographically feature white or other racial backgrounds of parents of mixed-race Japanese Americans.

These racial rules clearly divide those who are sufficiently Japanese American to represent the community as queen and those who are not. The debate about the racial rule and even the ability of mixed-race queens to represent the community has brought to the fore the changing understandings of race and ethnicity and certainly the relationship between them. We saw in chapter 3 how community members argued over whether a mixed-race woman who didn't look Japanese could be a Japanese American queen. How can she be queen if she doesn't physically represent the average Japanese American? Even in Hawaii, where there was no such issue before mixed-race women were allowed to run in the pageant, there was still much debate (1984, 1985, and again in 1993) and discussion about the possibility of allowing mixed-race women to run in the future and the impact that this would have on the pageant (Yano 2006, 304). All these debates end up illustrating the complex separations that local Japanese American communities make between race and ethnicity and the changing relationship between them. The very presence of mixed-race women and their participation or debated participation as queen highlights the very question of who *is* Japanese American? What is Japanese Americanness and increasingly what relationship does it have to the larger (usually white) society? The racial rules tap into the racial "we" and argue that bloodlines are essential for claiming Japanese Americanness. In this inscription of race, it is genes, familial ties, and bloodlines that determine physical appearance and are assumed to be racially determining. Racial rules, then, signal the embodiment of raciality where blood-quantum racial eligibility rules represent community spheres of control and possible places of resistance to the majority culture through debates about physical appearance, authenticity, and community ties.

Claiming Legitimacy for Pageants

By analyzing the pageant queens and their behavior, appearance, and deportment, we can see how versions of Japanese Americanness become deeply imbricated with gender and class meanings in the production of the queen as a good Japanese American girl. In the Los Angeles, San Francisco, Honolulu, and Greater Seattle Japanese American Queen pageants, organizers validated and legitimated themselves as the authentic Japanese American pageants because of their strong relationships and cultural exchanges across the regions. These social networks underpin the claim to racial/ethnic authenticity precisely through the contact of the queens. These networks explain how these links perpetuate the claim to authenticity and even legitimate rules and standards across pageants in each of the cities. They serve to make uniform the pageant form across all the cities without losing the particularly local character expressed within them.

These four pageants also make the claim to authenticity based on the fact that they are the ones chosen to attend the Miss Nikkei International pageant in Brazil, which also invites women of Japanese ancestry from Mexico, Canada, Peru, and all the "colonias" (regions) of Brazil in July. In 1995, when I was doing fieldwork, there was no trip to Brazil, but the past trips to Brazil are instructive as to how the Japanese communities in the U.S. cities, on the mainland and Hawaii, relate to Japanese Brazilians.

The trips to Brazil by earlier queens illustrate the different versions of Japaneseness (both racially and ethnically defined) that exist. The first cultural clash was language—Brazilians speak Portuguese, other Latin Americans (e.g., Peruvians) speak Spanish, most Japanese Americans don't speak Japanese or Portuguese—so communication is in Japanese if the queens can speak it or English, or there is no communication at all. Also, the cultural clash between North Americans and Latin Americans is particularly clear around gender roles and expectations of bodily display in the bathing-suit competition in the Miss Nikkei International pageant in São Paulo. The Japanese American girls from the four U.S. cities were mortified by the thong bikinis that they were given to wear. Since there is a decided de-emphasis on bathing suits and bare bodies in the United States, they found the Brazil experience too sexualized and revealing. They comforted themselves by thinking about the fact that they didn't know anyone in Brazil and would probably never be back there again after the pageant.

The clash is not just about gender but—because of the assumed link between body, race, and character—is also about different types of "morality" and "femininity." Debates about race then are not just about racial heritage, but instead about socially constructed cultural differences. These gender and sexuality differences that don't seem to be connected to race instead point out the diversity within the category Nikkei (of Japanese descent). Fundamentally, the cultural clash between Brazilian and North American understandings of Japaneseness are about different racial and gender norms regarding what is appropriate for Japanese-descent women.

The difference was most clear in terms of racial background. Queens from Los Angeles and Hawaii who had been to, and even won, the Miss Nikkei International spoke of the high rate of racial mixing in Brazil and indeed in other South American countries such as Peru. The North American queens were struck by how accepted the mixed-race queens of Japanese ancestry from all over Brazil or the "colonias" were in the pageant. They marveled at the fluidity of racial categorization in the pageants and that the mixed-race women from Brazil did not feel under pressure or embarrassed when they didn't speak Japanese. This may be an expression, even in a racially defined pageant such as the Miss Nikkei International, of the larger social context of racial meanings in Brazil which, for some, are based more on colorism or class differences than strict racial rules (Nobles 2000).

The cultural clash between different Japanese descent communities was also pointed out at the Nikkei 2000 conference held in San Francisco's Japantown in 2000. For example, youth representatives from Peru and Brazil were very concerned about their problems of *dekasegi* (return migrants), which is not a direct problem for the United States. Even so, the Nikkei 2000 conference displayed a broader recognition by local Bay Area Japanese American community leaders that the Nikkei community is global. Representatives from Canada, the Midwest, and Hawaii echoed each other that the understanding of Nikkei (of Japanese descent) has traditionally been a very hegemonic, West Coast understanding of Japanese Americanness. For example, the list "101 Ways to Tell If You Are Japanese American" published in the *Rafu Shimpo* (the Los Angeles local Japanese/English newspaper) listed predominantly Californian cultural experiences like going to Nisei Week or playing in the "Friends of Richard" basketball tournament. This hegemony of "West Coast" thinking about what it means to be a Nikkei was challenged at Nikkei 2000, when representatives from other cities, regions, and countries reported. For example, the Chicago-based Midwest representative, Jean Fujiu discussed openly the issues of mixed-race Japanese American members. She claimed that being mixed was not an issue in the Midwest due to the small size of the community and large rates of out marriage. She claimed that if someone was part Japanese American that person was Japanese American. This clearly marks multiracial people in the Midwest as part of the community while in other places, where the community may be larger and more exclusive, mixed-race Japanese Americans may be made to feel less a part of the community. These examples illustrate the diversity of definitions of Japanese Americanness, and that the pageants I studied perpetuated not just one version of Japanese Americanness, but many.

Queen Pageants in Japanese American Communities

Most people involved in the pageants keenly expressed what they felt to be the changing nature of the community in the interviews, but their remarks cannot be limited to the pageant. During fieldwork, every day that I was in the field, some reference was made to the relative size and power of the Japanese American community and the future of the community. Most expressed concern (although less so in Hawaii) about the shrinking nature of the community, the whitewashing or assimilation of Japanese Americans, or the changing composition of the community (with a particular focus on the role that mixed-race people played in the loss of cultural traditions). Most felt that the pageants, like other Japanese American organizations, were struggling to keep participation up due to the small size of the community. Likewise, most people saw the racial rule as being demographically driven. They explained that Hawaii could "afford" to have a 100 percent ancestry rule until the late 1990s because they have so many women who want to run in the pageant, whereas Los Angeles could not afford to do that because they would not get enough women to participate if they didn't allow women who were 50 percent Japanese to run. Pageant organizers in Hawaii also felt that "if we get enough to participate with it (the rule) this way, then why change? When we have to change to get more people, we will." And they did.

Table 8 summarizes racial eligibility rules and their social contexts. In San Francisco and Los Angeles there was recognition that the community was changing and they wanted to allow mixed-race women, who they saw as a part of the community, to participate. Even so, most people felt that the rule should stay at "one parent is of 100 percent Japanese Ancestry" and should not go to any less than that one grandparent was 100 percent. Most arguments in support of the rule mentioned that the queen should look Japanese in order to be effective. This seems to imply that race remains salient because race is supposedly correlated with how one looks. Others argued that the queen represents a racial/ethnic community and that if she didn't understand the culture or the community how could she represent them, thus implying that race is somehow a determinant of cultural prowess.

Finally, all the participants and interviewees felt that each queen uniquely reflected the city from which she came. The cities had reputations. For example, the Nisei Queen, who hails from Los Angeles, is known as being glamorous, sophisticated, and very "Hollywood." San Francisco's queen had the reputation of being smart, but not the most beautiful queen, which fit well with the more progressive nature of San Francisco's focus on speaking ability rather than beauty. Whether always true or not, the queen's type of Japanese Americanness was shaped nonetheless by the city from which they came, the type of pageant the city had, and the organizers and funders. They were also shaped by the local Japanese American community's perception of itself, including gender politics. What follows is a brief explanation of the history of the pageant in each city, the debates that have taken place, and the specific form of the ancestry rule and its implications.

Los Angeles, California: Hollywood, but Not Too Hollywood

Nisei Week in Los Angeles was the first Japanese American festival to have a queen to reign over the festivities. Started in 1934, Nisei Week tried to counteract the Depression by encouraging people to "buy in Lil Tokyo" (Kurashige 2002). A queen contest was added in 1935 to draw more people into Little Tokyo to spend money. Aimed at the

Table 8. Pageant information from four cities

City	Racial rule	First pageant	Japanese American population in 2000	Japanese Americans as percentage of local population in 2000	Number of applicants	Main criteria
Honolulu	50% (changed in 1999 from 100%)	1953	228,290	26.3	50 or more	beauty
Los Angeles	50%	1935	200,802	1.2	approximately 35	beauty, community service
San Francisco Bay Area	50%	1968	105,414	1.5	6–10	essay, community service, talent
Seattle	25% or less	1960	45,823	1.3	3–5	scholarship, talent

Note: Population numbers and percentages of the total population come from U.S. Census data, 2000. Population numbers for Japanese alone and in combination are done by metropolitan area because this reflects more accurately the areas from which the pageants draw their participants. These metropolitan areas are Honolulu, Los Angeles (Los Angeles, Riverside, and Orange County), San Francisco (San Francisco, Oakland, and San Jose), and Seattle (Tacoma and Bremerton). See http://factfinder.census.gov.

younger Nisei, the queen contest was and continues to be a major attraction in the Nisei Week Festival. Originally, the queen contest was done by merchandise ballot. For every dollar spent in a Little Tokyo shop, a customer would receive a ballot, which could be cast for any of the five candidates. This created quite a contest with people holding back their ballots until the last moment to create a surge of voting and sometimes a surprise winner. Basically a popularity contest, the queen pageant also helped to bring needed dollars into community businesses. Alice Watanabe was the first Nisei Week queen chosen in 1935 and she posed in her borrowed kimono for photos with the general chair, Clarence Arima, and various non–Japanese American officials. From interviews with early queens, I learned that they did very little public speaking, but felt it was their job to smile, look nice, and represent the Japanese American community to others, particularly the white dominant society. At this time the queen and her court didn't travel very far and their lives weren't that glamorous. As one past queen commented, "We got as far as the [San Fernando] Valley and we won a toaster at most!"

It must be said that while the Nisei Week Queen did not start out as a beauty contest but as a way to raise money, many of the early participants realized that it was their only outlet to affirm Japanese women, and themselves, as beautiful. Because of continuing discrimination against Japanese Americans, such as the Alien Land Law of 1913, which ruled that the Issei could not own land, or the Naturalization Act of 1790, which would not let them become citizens, Japanese American women could not participate in larger pageants such as the Miss California Pageant or the Miss America Pageant. The Nisei Week Queen Pageant was a way for young women who wanted to participate to do so. At the same time, the pageant represented an alternative model of beauty—one different from that prevalent in dominant society. To be Nisei Week Queen, one had to be a Japanese beauty, but also understand American culture. In this way, the Nisei Week Queen was not just a carbon copy of Miss America, but instead offered a different model of what a queen should be. We cannot assume that Japanese American standards of beauty were or still are the same as whites. This is not to say that Japanese American women were not influenced by western standards of beauty. In fact, the Nisei Week Queen was supposed to be as comfortable in a kimono as she was in an evening gown and heels so she clearly had an understanding of both western and Japanese beauty standards. The point is that the early Nisei Week Queen Pageant represented an opportunity to validate Japanese women and their model of beauty while at the same time recognizing Western beauty standards.

Other changes influenced the perceptions of beauty. By 1959 the ballot system had been replaced by private judging, usually done at a committee member's house. It was a very private, small affair and the queen was then announced and crowned at a coronation ball, which was a large and public affair. It was during this period that some of the judges started to come from the entertainment industry located in and around Hollywood. The introduction of these outsiders, mainly white, who were professionals in the show-business industry changed the nature of the pageant to make it less about support from the local community and more about glamour and beauty. This brought debates about which model of beauty the white judges would be imposing on the contestants.

The influence of the local community can be seen in every city and Los Angeles' Japanese American community was no exception. The presence of Hollywood and the entertainment industry can still be felt in the Nisei Week Queen Pageant and various other functions. Judges still come from the industry, the Mistress and/or Master of Ceremonies are celebrities, and professional dancers, singers, and musicians perform the entertainment during the pageant, even though it is attended mainly by local Japanese Americans. Unlike the other pageants, the Nisei Week pageant has a theme, which is wholly unrelated to the festival or things Japanese. For example, during my year of fieldwork in the mid-1990s the theme of the pageant was Carnival, and so there was a professional samba band, with professional dancers as the entertainment. As someone from Los Angeles explained to me, "Who would pay $100 a seat to see the contestants dance and sing? You have to give people something entertaining for their money." The outcome of the influence of the industry was that the pageant consisted of very little time for the contestants on stage and when they were on stage they were all dressed in the same dress, which caused one judge to ask jokingly, "They all look the same, don't they?" Clearly, the Nisei Week pageant comes the closest of any of the cities I studied to being like a conventional beauty pageant, as the script and actions of the participants are similar in many ways to mainstream pageants like Miss America.

In other ways, Los Angeles' pageant is unique. The pageant contestants, once they are named a part of the court, have matching designer clothes—donated by the designer to the court. There is a tremendous sense of production about the pageant and professional videos run during and before the pageant. The scale of the production is largest in Los Angeles and the link to the entertainment industry is clear. There also have been some links between the pageant and women making it into the entertainment industry. Some of the past Nisei Week queens have gone on to become models or journalists, or have worked in the entertainment industry in production and as actresses. Although the pageant is community driven and about reaffirming Japanese American women, it is also equally influenced by the community that surrounds it, that is, Hollywood, commercialism, and glamour. This brings in contact two different racialized models of beauty; the mainstream Hollywood (white) model and the community (Japanese American) model.

In addition, the geographic arrangement of Los Angeles influences the pageant, festival, and parade in interesting ways. On the drive toward downtown Los Angeles, it is readily obvious that the surroundings of Little Tokyo in 1995 are very different than they were fifty years ago. The area surrounding Little Tokyo (near First, Second, and San Pedro streets) is quite run down and populated most consistently by homeless people. The major renovations of Little Tokyo that took place in the 1970s and '80s were largely due to Japanese capital and investment by Japanese businesses. The hotel where the pageant was held, the New Otani, is very upscale and frequented by Japanese businessmen and tourists, but the surroundings are not congruent with the hotel itself. It is telling that the development and survival of downtown has been limited primarily to Little Tokyo and been done with Japanese money. The Japanese ownership brought sometimes tense relationships with local Japanese Americans, some of whom were involved in picketing the New Otani one year during the Nisei Week festivities for not allowing employees to unionize and not paying union-level wages.

In addition, the dispersion of Japanese American communities into various parts of Southern California has created smaller but viable Japantowns. As one participant explained, "People don't have to come into Lil Tokyo anymore. They can get their Japanese food in Gardena and it is safer than coming downtown." Particularly after the riots in

Los Angeles in 1992, many people were afraid to come down to the festival or even Little Tokyo for fear of being mugged. Participation in Nisei Week seems to have dropped off and the number of both participants and spectators in the parade, for example, seems to be shrinking. This has also affected the pageant in that they have trouble getting people to the pageant, which is almost always held in a hotel near Little Tokyo, and getting women to agree to run in the pageant, since they have to come downtown for many of the rehearsals. Where they once had ten or fifteen women vying for the title, they now only have about six candidates each year. The geographic arrangement of Los Angeles, with a very small central geographic downtown area and many sprawling suburbs, makes the centralization of Little Tokyo located in the downtown area hard to sustain. Merchants in the area likewise have found it difficult to keep going, while merchants like the Marukai market in suburban Torrance are expanding to shopping-mall proportions. All of this affects the pageant, its funding, and the number of people it can draw in to participate or attend. Interviewees most often interpreted this as the failure of Japanese Americans to remain a cohesive geographic community. When Nisei Week started in 1935, most Japanese Americans lived near or were willing to come into Little Tokyo to celebrate it. It was a time for the community to come together to help each other financially, but also to celebrate the culture and community. Today, the dispersion of economic and social centers for the Japanese American community is reflected in Nisei Week Queen proceedings. Even so, the contestants continued to be tied to the community in other ways such as through their sponsorship by local community organizations.

The rules guiding the principles of Nisei Week have also changed over time. No one I interviewed recalled there being racialized rules in the early years of Nisei Week, in the 1930s and just before and after World War II. One or two contestants were mixed, but for the most part it wasn't an issue. One interviewee said, "When they made these rules they didn't have to think about those kinds of things. Everyone was pretty much full Japanese." By the 1950s, there was a rule that "candidates be of Japanese ancestry, at least one half."[3] Even with this rule, still very few mixed-race women participated. One participant speculated, "They probably didn't really need that rule until maybe the 1960s." This may be because there were very few interracial marriages to produce mixed-race children before and after World War II.

It was illegal in California until 1948 for Japanese Americans to marry whites. By the time of the repeal of antimiscegenation laws nationally in 1967 with the *Loving v. Virginia* decision, the Japanese American out marriage rate was already on the increase. It wasn't until 1974 that the Nisei Week Queen was mixed. Elsa Akemi Cuthbert started a trend, which caused outrage, and for many she marked the beginning of the debate over the mixed-race queens. It seems clear that in the early stages of the Nisei Week Queen pageant there was really no need for racialized rules about who could and who could not participate in the pageant. It was assumed that everyone who wanted to partici- pate and everyone who did participate was 100 percent (full) Japanese even though there were mixed women participating. When the demo- graphics of the community started to change, the rules changed with it and allowed women who were 50 percent or who had one parent who was 100 percent to participate. It wasn't until mixed-race women started participating, even in some years becoming the majority of the contestants and at times the queen, that the debate over the racial makeup of the queen became an issue. There was no need to discuss race before, but with the racial ancestry of the queens changing, there was a full-scale, community-wide discussion about race. It was clear- ly acceptable to some that mixed-race women could participate, but when they started to win that was more difficult to accept. The pag- eant didn't just reflect racial politics or provide a field on which they took place—in this case it prompted the racial politics itself.

In 1982 a debate began shortly after the Nisei Week Queen for that year (Janet Barnes) was chosen. Linden Nishinaga of Monterey Park wrote in to the editor of the *Rafu Shimpo* newspaper, Los Angeles' largest Japanese/English paper, about what he perceived to be too many mixed-ancestry beauty queens. He wrote,

> It seems to me that for a Nikkei population of 261,822 in California alone, the vast majority of whom have full Japanese ancestry, a more representative group of beauties could easily have been selected. Of the nine candidates, four on the basis of surnames and Eurasian looks, were half Japanese and half Caucasian. This is a full 44 percent. Both the winner and runner-up were of (mixed parentage). This trend has been going on now for four years. Two years ago, for example, another half had won the event and "repre- sented" us while the runner-up, a full Japanese, later went on and won the Pasadena Rose Queen contest. This disproportionate selection and seeming infatuation with the Eurasian looks not only runs counter to what I consider pride in our Japanese ancestry but also to the very idea of the Nisei Week

Queen tradition itself . . . in order to appreciate the particular Japanese beauty one must look through a different set of glasses and discover the many other special qualities, features, and mannerisms one normally wouldn't be looking for in our often superficial commercialized Hollywood glamour model environment. Besides, why then should we stop with the half Caucasians? Why not half-Black women? Or why not wholes of other races, e.g., blondes? So in all seriousness, since the Nisei Week Queen is supposed to represent our Nikkei community which is still large, viable and strongly identifiable, our beauty representatives should at least be representative. For how else are we ever going to stop playing games and start becoming truly proud of being just what we really are, Japanese Americans. (Nishinaga 1982, 3)

There was a torrent of response in the form of letters to the editor of the *Rafu Shimpo* and many challenged the racial notions of Nishinaga's assumptions about who was Japanese and the use of the racial eligibility rules. Allys Mayumi Moreno, a mixed-race woman from La Puente, wrote:

Who is Mr. Nishinaga to say that because my parents were not both Japanese I should be less proud of being Japanese American than he is, or that I am less representative of the Nikkei population than he is? It saddens me considerably to read this type of prejudice because this is the kind of village-elder rigid dogma that I hoped we had left behind when we chose to call ourselves Japanese Americans. I had hoped after all we had suffered during and after World War II we had become a little more tolerant of others. (Moreno 1982, 3)

By invoking both the racial rules used during internment and the recollection of internment as a racially motivated collective crime against Japanese Americans, Moreno powerfully moves away from the assumed racial purity of the homeland Japan, which she hopes is "left behind" in the United States. Others wrote in to say that the racial eligibility rules recognized mixed ancestry as Japanese American, contradicting Nishinaga's implication that only full Japanese are really Japanese American and therefore representative. Jun Kawasaki wrote:

[I]f I recall correctly, a ruling was established by the Nisei Week Committee as long as one parent is Japanese, the aspiring young lady qualifies as a candidate. Secondly, the word *Nikkei* designate any person of Japanese (ancestry) lineage, And I feel that half Japanese qualifies. (Kawasaki 1982, 4)

To say that mixed-race queens were still Japanese American does nothing to challenge the concept of race as impermeable because it still

harkens back to lineage and blood. Others also disagreed with Nishinaga, but did little to question the assumption about blood or racial
rules in the first place. Y. Inouye from West Covina wrote:

> I was rather appalled by the myopic viewpoint expressed by this Oriental
> Archie Bunker. The only prerequisite for the contestants is that they be of
> Japanese ancestry and female, and the four girls singled out by Nishinaga
> were well qualified. If there is one drop of Japanese blood flowing in one's
> veins, that person is of Japanese ancestry. During World War II, the mixed
> ancestry individuals were incarcerated along with the full-blooded persons
> and these individuals have paid the price and have contributed to the prog-
> ress of all Japanese Americans in society. (Inouye 1982, 2)

The use of the "one-drop" analogy as applied during internment reinforces the community boundary to include mixed-race queens. Others
pointed the racial finger at Nishinaga himself, telling him that if he
wanted a pure festival to go to Japan, "where they really practice racial and ethnic discrimination. There treatment of Japanese of mixed
parentage is a disgrace" (Edgerton 1982, 2). Others moved away from
racial rules, drops of blood and other racial purity arguments to argue
for the embodiment of culture.

Cindy Miller from Sierra Vista, wrote:

> I feel the whole idea of the queen position is a representative for the spirit
> of Japan as well as its people. I feel that Eurasians have just as much right
> to be a representative as full blood . . . my opinion is that the representa-
> tive of Nisei Week is a personification of a feeling of pride in your heritage
> and culture. If that representative is half Caucasian, I feel that she shows
> her strength, love and pride of the Japanese culture just as much as a full-
> blooded Japanese who have not realized the struggles and meaning of what
> Japan is. (Miller 1982, 2)

While there is slippage between Japan and Japanese American in this
letter, there are clear echoes of the current contrast between "cultural
impostors" who are full, but don't fully understand what it means to be
Japanese, and the Eurasian who shows pride in her Japanese culture.

The debate came to an abrupt end when the 1980 queen, Hedy
Posey, a mixed-ancestry queen herself, wrote in to the editor:

> I think it's about time that one of the subjects of this controversy voiced
> her side as well. First of all, I may only be 50 percent Japanese, but I'm as
> proud of that 50 percent as I would be if I were 100 per cent . . . who's to
> say that I'm not as "Japanese" as any other Nisei, Sansei or Yonsei? What is
> the definition of a Japanese American anyway? I know a lot of full-blooded
> Japanese who know a lot less about heir heritage than some of my Eurasian

friends. I grew up in a Japanese neighborhood of Los Angeles, with Japanese food, culture and language in my home and attended Japanese school for 11 years . . . still some prejudiced Nisei and Sansei think that I am not "Japanese" enough to represent them. . . . During World War II, Nisei fought to be accepted as "Americans." Isn't it ironic that in this day and age, that I have to fight to be accepted as a Japanese American? Since I entered my first pageant over two years ago, I have travelled to Hawaii, San Francisco, Japan, and Brazil, not to mention all over Los Angeles, expressing my pride to be representing the Japanese American community of Los Angeles. It breaks my heart to think that the very people that I have been so proud to represent aren't proud that I'm representing them. (Posey 1982, 2)

Hedy Posey clearly was culturally proud and had the culture (language, food, neighborhood) to back up her claims to Japanese Americanness. Her voice for the Eurasian queens put an end, for the time being, to the debate about mixed-race queens in Los Angeles. However, the debate revealed publicly the increasing anxiety about intermarriage and multiracial people, the deep entrenchment of racial rules and concepts (drops of blood, rules about race), and the ongoing debates about who the queen really represents and how that collectivity (Japanese American) will be defined. The impact though was that the ancestry purity tests in the form of racial eligibility rules would endure for much longer.

In the 1990s these racial ancestry rules were often mentioned to me as discriminatory and that the U.S. government had used them during internment. One former queen said, "If you were one sixteenth Japanese even they sent you to camp. You would have to go there, but you can't be Nisei Week Queen. Why should Nisei Week be any different?" Others felt that the racial rules were suspect, but that they were very much a part of the tradition of the Nisei Week Queen. Some speculated that the rule would eventually have to change to incorporate Japanese Americans with less than 50 percent Japanese ancestry. "Maybe we will be like the Indian Reservations. If you are one thirty-second then you are in." Others felt that the rule would not change and would hold steady at 50 percent Japanese. They argued strongly that if the rule had to be changed to 25 percent, then the organizers would just "close up shop" rather than change the rule. "I doubt they will ever change the rule. I think they will shut it down first. Not even thinking they were being racist or anything. It would be like 'Oh darn, we ran out of candidates.' We faded away. Maybe that would be time for the pageant to fade away." Still others felt that the rule should change, but none said that they should do away with the rule altogether. They felt that the rule had to change due to the demographic changes in the community. "There are so many mixed marriages today that the only way you are going to get a pure Japanese nowadays is if somebody from Japan comes over. But you also want it to be a Japanese American thing. I would rather a one-quarter Japanese than a pure Japanese from Japan." This person also agreed that "It is called Nisei Week and I really think it should stay that you have to have some Japanese ancestry. A quarter is better than none." They held strongly to the idea that the queen, because she represents the community and not just culture, should be racially Japanese. They did not even entertain the idea of having the pageant with no racial rules. Clearly, race remains a salient criterion and is part of the Nisei Week Queen role. A queen without her crown, we saw in the last chapter, is not the queen. Likewise, a queen without race is not queen either. So, while she can be mixed, she can't be too mixed and still represent the community well.

Since 1935, there have been Nisei Week Festivals each year (with breaks for seven years during World War II) and much has changed. Now, there are larger prizes and trips to other places to represent the Japanese American community of Southern California, but the debate about race continues. After the large-scale debate in the 1980s, and the increasing number of hapa candidates, one would have thought that the debate would die down. In 1995, when I did fieldwork, though, both of the Nisei Week Queens (1994 and 1995) were of mixed descent. This made small ripples in some ways. *Face* magazine (an Asian American beauty magazine) in 1996 ran a small article on the inside of their front cover which pictured the current Nisei Week court getting ready for a makeover with the question "Are we insecure about our beauty?" over the top of the photo. The accompanying caption read, "Blame It on WW II. You be the judge." The article then continued to bemoan the fact that the crown went to the only hapa contestant among the court. The article implied that it was something other than beauty they were judging in the pageant, but concludes, "Maybe the judges simply felt apologetic about the beauty of full blooded Asian women" (*Face* 1996, 10). The tone of this article was particularly bold, but reveals the feelings that some have toward the continuing participation of mixed-race women in the Nisei Week Queen Pageant. The implications are that the mixed-race candidate shouldn't have won, that is, she was not qualified enough to win (in part because she is not monoracial); the only reason she won is because the judges are deluded by images that claim white is more beautiful; and by having a mixed-race queen, the Japanese American community of Southern California hurts other Asian women's self images. When I asked the queen about this incident she admitted to me that the photo was taken and printed without the Nisei Week court's permission and that the reporters never identified themselves or even asked questions of the queen and court. She also understandably was hurt by the targeting of herself as the only mixed-race candidate and angry that they felt she was not worthy of winning. She added later that she did not feel being mixed had helped her. She actually felt the opposite—that being mixed made it harder to be chosen as the Nisei Week Queen precisely because of people "like the *Face* [magazine] people."

Honolulu, Hawaii: Bridging Back to the Homeland

Akira "Sunshine" Fukunaga was visiting a buddy in Los Angeles in 1949 when he attended his first Nisei Week Festival. Thinking the festival a great idea, he returned to Honolulu to start planning the first Cherry Blossom Festival in Hawaii. Sunshine was the first vice president of the Honolulu Japanese Junior Chamber of Commerce (Jaycees) in 1949, and thought Cherry Blossom would be a good project for the Jaycees. According to the Forty-fourth Cherry Blossom Festival booklet, "Sunshine explained that this festival could help to perpetuate and promote the Japanese culture in Hawaii, as well as provide members with the opportunity to gain valuable leadership skills."

The first festival faced the usual obstacles. They needed to raise money, get the community involved, and "convince women that the Queen contest was worth the effort of entering." Like Nisei Week, the Jaycees Cherry Blossom Queen pageant was done by ballots. Businesses were asked to purchase ballots. "In exchange for making purchases at these establishments, customers would be given the ballots to vote for their favorite contestant. In that first year nearly 3,000,000 ballots were distributed." They managed to convince women to participate by explaining to them that beauty was not the main criteria for the queen, but instead the goal was to "select a young woman who would represent Hawaii and the Japanese community well."[4] In 1953 seventy-two women came forward to vie for the title of Cherry Blossom Queen in Honolulu and Violet Niimi was crowned the first queen. Since then, the Cherry Blossom Queen Pageant in Honolulu has been the largest and most competitive Japanese American pageant.

Like the Nisei Week Queen Pageant, the Cherry Blossom Pageant and Festival in Honolulu reflects influences of local culture and demographics. First and foremost the Japanese community in Hawaii is much larger than the one in Southern California. In 1990 the majority of the population in Hawaii was Asian/Pacific Islander, making up 62 percent of the total population. In 2000, of all Asian Pacific Islanders, the Japanese were by far the biggest group at 228,290, which was roughly 26.3 percent of the total population of Honolulu and surrounding areas. This creates a racial hierarchy in Hawaii that is unlike others on the mainland because in Hawaii there is such a small black population (2.5 percent of the population) and whites are not the majority (only 33 percent of the population).[5] In addition, a majority of these Japanese live in Honolulu with a 1990 population of 195,149 Japanese. The relative size of the Japanese community has also allowed the Japanese to rise into prominent places of power and politics. In addition, the presence of racial rules within a Japanese American pageant in Hawaii takes on particular meaning as Hawaii, although argued to be a "multiracial paradise," and very tolerant of racial mixing, in fact has "a unique system of representation with a strong *cultural* component; consequently, cultural symbols sometimes trump "ethnic" and "racial" symbolization" (Edles 2004, 60). With racial identity more subtle and perhaps integrated with a "local" identity, identity politics takes on an interesting twist as the Japanese American community within this "multiracial paradise" so tolerant of racial mixing was the longest to maintain racial eligibility rules of 100 percent (until 1999).

The size and power of the community is again reflected in the queen pageant where the queen is crowned at a large and very extravagant coronation ball by the governor of the state of Hawaii (who in the past has been Japanese American). The attention paid to the queen and pageant is also much larger than on the mainland. The queen pageant is larger (attendance of 1,500) than most (Los Angeles 800, San Francisco 300, Seattle 150) and gains quite a lot of media attention. In 1996 the queen had several live TV interviews the day after the pageant, which aired on the local news. In other cities, such as San

Francisco, the entire festival might not make the local news and the queen would not be interviewed. This attention reflects the larger audience of the Japanese American community in Hawaii and the queen is more visible because of that. One Hawaiian said, "It (the pageant) is much more competitive and it is very high profile. The posters are all over and you see the books (program booklets) and everyone sits there and reads it like ten times." Several of the queens talked about having to get ready every time they went out of their house for fear that they would be recognized by people as the queen and embarrassed lest they not look well dressed enough or not have their makeup on. This is in stark contrast to the relative anonymity of the queen in Los Angeles or San Francisco who could move around relatively freely without ever being noticed, unless in Japantown or Little Tokyo "where people might know them."

The relative size of the community is also reflected in the fact that there are not separate and special organizations focused only on Japanese people in Hawaii. San Francisco, for example, has several Japanese American basketball leagues. Started in an era when many Japanese Americans could not play on their local school teams because of their race and later maintained due to different skill (and height) levels, the Japanese American leagues gave Japanese American kids a place to play basketball. These Japanese-only or Japanese-dominated leagues do not exist in Hawaii because as one interviewee said, "Everyone can play basketball. Especially if you go to one of the schools where there are a lot of Japanese living in the area you are going to get on the basketball team."

The predominance of Asian Pacific Islanders and the Japanese in particular in Hawaii, has afforded the Japanese population there to be a part of the majority and not a separated minority group. Another interviewee said,

> In Hawaii there is really no "Japanese American community" that I can think of. There isn't a core group of Japanese Americans who get together and are involved in everything. There are more people and so in some ways there is a less of a need (to have separate Japanese American organizations). You want to see Japanese Americans, look at your high school class, there is probably lots. Because they are everywhere, there isn't as much need to associate.

The mainstreaming of the Japanese in Hawaii, including Japanese culture and food, makes the Cherry Blossom Queen also more mainstream. It is ironic that the place where there is "no Japanese

American core community" is the place that maintains the community boundary most strongly via the ancestry rules. One might expect because so much racial mixing has gone on in Hawaii that there was a more tolerant racial atmosphere in Honolulu, but this was clearly not always the case—particularly in the Cherry Blossom Queen Pageant.

The power that the Japanese have economically and politically also has an impact in the Cherry Blossom Queen Pageant. By being crowned by the governor, and attended by the mayor and other politicians, the Cherry Blossom queen is in the public eye. As she is waltzed around the floor on her first dance by the governor, the queen is toasted by a virtual "who's who" of Hawaii, many of whom are Japanese American but a large number are not. The fact that the Jaycees and the pageant can command the attention and time of the governor, not only for coronation rehearsals but other visitations and events shows how much power the pageant organizers have. In addition, this translates into money for the pageant, the Jaycees, and the organizers themselves. This fits with the goal/rationale of the putting on the pageant by the Jaycees. The Japanese Junior Chamber of Commerce sees itself as putting on the pageant in order to give their younger businesspeople the leadership experience they will need to be successful in the future. More than one business deal has been made during the planning and implementation of the festival. The queen pageant is by far the biggest event that the Jaycees plan and it remains their main moneymaker.[6] Money, then, has a large role to play in the support of the Jaycees and the pageant, and one can feel that the Hawaii Cherry Blossom Queen has more money behind her than the queens from other cities. Her transportation, dresses, and many of her meals are paid for by hosts, businesses, or the Jaycees. The contestants themselves do generate a portion of the income, and as we saw in the last chapter, one of the titles (Miss Popularity) is directly related to how many program booklets and tickets the contestant sells. This moneymaking aspect and the ability to make political and business connections is openly part of the pageant and the queen herself has often been encouraged by her employer to run as a way to make the business look better or to get free publicity.

There is an interesting relationship between the pageant, the Jaycees, the queen, and Japanese nationals. There are many Japanese nationals present in Hawaii for business reasons and they are known to be major property owners on the islands. These Japanese companies provide significant financial backing for the festival and the Jaycees. The Japanese Culture and Community Center of Hawaii, built in 1994, was made possible in part by donations from Japan. This closer relationship that Hawaii has with Japan seemed at times to be very cordial and well oiled and at other times to be strained. There did seem to be some resentment in general that the Japan Japanese were buying up everything in Hawaii and nothing would be left for the natives (meaning other people in Hawaii, not just native Hawaiians). There also, however, seemed to be tremendous cooperation between the Japan Japanese and the Hawaii Japanese. I noted that the Hawaii Japanese referred to themselves primarily as Japanese and not Japanese American. When questioned about it, one interviewee said, "We are not so uptight about proving that we are American. We know we are American, so no need to say it all the time." This is a significant difference between Hawaii and the mainland. Since Japanese in Hawaii were not interned during the war, there seems to be less of a need to remind people that they are American as well.

In addition, not being a minority group they don't feel the need to try to assert power. They have lots of power economically and politically relative to other groups in Hawaii. The Japanese in Hawaii see the islands as different and more under their influence than the mainland, and it is true they do have a tremendous influence. There was also realistic recognition in Hawaii, however, that Japanese Americans in Hawaii and all people in Hawaii were and will continue to be dependent on the Japan Japanese economically. Closeness to Japan, whether economically, culturally, or geographically, influenced the pageant. The Hawaii Japanese described their own pageant as being more real Japanese or more traditional than pageants of the other cities. By this, they meant that their stage and sets were more sparse than others and the pageant more formal, which people in Hawaii felt was more like Japan, more authentically Japanese than the others. In addition, many of the contestants in Hawaii still had family, often parents, in Japan and therefore were of a different generation than their mainland counterparts. Again, this symbolizes the closer ties to Japan, but also gives these contestants something to hold on to that they felt made them more authentically Japanese.

Many people I interviewed in Hawaii used the racial rule as the main rationale for keeping the pageant culturally more Japanese. They explained that there was certain resistance or reluctance to change the rule because of relations with Japan, reasons of purity and authenticity. For example, tremendous emphasis was placed on the kimono section (or Eastern section) of the pageant and the kimonos were chosen for each individual contestant to wear. During this section of the pageant, the commentary was done both in Japanese and English (unlike the other parts of the pageant which were only in English) and each kimono title and explanation was given.[7] This was a very formal and controlled part of the pageant. There was no cheering or flash photography, and it was very slow moving. The Hawaii court seemed to be proud and felt that their pageant was more authentic than the others.

In addition, they felt that they had learned about the Japanese culture through participating in the pageant. If they already had familiarity with Japanese culture, the contestants were sure to say so in their applications and speeches. Many of them mentioned Japanese cultural arts such as ikebana, *odori* (traditional dancing), *obi* (tying the "belt" around the kimono), or the tea ceremony. The further emphasis on cultural arts was evident because Hawaii was the only city in which the contestants were given instruction on Japanese cultural arts such as the tea ceremony and ikebana. When I first heard about these cultural classes I was intrigued and wanted to know more about how they went about teaching someone about their own culture. Such a big deal was made of these classes as a way for the Hawaii pageant to set itself apart as more cultural that I assumed that the classes went on for a long time over the many months of preparation. I was more than a little surprised to hear that the contestants have a total of one ikebana lesson and one tea ceremony lesson in the whole year. One contestant told me, "You know honestly, the girls say that they want to learn about their Japanese culture in the pageant, but they don't really (learn about it). We get one hour of ikebana and one hour of tea ceremony. I didn't learn anything. What did I learn that I didn't already know?"

It seems that the importance of the classes was not the content of the classes themselves or how much the contestants learned, but their symbolic importance. It was necessary to set the Hawaii pageant apart as more cultural in order to make authenticity claims that superseded others. But culture seemed to vary from contestant to contestant and queen to queen. Even though all of the contestants were 100 percent Japanese racially, they still were thought to need to learn about the

Japanese culture, that is, they didn't have it already. Seeing as Hawaii had such tight racial rules about Japanese ancestry, I didn't think that the racial rule would be important, but the most discussed issue about the pageant while I was in Hawaii was the racial rule about who can and cannot participate.

Hawaii as a society is very racially mixed, but the Cherry Blossom Queen Pageant was not until 1999. Even the Jaycees who put on the event are themselves of various Asian ethnic backgrounds, but the queen pageant remained carefully guided by ancestry rules. Again, the size of the Japanese American community in Hawaii was given as the reason why they could demand that the Cherry Blossom Queen pageant contestants were of 100 percent, provable, Japanese ancestry until 1999. As one person put it, "You can find full Japanese people everywhere, so you can afford to keep it 100 percent." Or this person who said, "They will be able to keep the 100 percent rule a lot longer there [Hawaii] than here [Los Angeles] just because of the population. There is not as much intermarriage as here. They will be able to hold out longer just for sheer numbers." Others felt that the rule helped to narrow so many candidates down. "They say that they do that because there are so many Japanese people in Hawaii that they have to limit it somehow. They have so many candidates." There was discussion of changing the rule in the past, but they didn't change to incorporate multiracial women formally and with significant resistance until 1999.

Several people on the mainland had their reasons why it was changed in 1999. "When it gets tougher to find 100 percent, they will back down." When I asked the general chairman in the mid-1990s about the rule he had this to say,

> We're very, very, very frank about it. We said those have to be 100 percent and that was it. It's not as important an issue here in Hawaii, and believe me if it was an important issue, we wouldn't have twenty-one sponsors. We wouldn't have the pageant for forty-four years virtually unchanged. And so in a sense, one may say it's racist, but on the other hand, maybe it's not, because people would not say "okay" if it were.

Another past participant said:

> This issue comes up every now and again, it's kind of this controversy, and my stand is that I feel that as long as they have enough participants, then they should keep it the way it is. Once participation starts to diminish then look at other options, one of which is to allow people of other ethnicities to participate in the pageant.

The assumption is that people who are half Japanese or anyone who is not full Japanese is not really Japanese but really their "other ethnicity" and therefore just not eligible. One organizer suggested to me that hapa women just didn't want to run and that they (the Jaycees) didn't get that many mixed women applying. This seemed a relatively weak rationalization when in fact the rules were public and they stated that the candidates had to be 100 percent. But things were changing. Where the Jaycees used to be able to get many, many candidates and they would accept only the first fifty applicants, they received fewer applications and had to recruit more and more women. From the fifty applicants they interviewed in 1996, they screened out all but fifteen to be considered for the Cherry Blossom Queen. Each family was interviewed and the parents were intimately involved in the pageant process. But the interview, as we saw before, also served to allow the organizers to confirm that the contestant was 100 percent Japanese.

The possibility of hapas running or being allowed to run in the pageant revealed some interesting results. Most of the members of the court in 1995 said that if they let hapas run they themselves would not have run in the pageant that year. They explained that if hapas were allowed to run, they would win because they were prettier. This is an interesting assertion given that in Los Angeles, the mixed-race queen felt that being mixed and looking more white than the other candidates worked against her. In Hawaii some interviewees explained to me that hapa people were considered better looking in general because their racially blended features were popular. However, this same interviewee didn't know how hapa candidates would go down within the Cherry Blossom Queen Pageant in Honolulu. She hypothesized that while hapas were generally considered cute in Hawaii, they wouldn't do as well in the context of the pageant because it was about representing the Japanese of Hawaii. It is difficult to say since mixed-race women at that time were not allowed to participate in the pageant in Honolulu.[8]

Current participants also explained that if scholastic achievement or grades (as in Seattle) or talent (as in San Francisco) were to factor into the score that they wouldn't run either because they didn't have the talent or the grades. They liked the fact that their pageant was based on poise, beauty, and ability to speak publicly—in their mind what the job of queen entails and not talent and grades which the queen has no time to exhibit. They argued with me. "Why how well she sings? The queen doesn't sing during her reign!"

It is clear that the size of the Japanese community in Hawaii is thought to be the reason why the pageant is so big that the organizers could, in the past, afford the 100 percent racial rule, and the racial rule remained until 1999 officially unchanged and unchallenged. This is very different from Nisei Week, which set out in the early stages to show to the larger, dominant white society how nice Japanese Americans were. The need for Japanese festivals was heightened on the mainland because of the small size, minority status, and discriminatory treatment of the community compared to the community in Hawaii, which became powerful in numbers, politics, and finances over time.

Changing the Racial Rules in Hawaii

In 1999 Hawaii changed its racial eligibility rules from 100 percent Japanese ancestry to 50 percent. Keith Kamisugi, then the president of the Honolulu Japanese Junior Chamber of Commerce, was responsible for the rule change amid much criticism. His rationale was both due to demographic pressures and the cultural shift to recognize multiraciality more openly in the pageant. He felt that they should do it to encourage more women to participate in the pageant, but also because it was the morally right thing to do. He argued,

> At the point where we were close to finalizing the contest rule change, a few people asked if we would still require a Japanese surname, based on the false notion that the queen and court visit to Japanese would be less than ideal if the queen had a "haole" [white] last name (a few individuals really said this to me). Absolutely not. A Japanese American woman named Toth is no less or more Japanese than a woman named Matsumoto. Pride in our Japanese heritage does not come from our birth certificate. It comes from our family, our community and our experiences as participants in that culture. I'm gratified that the Cherry Blossom Festival has achieved such diversity in the queen contest. It is a true reflection of our Japanese American community. (Kamisugi 2001, 1)

This move preserved the belief in racial ancestry as crucial to Japanese Americanness while increasing flexibility in community membership criteria in terms of names and physical appearance. It also drew attention to the preservation of race, while expanding community membership based on family, community ties, and cultural experiences.

This again preserved the arena of race while expanding cultural social networks. However, there was concern that there would be a racial reaction in Japan. Keith explained the concern in an interview with Chris Yano (2006). He said,

> That was also one of the arguments of the opposition: our relationships with the five sister chapters, Jaycee chapters in Japan, and our relationship, I guess you could call it, with the Imperial Household, 'cause the Cherry Blossom Queen visits the Imperial Household, usually with the second or the third princess or whomever. And what would they think? (Yano 2006, 318)

He claimed he didn't mind if the visit to the Imperial Household was taken off the visitation schedule because of the rule change. He also, ironically, was criticized after changing the ethnic and racial rule when hapa contestants didn't make it onto the court. He explained his response:

> The change in the ethnic requirement does not automatically raise multi-ethnic contestants to any different level. Meaning that once you're in the door, if you are a multiethnic contestant, you're just like everybody else. So multiethnicity has nothing to do with the Queen and Court . . . . just because you're *hapa* doesn't mean you're gonna get more or less of a chance. (Yano 2006, 320)

The change in the racial eligibility rules, according to the 1999 Honolulu Cherry Blossom Queen Program Booklet, was also accompanied by the removal of "physical beauty" as a judging criteria and an increase in the number of culture classes from 5 to 12. Removing the official category of physical beauty and the removal of the 100 percent rule would deflect attention away from racial appearance. It still took a few years for the first multiethnic queen, Vail Matsumoto, of Italian and Japanese ancestry (2000), the first queen with a non-Japanese last name, Catherine Toth, of Japanese, Hungarian, Portuguese, German, and Dutch ancestry (2001), and the first part-Hawaiian queen, Lisa Okinaga (2002), to win.

While race and ethnicity are certainly looser in relation to each other than they were, the continued use of the racial rules and the concern about what others (particularly sponsors) will think is interesting. If Hawaii moves to lowering the rule to 25 percent or if there are "too many" mixed-race queens, as the debate in Los Angeles claimed, it will be interesting to see just how loose racial boundaries actually

Figure 4. 2000 Honolulu Cherry Blossom Queen, Vail Matsumoto, the first multi-ethnic queen in Honolulu. Photograph courtesy of Earl Mostales.

Figure 5. 2001 Honolulu Cherry Blossom Queen, Catherine Toth, the first Honolulu Cherry Blossom queen with a non-Japanese surname. Photograph courtesy of Earl Mostales.

are in the Honolulu Cherry Blossom Queen Pageant. There was still concern that the "change to allow half Japanese women into Hawaii's longest running ethnic festival . . . would see the pageant's purpose of cultural identity thinning with the blood requirements" (Tighe 1999, A3).

Seattle: Scholarship, Not Race?

Although the Seattle Japanese American community had a few pageants throughout the 1940s and 1950s, the current pageant wasn't started until 1960 when Nancy Sawa was crowned the Greater Seattle Japanese Community Queen. The Seattle pageant, like Los Angeles and Honolulu, has undergone changes over time and is reflective of the local social context; it seems to have done away completely with racial rules and instead substituted community and geographic rules about who may participate.

The Seattle Japanese Community Queen Pageant is the only pageant that is a scholarship pageant. While this difference may seem subtle at the outset, it has a profound impact on the type of queen the pageant chooses and also who in the community would come forward to be involved in the pageant. The grades that each contestant earns in school are considered part of the criteria for judging and constitute 20 percent of the score that each candidate receives.

In 1995 Seattle, unlike Hawaii, was clearly struggling just to keep the pageant going. The low turnout, both in terms of contestants (five each year that I was doing research) and in terms of community support, actually meant that the pageant was canceled in 1996–97 as I was leaving the field. The reported reason for the cancellation was a lack of contestants who met the competition criteria. One of the organizers said, "If we included everyone who wanted to participate, we would have gone ahead with it, but there are certain restrictions that we have" (Uyeno 1996b, 1). By "restrictions," they were not referring to the racialized rule about how much Japanese ancestry a woman must have in order to participate. The main criteria that the contestants didn't meet was the geographic one. The Seattle pageant requires that the queen candidate "must be attending school in the Greater Seattle area *and* must have family residing in the greater Seattle area" (Northwest Nikkei 1996, 8). The women who wanted to participate but couldn't were from out of state. Seattle clearly is defining who has a right to represent the Japanese community using geographic and family ties as criteria. They are making a racial argument through a geographic one. One queen originally from Hawaii was allowed to participate because her grand-parents lived locally. This is different from Nisei Week in Los Angeles, which has a racial definition, but not a geographic one. Los Angeles has no requirement that a woman must be originally from Los Angeles and several Nisei Week queens have not been from Los Angeles, but from San Francisco and just attending college in Los Angeles. A contestant from Los Angeles said, "If you change the rule, though, too much then you go to one fourth, one eighth, one sixteenth, then what is the use? Why not just have everyone from Southern California pageant?" Seattle seems to have done away with the racial rule as she suggests and substituted a community rule instead.

This is an interesting criterion given the geographic nature of the Seattle Japanese American community. A small community by Hawaii standards, there were 45,823 Japanese Americans (1.3 percent of the total population) in the Seattle, Washington, area in 1990.[9] Where once the Japanese American community was concentrated primarily in the Beacon Hill area of Seattle, now Japanese Americans can and do live scattered all over the greater Seattle area. Since the dispersement of the community, there is no central geographic area of Japanese busi-nesses or residential area like Japantown in San Francisco or Little Tokyo in Los Angeles. Instead, with the decline of Japantown and Chinatown in Seattle, there has been an effort to blend the remaining businesses in the area together with emerging southeast Asian Businesses to form what is now call the "International District." This dispersement and loss of a distinct geographic area either for Japanese businesses or resi-dences is evidence of the change that the community is going through. And while the international district promoting "pan Asian" identifi-cation has worked for the business district, the same tactic has not been used in the pageant.[10]

In 1995 the pageant was small by Hawaiian standards and attended by approximately 150 people. It was a simple but elegant affair with beautifully and carefully custom-designed stage decorations and po-dium. The number of candidates was small and the talent and scholar-ship criteria ensured that the women who participated were not just attractive but also well rounded, having diverse interests and accom-plishments. All were participating in part for the scholarship money (totaling $3,200 in 1994) that each would receive regardless of who was chosen queen. This focus of making it a scholarship pageant to draw in more women to participate was being considered by the San Francisco pageant, but some worried that it would just draw women who wanted the money for school and did not want to do it as a service to the community. This moved the focus away from racial and ethnic criteria and toward academic criteria. There was also the implication that if these criteria were applied elsewhere, it would reduce the numbers of participants in other cities.

Likewise, the pageant reflects the progressive political context of Seattle. For example, between 1971 and 1975, there was no pageant due to the stigma attached to pageants. At the height of the women's movement, Seattle decided to not have a pageant. It came back in 1976 and many welcomed its resurgence, in part because they wanted the Japanese American community in Seattle to be represented at the SeaFair Festival in which the Greater Seattle Community Queen participates along with queens representing the different communities in Seattle. The winner of the SeaFair Queen title the year that I was doing research was a physically challenged wheelchair user and many felt that this reflected values in Seattle where they would be making a positive political and social statement by choosing her as the SeaFair Queen.

In 1996 the Seattle pageant had no stated racial rules.[11] However, the organizers did seem to have some ways to assure that the queen would be racially Japanese in order to represent the community. They may have been able to get around not having racial rules by creating a requirement that the candidates must have family (assumed to be biological and Japanese American) residing in the geographic area and by having the word "Japanese" in the title of the pageant. This would encourage those who were not Japanese to select themselves out, but what about mixed-race women? The Seattle pageant was known to have had a queen who some speculated was only one-sixteenth Japanese. They argued that because she was mostly Korean, it was hard to tell, but many were convinced that a candidate could be only a little or a drop Japanese and still be queen in Seattle. The mixed-race rule, though, did not seem to be that much of an issue in Seattle. They were more worried about just continuing the pageant itself. One organizer said, "We don't have a Japantown or a Little Toyko, so I think the fabric of the community lies in the different organizations. With the demise of the organization, the community gets smaller" (Uyeno 1996b, 2).

Seattle is struggling with a dispersed community and a lack of support for the pageant, and the racialized rules have been less salient.

San Francisco: Multiraciality as a Survival Strategy

San Francisco has had a racial eligibility rule of 50 percent Japanese ancestry. San Francisco's pageant also reflects the progressive and multicultural nature of the city itself. Unlike Seattle, San Francisco did not geographically limit the candidates to having to have relatives in the Bay Area, so many of the participants are not originally from the Bay Area and do not have family there. In addition, unlike Los Angeles, there has not been that much argument over the racial rule in San Francisco, and they were the first pageant to change their racial rules in 1996 from "one parent must be of 100 percent Japanese ancestry" to "you must be of at least 50 percent Japanese ancestry." They made this change because they felt that in saying one parent had to be 100 percent Japanese ancestry, they might be leaving some people who were 50 percent out. One committee member told me that he had a friend who had two parents who were each half Japanese and that she should be able to run no matter what her combination as long as she had 50 percent Japanese blood. Another committee member said, "Realistically, our community, being a smaller community, and also a community that has a large rate of interracial marriages, feels that as long as the candidate is 50 percent then that is fine. We might be depriving a lot of people of the chance to participate. We couldn't get away with this in Hawaii or Los Angeles because the populations are so large." Again, this was attributed to the demographic size of the community, which allowed the larger pageants to keep out mixed-race Japanese Americans. San Francisco couldn't afford to do it due to a small community. The main reason cited when I asked people why they couldn't get more women to participate was the racial rule. They argued, "One parent has to be Japanese. I think it is difficult these days to try to find people who are even half Japanese" or "It is getting harder because there is not as many full Japanese" or "there is not that many pure Japanese anymore . . . or pure anything anymore."

There also seemed to be a much more relaxed attitude about mixed-race candidates and there were more in San Francisco than in most of the other cities studied. The fact that the majority of the candidates were mixed in 1995 and 1996 made San Francisco a particularly in teresting place to do research to see how the impact of mixed-race people was being understood. For the most part, most people involved and watching the pageant took it for granted that "our" (the Japanese American) community was changing and that we have mixed candidates and queens now because that reflects the change in the community. Even so, many felt that while the rules eventually would have to change to allow people who were 25 percent to run for Cherry Blossom Queen they weren't sure about doing away with the rule altogether. Again, many felt that it was related to getting a bigger pool of women to participate. "For them to pull a larger group of girls it will need to go to 25 percent" or "It is good that they've got it down to 50 percent now, but they will have to change that as time goes on in order to attract girls." Another one of the participants said, "I only know 10 full Japanese girls. Everyone is mixed and the rules will have to change, but I don't think we should go below a quarter."

Most felt that there should be some floor on how "low we go" because the festival and the pageant, particularly the queen, "stood for something culturally" and that the "cultural something" wouldn't come through if the queen were less than 25 percent Japanese racially. "I think it is important that rule because if you're just slightly Japanese you are probably going to have less knowledge of the community" or "By reducing the amount of Japanese in the candidate, they take away from the Japanese culture base of the festival." They clearly think that race is partly determinant of ethnicity. Others felt that the rule was there because people still needed to be able to racially recognize the queen.

> There are mixed people who are active in the community way more than the people who are 100 percent. I think we will have the percentage rule because of the way it looks. They don't want people to question "how can she be queen if . . . " I think it has to do with older people who are not ready to accept that. For me it was okay because they might not be able to tell (I'm mixed). But, I think they just don't want to have to deal with explaining "she is really active in the community even though she doesn't look it."

Race was still a salient part of the "job" and therefore a continuing criterion for the queen.

Unlike Los Angeles, the main debate in San Francisco was over feminism rather than the racial rule, although there were racial undertones to the debate as we saw in the last chapter. One can see the progressive political nature of the Bay Area local community through the impact that feminism has had on the pageant. First, the pageant participants and organizers in San Francisco were more aware of feminism and the feminist critique of pageants than in the other cities. Every person I interviewed, when asked about why women would not want to participate in pageants, gave an answer in relation to feminism. Many argued that the pageant got a "bad rap" as not valuing women and they felt that this was unfair. They felt that the pageant in San Francisco was a community pageant and not a beauty pageant. The mantra "it's not a beauty pageant" was evident in almost all aspects of the pageant and the organizers worked hard to maintain that it was about affirming young women in the Japanese American community. This response about it not being a beauty pageant illustrates that the participants and the organizers were very familiar with feminism and many considered themselves feminists. They, without being prompted, talked about how the pageant allowed women opportunities to speak out, be seen and heard, and meet powerful people. This automatic response to the pageant as "not just about beauty" is an indication of how deep feminism has sunk into the local Japanese American community so that even the pageant, which is not particularly known as a feminist institution, has feminist underpinnings.

For example, the committee members insisted that the press calls the participants "candidates," not "contestants," to try to do away with the image that this is strictly a beauty contest and therefore competitive. In addition, the committee also tried very hard to refer to the candidates as "ladies" or "women" and not "girls." However, the candidates called themselves "girls"—thus, it seemed, infantilizing themselves in the context of the pageant. The conflict then between referring to them as girls and as women often was remarked upon, once again illustrating the impact that feminism had and continues to have on the pageant in San Francisco. The debate in San Francisco was about race, but also about feminism. Therefore debates about mixed-race women being prettier, which were common in Hawaii, didn't occur with the same frequency in San Francisco because the object of the pageant was not supposed to be about beauty in the first place.

Conclusion

Unlike international pyramid pageants, the Japanese American community pageants are local community festival pageants. While the community pageants have much in common, the queen has come to symbolize, represent, and reflect the unique nature of each of the local Japanese American communities. This means different things in different contexts. We saw how in Los Angeles the influence of the entertainment industry has made the pageant and, therefore, the queen "more Hollywood." This has given rise to debates about the introduction of mixed-race contestants in Nisei Week as having a better chance because they conform more to the dominant model of beauty. In Hawaii, the racial rule remained unchanged longest and the size of the community allows it to continue to exclude some mixed-race women from being eligible to represent the Japanese community of Hawaii. Again, the local context of Hawaii and its relationship with Japan as well as with the United States has shaped the pageant to be more traditional and about culture and race rather than speaking ability and intelligence. Seattle is by far the smallest and most struggling community. Having defined Japanese American community membership in terms of geography and social networks of relatives, they face having few to no women eligible and willing to participate in the pageant. San Francisco reflects the more progressive and tolerant culture of the Bay Area when it willingly accepts and encourages participation by mixed-race women in the Cherry Blossom Queen Pageant. They also deal most extensively with feminism even in a traditionally nonfeminist context.

These different Japanese American communities are dealing with different issues related to the power that the community can wield; the relationships it has with other, predominantly majority, communities; and the way that they see the community moving. Even so, all are dealing with the issue of the impact of increasing rates of interracial marriage and mixed-race Japanese Americans. All have racialized rules and all, I would argue, are in flux. They are having to negotiate what this means in terms of who is Japanese American and who is not. They define Japanese Americanness in multiple ways using race/blood quantum (Hawaii), family (Seattle), residence (Seattle), and culture (Los Angeles) to measure up who can be eligible to be queen. This also, because it is about multiraciality, begs the question of who will be allowed to participate now that Japanese Americans have familial relationships both individually and collectively with whites and other Asians.

It appears that both Los Angeles and San Francisco are trying to mediate between a racial and ethnic vision of who is a Japanese American. Hawaii, on the one end, had an almost entirely racial definition of who can qualify to represent the community and therefore who can be a part of the community until recently. Seattle, at the other extreme, has an almost exclusively cultural definition of who is Japanese American and seems to have let the racial component of the rules/criteria for the queen fall away. This chapter has illustrated that different Japanese American communities in Los Angeles, Hawaii, San Francisco, and Seattle are renegotiating racial and ethnic meanings and demographic shifts within their local contexts in creative forms. All, except Seattle, continue to openly advertise racial eligibility rules and thus are all working race in context-specific and unique ways.

Conclusion

Japanese Americanness, Beauty Pageants, and Race Work

THE JAPANESE AMERICAN BEAUTY PAGEANTS in the four cities of Los Angeles, San Francisco, Seattle, and Honolulu share many similarities, but this book has focused on how race is conceptually made and remade through race work in unique ways in each of the four social contexts. The racial projects that spring from each of these contexts have been different, but they are united by racial eligibility rules that determine in this particular cultural institution of beauty pageants who can and cannot symbolically represent the Japanese American community as queen. This is not to say that the pageants are necessarily a good or even representative example of how the majority of Japanese American communities are feeling about the future of their community or Japanese Americanness itself. Japanese American beauty pageants are, in fact, a contrived and overproduced version of Japanese Americanness but are an important arena for conversations about Japanese Americanness and how it is changing in the face of increasing interracial marriage and growing numbers of multiracial people. The uniformity of blood quantum and eligibility rules in the Japanese American beauty pageants points to the ongoing importance of race as a concept within this racial and ethnic community.

The pageants provide an example of how race, ethnicity, and culture come to be embodied through a process of producing and training the queen each year. As the queen has racially changed, so too have the community's racial definitions of itself. The racial eligibility rules can also be used as a gauge to give an account of Japanese American racial meanings and racial states, their relationships to Japan Japanese racial meanings and states, and the larger racial context of the United States. The queen as a symbol moves between these racial meanings representing Japanese Americans to themselves, to the larger majority (white) American society, and to the Japanese in Japan.

The case study of the mixed-race queen has highlighted the complexity of racial negotiation, claims to authenticity, and the hierarchy of those claims. While it was clear that the mixed-race queen candidates were using all types of strategies, including ethnic ones, to make racial claims, I argue that this in and of itself does little to undermine the concept of race and its assumed relationship to biology. Asserting mixed race, but then couching it in the terms of the blood-quantum rules of 50 percent Japanese American and 50 percent white or "half this and half that," does nothing to undo race or to try to live in a postracial or even multiple-racial world. Even with the ontological experience of being mixed-race and understanding that race is socially constructed, the mixed-race candidates, in the context of the pageant, complied with racial eligibility rules and reified race in their efforts to make racial claims. The blurring of the racial boundaries, which the mixed-race queens highlighted both in Los Angeles in the 1980s and in Honolulu in the 1990s, made race work more, not less, important as the racial boundaries became looser and less defined. People engaged furiously in dedicated race work, to repair the relationship between race and ethnicity. As the boundary of who is Japanese American enough to represent the community as queen was debated in Honolulu, the boundaries of what is Japanese American became reinscribed racially—now 50 percent instead of 100 percent.

In the last chapter, we saw why Honolulu was the last one to change the racial eligibility rules by looking at the community's overall political and economic power. In chapter 5 we also examined the micro politics of control over the queen candidates in terms of the linking of gender politics and racial claims. The debate about the future of the community and its racial make up was clearly pinned onto the future mothers of the "race"—young women in the pageant. The queen, as the symbol of the community, was a racialized object or symbol used to advertise companies, the community, and the festival itself. She then became an arena for debate including Japanese American anxieties about the community, culture, intermarriage, gender, and mixed-race children.

The central contribution of this book has been to show that race continues to be a socially real process through which people guide their actions. Race is work—with all of its connotations. In work, we learn from and are enriched by the process, but it is something that is serious and takes effort. Nonetheless, this is not forced (although may be strongly shaped) labor that takes little or no skill. Race work builds on the contributions of theorists of race, class, and gender, who have highlighted the "doing" of race in social context as an interactional accomplishment (West and Fenstermaker 1997). Critiques of this symbolic interactionalist understanding of the processes of racial formation have rightly found that these types of theories leave out the recognition of the institutional and structural constraints of that "doing" (Collins 1997). The "doing" of race happens as we have seen throughout the book, in very specific socially grounded contexts, which inextricably shape that same doing. Without the social context, there are decontextualized claims that race can and should be undone. However, the theory of race work, as I have put forward throughout this book, is a different way to think about race, not just as a situated interactional accomplishment, but instead as an effort or labor of practice.

This race work, or effort by social actors, allows us to recognize that people are acting toward or against racial rules, projects, and formations and hence institutions and structures, which are also themselves racially filled. Race work, then, is analogous to other understandings of labor processes (Burawoy 1985) where exerted effort in social interactions sustains beliefs in the racial production process itself and where actions are oriented to substantiating racial claims within specific racial projects or relations and regimes of racial production.

Why is this renegotiation of race happening now? The Japanese American beauty pageants produced a certain type of Japanese Americanness that tries hard to maintain a particularly antiquated and nostalgic sense of Japanese Americanness—once racialized by others in internment and now imposing race itself, not as self-delusion or self-hate, but as a form of self-preservation. The queen is the representation and symbol of that understanding and her actions therefore matter—but so too do the political, economic, and cultural community institutions that shape not only who, but what, the queen comes to represent. While this study may seem frivolous and apolitical to many, it ends up revealing much about the power relations within the community and the political relationships that Japanese American communities have with each other, with Japan, and with dominant American society and whiteness. While it doesn't focus specifically on material inequities, it does provide data for us to discuss how material inequality can impact the way individuals and others come to see themselves through their collective symbols such as beauty queens. Even though many, though not all, Japanese Americans may have "made it" in socioeconomic terms, the study shows that this is not enough for them to "out white the whites." They are still profoundly racialized as Japanese Americans and they know it.

This book also provides important empirical evidence of the complexity of what has been termed integration or assimilation. As the majority Japanese American communities move from being monoracial to being multiracial, the group boundaries change over space, time, and context. However, the concept of race is hard to move. The racial rules continue to signify race as biological and to promote the use of biology (or assumed biology) to define culture. Even internalized notions of biological race are deeply seated social actions.

Like labor process theories, then, race work is not only about relations of racial production within individuals, but also about relations of production between and among social actors. In fact the production of the queen as a racial project depends upon collective and interactional racial meanings. The queen pageant also creates a hub around which such relations are constructed. The relations *of* racial production then are the work of race. But these relations happen within a structure of race—relations *in* racial production, which are also producing racial meanings (see Burawoy 1985). Mixed-race bodies challenge both the biological underpinnings of race—as they may or may not "look" Japanese American—but they also challenge the relations in racial production. They challenge (as in the case of Honolulu) or they reinscribe (as in the case of San Francisco) race. Individual relations of racial production, within mixed-race individuals, radiate out into their families and local communities, but these also impact, by their very presence, larger racial regimes within the pageants and in other areas with racial eligibility rules such as Japanese American basketball leagues. This process of relations *of* and *in* racial production, codify the process of racialization into the concept of race. This productive process, I argue, is analogous to the labor process and as such, "must itself be seen as an inseparable combination of its economic, political and ideological aspects" (Burawoy 1985, 25).

This leads back to the levels at which we have been examining race work. At the first level, there are relations in racial production (race work) where actors are relating to themselves in bodily ways, responding to the physicality of their racial selves as pointed out by other social actors which harkens back to biological understandings of race. An example of this would be the proving that mixed-race candidates feel they must do in the pageant to authenticate themselves as Japanese Americans. At a more meso-social interactional level, there are relations of race work where social actors relate to one another and the basis of those social relations is a presumed racial one. They are tied together as the producers of the queen, which involves the committee, the festival sponsors, the families, and the women themselves. Not all these racial producers have the same amount of power or say in the process, but are embedded in social relations tied together by racial productive relationships. The concept of the queen as an ambassadress, connecting the local Japanese American communities, illustrates the high levels of agreement about the racial conditions of her production. Perceived racial commonalities produce social relations of race. An example of this was when in the course of fieldwork one committee member questioned me about my own racial background. Upon learning that I was part Japanese American, his exclamation, "Oh, you are one of us. You are a sister!" belied the racial commonality he then recognized that we shared.

On a larger, macro level, these relations of racial production are related to racial regimes, structures, and racial projects which themselves carry codified (past) understandings of race within them which shape, encourage, or sometimes limit the racial production going on within them. This is the structure of race or racial formation, which strongly determines which racial meanings can be produced, and by whom. The racial eligibility rules embedded deeply in each pageant reflect the operation of these regimes.

Table 9. Race work interactions

Social levels of interaction	Types of interactions	Concepts of race perpetuated
Relations in race work	Social actors relate to the body/physical nature	Biological race
Relations of race work	Relations to one another are social relations of racial production	Social race
Race work regimes	Relations to structures and larger racial projects	Racial formation

As the racial bodies within the community changed, the relations in race work also changed. This produced changes in the social relations, which produced racial meanings. For example, there were now Japanese Americans who had mixed-race nephews and nieces who they wanted to participate in the pageant and who they now recognized and accepted as Japanese Americans. This shifted the racial structures of the racial eligibility rules in places like Los Angeles and later Honolulu. The pageant as a particular racial project in a particular community produces and reproduces consent to the racial eligibility rules and corresponding belief in certain biologically driven notions of race every year. It is difficult to participate in the pageant and question race. Mixed-race bodies have obviously produced their own ideas of race and then those ideas have become incorporated in the racial project of the pageant and become part of the racial control regime. In Honolulu, they changed the blood-quantum rule from 100 percent to 50 percent, but they didn't get rid of it altogether and all the pageants continue to use ethnicity, community participation, or family ties as ways to keep racial ideas in the pageant. The racial challenge to Japanese American racial understandings in this book have intensified race work, not eliminated the concept of race.

In fact, many of the pageants now face the challenge of whether to continue at all. Criticized both from within the community by groups such as the Women's Concerns Committee in San Francisco, and from without, by growing critiques of pageants generally (Giroux 2000), what is the future of the pageants themselves? Will they reduce the racial eligibility rules or discontinue the pageant altogether? As long-standing cultural institutions, Japanese American beauty pageants in the short term seem to be surviving. They continue to recruit and produce the queen each year. They continue to draw sponsorship and audiences for the pageant and the festival, but they are clearly in decline from ten or even twenty years ago. As Japanese Americans move to try to reinvigorate their communities by building gyms for basketball (in Los Angeles) or new community centers (in Honolulu) the fundamental position of Japanese Americans is in question. The power of race still looms large though and the interviewees put it well when they told me that Japanese Americans would just 'close up shop' on the pageant before they would let just any racial body be the queen.

This look at Japanese American beauty pageants shows us that race continues to be a social fact, guiding social actors in their behavior and orientation to the world. While the belief in biological race may or may not be the underpinning of this social action, a crucial part of the social belief in race is the belief that race is embodied and inextricably linked to culture and ethnicity. However, race is a social construction as well as a social fact and there is "work" and effort that must be expended in order to produce the race/ethnicity/culture nexus. The theory of "race work" adds a conceptual link. It allows us to see that "race work" occurs at multiple interactional levels and this book tries to illustrate that at each level, intra- and interpersonal (chapter 4), collective (chapter 6), and comparative (chapter 7).

Race work produces the link between race and ethnicity at these different levels, but because it is a socially constructed production and connection, there is room for a variety of racial projects. There are crucial spaces across these levels for new racial politics to emerge. The locus for changing racial meanings then may be at the more micro level as the space for racial innovation seems to narrow as actors move from the micro to the macro levels. Japanese American beauty pageants bring together prime examples of race work with the possibilities that they contain for a remaking of the racial order from the ground up. Beauty pageants continue to be significant cultural forms both in Japanese American communities and larger society, and are an important location of race work and politics.

Notes

Introduction

1. A number of popular publications published statistics on this topic such as *Time* (Fall 1993): 14-15, and *USA Today*, Dec. 11, 1992, A7. For more scholarly work, see Larry Shinagawa's "Intermarriage and Inequality: A Theoretical and Empirical Analysis of the Marriage Patterns of Asian Americans," diss., University of California, Berkeley, 1994, or O'Hare and Felt 1991.

2. Numerous institutions, such as churches and cultural groups, are concerned about the changes in the Japanese American community. One example is the Japanese American Consortium of Community Related Organizations (JACCRO), made up of eighty community-based organizations in Northern California, which gathered together in 1997 to do a community-based research project exploring the future for these organizations given their declining membership base. In addition, conferences such as the Ties that Bind (1998) and the Nikkei 2000 examined the future of the Japanese American Community.

3. "History of the Cherry Blossom Festival" from Forty-fourth Cherry Blossom Festival booklet, Honolulu, Hawaii, 16.

4. For a more detailed account of the Cherry Blossom Queen Pageant and Festival in Honolulu see Yano 2006.

5. All participants' names have been changed.

2. The Japanese American Community in Transition

1. This is a cultural school in the East Bay of the San Francisco Bay Area, which focuses on teaching (mostly Japanese American) children about Japanese American culture, and teaching Japanese-language classes. There are other such schools in other locations such as the Jan Ken Pon No Gakko in Sacramento.

2. This is not to imply that all of these marriages produced mixed children or that there were not mixed children born out of marriage, but this is the group, mixed marriages with children, about which there was the most data available.

3. Japanese American Beauty Pageants in Historical Perspective

1. For an excellent and more detailed historical analysis on the context of Nisei Week, see Kurashige 2002.

2. For a short time, there were bathing-suit competitions in Los Angeles, but they were discontinued in the 1970s.

4. Cultural Impostors and Eggs

1. I thank Rona Halualani for this insightful suggestion/comment and for introducing me to the concept of hierarchies of authenticity.

2. These are physical characteristics that interviewees said they felt constituted "looking Japanese."

3. I use the term *hapa* here to describe women who were of mixed Japanese ancestry. The term comes from the Hawaiian phrase "hapa haole" meaning half white or foreigner (without breath). Although the term has been deemed derogatory by some, most of my interviewees referred to themselves as half or hapa or mixed. For more information about the term, see http://www.hapaissuesforum.org.

4. All the names have been changed to try to protect anonymity. When the pseudonyms were developed, I attempted to try to keep the ethnic nature of the name intact so I replaced Japanese last names with other Japanese last names and Anglo first names with other first names.

5. There is quite a debate today about Asian American women who actually have their "eyes done," that is, have the fold in their eyelid removed to have "bigger" (more Caucasian-looking) eyes. I have only heard of one case in the pageants where a mixed-race woman had her eyes and face "done" not to make her look more Caucasian, but to make her look more Japanese, that is, inserting an epicanthic fold into her eyelids.

6. Seattle Japanese Community Queen Pageant program booklet, 1996.

6. The "Ambassadress" Queen

1. The women participating in the pageant call themselves "girls." In the direct quotes, I have tried to use the participants exact words or I put the word "girl" in quotes to signal that this is the language that they use to describe themselves. However, I felt that this term was being used to infantilize women (ages 18–26) who in my mind were clearly women. Therefore, when referring to them as a group I use the terms "women," "candidates," or "participants."

2. This sentiment is interestingly also true for some of the Japanese sociologists who I met at the American Sociological Association meetings in 1997 who were interested in Japanese Americans. They were studying the assimilation of Japanese Americans; they wanted to know if Japanese Americans are really Japanese anymore—whether they have managed to hold onto any culture or not.

7. Percentages, Parts, and Power

1. Forty-second Annual Honolulu Cherry Blossom Queen Rules and Regulations. San Francisco Rules and Regulations, 1996. Fiftieth Annual Nisei Week Japanese Festival, Nisei Week Queen Pageant, Applicant Qualifications, 1996; Northern California Cherry Blossom Queen Pageant Qualifications; and Japanese Community Queen Candidates Wanted advertisement, in *Northwest Nikkei*, August 1996, 8.

2. Most birth certificates in the United States of these participants born in the 1970s and 1980s had "mother's race" and "father's race" on the birth certificate.

3. 1954 Nisei Week Queen Committee Report, Queen Candidates Eligibility.

4. All above quotes from "A Lifetime of Giving," a festival profile of Mrs. Lillian Tajima from the "Forty-fourth Annual Cherry Blossom Festival Booklet," 1996, 63.

5. All this data comes from 1990 Census of Population and Housing Summary Tape File 1C.

6. For an excellent historiography of the pageant in Honolulu and the role of the Jaycees in organizing it, see Yano 2006.

7. Ironically, this Japanese and English commentary was given not by the Mistress of Ceremonies, but instead by a Jaycee, who was a Japanese national woman, and her husband, also a Jaycee, who was a Caucasian man. They both spoke Japanese and translated this section of the pageant for the audience while the MC, a past queen and Japanese American herself, commented throughout the ceremony how "bad" her Japanese was and how she hoped that she hadn't offended anyone.

8. This is further complicated by the fact that Miss Universe (1997), Brooke Lee, was a hapa (part Chinese and Korean) from Pearl City, Hawaii and may have won her title in part because she was mixed-race. This may signal that "mixed" looks are popular in a wider context of the world and not just in Hawaii.

9. From the 1990 Census of Population and Housing Summary Tape File 1C (entry 400).

10. Ironically, this meant that when the Seattle court visited San Francisco, they were keen to buy *0-manju* (Japanese rice cakes with sweet red beans inside) because they could no longer buy it "fresh" in Seattle because there were no shops that made it anymore. They could only get it via "importing" it from other Japanese American centers.

11. The rules as they were listed in the announcement for candidates in the newspaper and in the program did not say that she must be "of Japanese ancestry."

Bibliography

Alba, Richard. 1996. Italian Americans. In *Origins and Destinies*, ed. Sylvia Pedraza and Ruben Rumbaut. New York: Wadsworth.

Ali, Suki. 2003. *Mixed-Race, Post-Race: Gender, New Ethnicities and Cultural Practices.* Oxford: Berg.

Amy Kimura crowned first Cherry Blossom Queen of the millennium. 2000. *Nichi Bei Times.* http://www.nichibeitimes.com/news/queen.html.

Anderson, Benedict. 1991. *Imagined Communities: Reflections on the Origin and Spread of Nationalism.* London: Verso Books.

Anzaldúa, Gloria. 1987. *Borderlands, La Frontera: The New Mestiza.* San Francisco: Aunte Lute Books.

Armstrong, Bruce. 1989. Racialisation and national ideology: The Japanese case. *International Sociology* 4, no. 3:329–43.

Ashkenazi, Michael. 1993. *Matsuri: Festivals of a Japanese Town.* Honolulu: University of Hawaii Press.

Aspinall, P. J. 2003. The conceptualisation and categorisation of mixed race/ethnicity in Britain and North America: Identity options and the role of the state. *International Journal of Intercultural Relations* 27:269–96.

Balibar, Etienne, and Immanuel Wallerstein. 1991. *Race, Nation, Class: Ambiguous Identities.* New York: Verso.

Banet-Weiser, Janet. 1999. *The Most Beautiful Girl in the World: Beauty Pageants and National Identity.* Berkeley: University of California Press.

Banner, Lois. 1983. *American Beauty.* Chicago: University of Chicago Press.

Banton, Michael. 1977. *The Idea of Race.* London: Tavistock Publications.
———. 1987. *Racial Theories.* New York: Cambridge University Press.
Barbaree, Erin Toki. 1995. Wake up! Unpublished essay. April 21, 1995.
Barnes, Jessica S., and Claudette E. Bennett. 2002. The Asian population. *Census 2000 Reports.* February 2002. http://www.census.gov/prod/2002pubs/c2kbr01-16.pdf.
Barrett, Michele. 1987. The concept of difference. *Feminist Review* 25:29–41.
Barringer, Herbert, Robert W. Gardner, and Michael J. Levin. 1993. *Asians and Pacific Islanders in the United States.* New York: Russell Sage Foundation.
Barth, Frederick. 1969. *Ethnic Groups and Boundaries: The Social Organization of Culture Difference.* Boston: Little Brown.
Beech, Hannah. 2003. Eurasian invasion. *Time Asia.* Oct. 29. http://www.time.com/time/asia/news/html.
Bennett, Claudette, Nampeo R. McKenney, and Roderick J. Harrison. 1995. Racial classification issues concerning children in mixed race households. In *Racial Statistics Branch of the Population Division of the Bureau of the Census.* Washington, D.C.: Bureau of the Census.
Blauner, Robert. 1972. *Racial Oppression in America.* New York: Harper and Row.
Blumer, Herbert. 1958. Race prejudice as a sense of group position. *Pacific Sociological Review* 1:3–7.
Blumer, Herbert, and Troy Duster. 1980. Theories of Race and Social Action In *Sociologica: Theory: Race and Colonialism.* Paris: UNESCO.
Bobo, Lawrence, and Vincent L. Hutchings. 1996. Perceptions of racial group competition: Extending Blumer's theory of group position to a multiracial social context. *American Sociological Review* 61:951–72.
Bonilla-Silva, Eduardo. 2002. "We are all Americans!" The Latin Americanization of racial stratification. *Race and Society* 5, no. 1:3–16.
Bordo, Susan. 1993. *Unbearable Weight: Feminism, Western Culture and the Body.* Berkeley: University of California Press.
Bradshaw, Carla K. 1992. Beauty and the beast: On racial ambiguity. Pp. 77–88 in *Racially Mixed People in America,* edited by Maria P. P. Root. Newbury Park, Calif.: Sage.
Brunsma, David L. 2003. Regional differences in the bi-racial experience. Paper presented at the American Sociological Association Conference, Atlanta, Ga.
Bryman, Alan. 2004. *Social Research Methods.* 2d ed. Oxford: Oxford University Press.
Burawoy, Michel. 1985. *The Politics of Production.* London: Verso.
Burawoy, Michael, et al. 1991. *Ethnography Unbound: Power and Resistance in the Modern Metropolis.* Berkeley: University of California Press.
Burkhardt, William R. 1983. Institutional barriers, marginality, and adapta-

tion among in the American Japanese mixed bloods in Japan. *Journal of Asian Studies* 7:510–44.

Butler, Judith. 1999. *Gender Trouble: Feminism and the Subversion of Identity.* New York: Routledge.

Calhoun, Craig. 1994. *Social theory and the politics of identity.* Oxford: Blackwell.

Callahan, William. 1998. The ideology of Miss Thailand in national, consumerist and transnational space. *Alternatives* 23, no. 1:29–61.

Census 2000 Data. http://factfinder.census.gov/bf/_lang=en_vt_name=DEC _2000_PL_U_QTPL_geo_id=04000US15.html

Chan, Sucheng. 1991. *Asian Americans: An Interpretive History.* Boston: Twayne.

Chang, Diane Yukihiro. 1996. Beauty queens don't deserve the adulation. *Honolulu Star-Bulletin*, March 8.

Chapkis, Wendy. 1986. *Beauty Secrets: Women and the Politics of Appearance.* Boston: South End Press.

Chen, David W. 2001. Little Tokyo journal: Charting revival through basketball. *New York Times,* Nov. 5, 2001, sec. A:15.

Chen, Victoria. 1992. The construction of Chinese American women's identity. In *Women Making Meaning, New Feminist Directions in Communications Research,* edited by Lana Rakow. New York: Routledge.

Chew, Kenneth S. Y., David J. Eggebeen, and Peter R. Uhlenberg. 1989. American children in multiracial households. *Sociological Perspectives* 32:65–85.

Christian, John, Nicholas J. Gadfield, Howard Giles, and Donald M. Taylor. 1976. The multidimensional and dynamic nature of ethnic identity. *International Journal of Psychology* 11:281–91.

Cohen, Colleen Ballerino, Richard Wilk, and Beverly Stoeltje, eds. 1996. *Beauty Queens on the Global Stage: Gender, Contests, and Power.* New York: Routledge.

Collins, Patricia Hill. 1990. *Black Feminist Thought: Knowledge Consciousness and the Politics of Empowerment.* Boston: Unwin.

———. 1997. On West and Fenstermaker's "Doing difference." Pp. 73-75 in *Women, Men and Gender: Ongoing Debates,* edited by Mary Roth Walsh. New Haven: Yale University Press.

Cornell, Stephen, and Douglass Hartmann. 1998. *Ethnicity and Race: Making Identities in a Changing World.* Thousand Oaks, Calif.: Pine Forge Press.

Craig, Maxine Leeds. 2002. *Ain't I a Beauty Queen? Black Women, Beauty and the Politics of Race.* New York: Oxford University Press.

Creef, Elena Tajima. 2004. *Imagining Japanese America: The Visual Construction of Citizenship, Nation and the Body.* New York: New York University Press.

DaCosta, Kimberly Ann. 2000. Remaking the colorline: Social bases and implications of the multiracial movement. Diss., University of California, Berkeley.

Dalmage, Heather M. 2000. *Tripping on the Colorline: BlackWhite Multiracial Families in a Racially Divided World.* New Brunswick, N.J.: Rutgers University Press.

———, ed. 2004. *The Politics of Multiracialism: Challenging Racial Thinking.* Albany: State University of New York Press.

Daniels, Roger. 1988. *Asian America: Chinese and Japanese in the United States since 1850.* Seattle: University of Washington Press.

Davis, F. James. 1991. *Who Is Black? One Nation's Definition.* University Park: Pennsylvania State University Press.

DeBonis, Steven. 1995. *Children of the Enemy: Oral Histories of Vietnamese Amerasians and Their Mothers.* Jefferson, N.C.: McFarland and Company.

Degler, Carl N. 1971. *Neither Black nor White: Slavery and Race Relations in Brazil and the United States.* New York: Macmillan.

Dill, Bonnie Thornton. 1988. Our mother's grief: Racial ethnic women and the maintenance of families. *Journal of Family History* 13, no. 4:415–31.

Dower, John W. 1986. *War without Mercy: Race and Power in the Pacific War.* New York: Pantheon Books.

DuBose, Herman L., and Loretta I. Winters. 2002. *New Faces in a Changing America: Multiracial Identity in the Twenty-First Century.* Newbury Park, Calif.: Sage.

Dyson, Michael Eric. 1996. *Between God and Gangsta Rap: Bearing Witness to Black Culture.* New York: Oxford University Press.

Edgerton, Roger. 1982. Letters to the editor: More re: mixed-ancestry beauty queens. *Rafu Shimpo*, Sept. 8, 2.

Edles, Laura Desfor. 2004. Rethinking "race," "ethnicity," and "culture": Is Hawaii the "model minority" state? *Ethnic and Racial Studies* 27, no. 11:37–68.

Emerson, Robert M. 1983. *Contemporary Field Research: A Collection of Readings.* Prospect Heights, Ill.: Waveland Press.

Epstein, A. L. 1978. *Ethos and Identity: Three Studies in Ethnicity.* London: Tavistock.

Eschbach, Karl. 1995. The enduring and vanishing American Indian: American Indian population growth and intermarriage in 1990. *Ethnic and Racial Studies* 18:89–108.

Espiritu, Yen Le. 1992. *Asian American Panethnicity : Bridging Institutions and Identities.* Philadelphia: Temple University Press.

———. 1997. *Asian American Women and Men.* Thousand Oaks, Calif.: Sage.

———. 2003. *Homebound: Filipino American Lives across Cultures, Communities, and Countries.* Berkeley: University of California Press.

An ethnic pageant that has clung to custom will now allow women who are not 100 percent Japanese to compete. 1999. *Honolulu Star Bulletin*, February 2. http://Starbulletin.com/1999/02/02/features/story1.html.

Face. 1996. Spring issue, 16:10.

Feagin, Joe R., and Hernan Vera. 1995. *White Racism: The Basics.* New York: Routledge.

Feagin, Joe R., and Clarice Bosher Feagin. 2003. *Racial and Ethnic Relations.* 7th ed. New York: Prentice-Hall.

Fernandez, Carlos A. 1996. Government classification of multiracial/multiethnic people. Pp. 15–36 in *The Multiracial Experience: Racial Borders as the New Frontier,* edited by Maria P. P. Root. Newbury Park, Calif.: Sage.

Fernandez, Enrique. 1993. The Latin whitewash. Pp. 70–74 in *Allure.*

Fields, Barbara Jeanne. 1990. Slavery, race and ideology in the United States of America. *New Left Review* 181:95–118.

Fong, Dexter. 1973. A sociohistorical study of the California Nisei Athletic Union "AA" North–South Basketball championship games for men from 1934–1971. Thesis, California State University, Sacramento.

Foucault, Michel. 1979. *Discipline and Punish: The Birth of a Prison.* New York: Vintage.

Frankenberg, Ruth. 1993. *White Women, Race Matters: The Social Construction of Whiteness.* Minneapolis: University of Minnesota Press.

Freedman, Rita. 1986. *Beauty Bound.* Lexington, Mass.: D. C. Heath.

French, Howard W. 2000. Still wary of outsiders, Japan expects immigration boom. *New York Times International,* March 14, 2000, A1, A11.

Fugita, Stephen S., and David J. O'Brien. 1991. *Japanese American Ethnicity: The Persistence of Community.* Seattle: University of Washington Press.

Gallagher, Charles A. 2002. Interracial dating and marriage: Fact, fantasy and the problem of survey data. Pp. 240–53 in *The Quality and Quantity of Contact: African Americans and Whites on College Campuses,* edited by Robert M. Moore III. Lanham, Md.: University Press of America.

Gamson, Joshua. 1995. Must identity movements self-destruct? A queer dilemma. *Social Problems* 42:390–407.

Gans, Herbert J. 1979. *On the Making of Americans: Essays in Honor of David Reisman.* Philadelphia: University of Pennsylvania Press.

Gardner, Robert W., Bryant Robey, and Peter C. Smith. 1989. *Asian Americans: Growth, change and diversity.* Washington, D.C.: Population Reference Bureau.

Garfinkel, Harold. 1967. *Studies in Ethnomethodology.* Englewood Cliffs, N.J.: Prentice-Hall.

Gibbs, Jewelle Taylor, and Gloria Moskowitz Sweet. 1991. Clinical and cultural issues in the treatment of biracial and bicultural adolescents. *Journal of Contemporary Human Services* 72, 1:579–92.

Gilroy, Paul. 2000. *Between Camps: Nations, Culture and the Allure of Race*. London: Penguin Books.

Gimlin, Debra L. 2002. *Body Work: Beauty and Self-Image in American Culture*. New York: Columbia University Press.

Glazer, Nathan, and Daniel P. Moynihan. 1975. *Ethnicity: Theory and Experience*. Cambridge: Harvard University Press.

Glenn, Evelyn Nakano. 1986. *Issei, Nisei, Warbride: Three Generations of Japanese American Women in Domestic Service*. Philadelphia: Temple University Press.

———. 1992. From servitude to service work: Historical continuities in the racial division of paid reproductive labors. *Signs* 18:1–43.

Goffman, Erving. 1959. *The Presentation of Self in Everyday Life*. New York: Anchor Books Doubleday.

———. 1963. *Stigma: Notes on the Management of Spoiled Identity*. Englewood Cliffs, N.J.: Prentice-Hall.

Goldberg, David Theo. 1997. *Racial Subjects: Writing on Race in America*. New York: Routledge.

———. 2002. *The Racial State*. Oxford: Blackwell.

Gould, Stephen Jay. 1994. The geometer of race. *Discover* 15/11 (November): 65-69.

Gregory, Steven, and Roger Sanjek, eds. 1994. *Race*. New Brunswick, N.J.: Rutgers University Press.

Grindstaff, Laura. 2002. *The Money Shot: Trash, Class, and the Making of TV Talk Shows*. Chicago: University of Chicago Press.

Guss, David M. 2000. *The Festive State: Race, Ethnicity and Nationalism as Cultural Performance*. Berkeley: University of California Press.

Hall, Christine Iijima. 1996. 2001: A race odyssey. Pp. 395–410 in *The Multiracial Experience: Racial Border as the New Frontier*, edited by Maria P. P. Root. Newbury Park, Calif.: Sage.

Hamamoto, Darrell Y. 1994. *Monitored Peril: Asian Americans and the Politics of TV Representation*. Minneapolis: University of Minnesota Press.

Hamill, James F. 2003. Show me your CDIB: Blood quantum and Indian identity among Indian people of Oklahoma. *American Behavioral Scientist* 47, no. 3:267–82.

Haney Lopez, Ian F. 1996. *White by Law: The Legal Construction of Race*. New York: New York University Press.

Harding, Sandra. 1987. *Feminism and Methodology*. Bloomington: Indiana University Press.

Harris, Angela P. 1990. Race and essentialism in feminist legal theory. *Stanford Law Review* 42:581–616.

Harris, David. 2002. In the eye of the beholder: Observed race and observer characteristics. Population Studies Center Report No. 02-522 August. In-

stitute for Social Research, University of Michigan. http://www.psc.isr
.umich.edu/pubs/pdf/rr92-522.pdf.

Hata, Donald Teruo, Jr. 1978. *Undesirables: Early Immigrants and the Anti-
Japanese Movement in San Francisco 1892–1893, Prelude to Exclusion.* New
York: Arno Press.

Hatfield, Elaine, and Susan Sprecher. 1986. *Mirror, Mirror . . . The Importance
of Looks in Everyday Life.* Albany: State University of New York Press.

Henry, Sheila E. 1978. *Cultural persistence and socio-economic mobility: A comparative study of assimilation among Armenians and Japanese in Los Angeles.*
San Francisco: R and E Research Associates.

Herman, Melissa R. 2003. The black-white-other test score gap: Academic
achievement among mixed race adolescents. Paper presented at the American Sociological Association Conference, Atlanta, Georgia.

Hirabayashi, Lane. 1993. Is the JA community disappearing? *Pacific Currents,*
B15-16.

Hochschild, Arlie Russell. 1994. The commercial spirit of intimate life and
the abduction of feminism: Signs from women's advice books. *Theory,
Culture and Society* 11:1–24.

———. 2003. *Managed Heart: Commercialization of Human Feeling.* 20th anniversary ed. Berkeley: University of California Press.

Hollinger, David. 1995. *Postethnic America: Beyond Multiculturalism.* New
York: Basic Books.

Holmes, Steven A. 1996. Black–white marriages on rise, study says. *New York
Times,* July 4, A10.

Honda, Harry K. 1993. Asian American talk about pressure of out marriage.
Pacific Citizen (16 April): 3.

———. 1995. "Color JACL's future multicultural" say JACL leaders. *Pacific
Citizen* (4–17 August): 9.

hooks, bell. 1992. *Black Looks: Race and Representation.* Boston: South End
Press.

Hosokawa, Fumiko. 1978. *The Sansei: Social Interaction and Ethnic Identification among Third-Generation Japanese.* San Francisco: R and E Research
Associates Inc.

Hwang, Sean-Shong, Rogelio Saenz, and Benigno E. Aguirre. 1994. Structural and individual determinants of outmarriage among Chinese, Filipino and Japanese Americans in California. *Sociological Inquiry* 64:396–414.

Hyena, Hank. 2000. Beauty and the beak. *Salon.com,* Jan. 27, 2000. http://
archive.Salon.com/health/sex/urge/world/2000/01/27/noses/print.html.

Ignatiev, Noel. 1995. *How the Irish Became White.* New York: Routledge.

———. 2004. Race in a post–civil rights era. Keynote address, Ethnic and
Racial Studies, Trinity College Dublin, Jan. 19.

Inouye, Jon. 1977. A major ethnic disaster. *Pacific Citizen* (March 25): 9.

Inouye, Y. 1982. "Letters to the Editor." *Rafu Shimpo* (Sept. 4): 2.

Iwasaki Mass, Amy. 1992. Interracial Japanese Americans: The best of both worlds or the end of the Japanese American community. Pp. 265–79 in *Racially Mixed People in America*, edited by Maria P. P. Root. Newbury Park, Calif.: Sage.

JACL women request end to beauty queen sponsorship. 1985. *Hokubei Mainichi*, April 2.

Jewell, K. Sue. 1993. *From Mammy to Miss America and Beyond: Culture Images and the Shaping of U.S. Social Policy*. London: Routledge.

Jiobu, Robert M. 1988. *Ethnicity and Assimilation: Blacks, Chinese, Filipinos, Japanese, Koreans, Mexicans, Vietnamese, and Whites*. Albany: State University of New York Press.

Kalish, Susan. 1992. Interracial baby boomlet in progress? Washington D.C.: Population Reference Bureau.

———. 1993. Demographics: Interracial baby boom. *Futurist* (May-June): 54–55.

Kamehameha grad wins pageant title. 2002. *Honolulu Advertiser* (April 4).

Kamisugi, Keith. 2001. Multiethnic queen is the right thing in Hawai'i. *Honolulu Advertiser*, March 27, 2001.

———. 2002. Honolulu Cherry Blossom turns 50. *Nichi Bei Times*, February. http://www.twojapaneebruddahs.com/.

Katz, S. H. 1995. Is race a legitimate concept for science? Pp. 1-6 in The AAPA Revised Statement on Race: A Brief Analysis and Commentary, University of Pennsylvania, 1-6.

Kawasaki, Jun. 1982. "Letters to the Editor: More Re: Mixed-Ancestry Beauty Queens." *Rafu Shimpo*, Aug. 31, 4.

Kendis, Kaoru Oguri. 1989. *A Matter of Comfort: Ethnic Maintenance and Ethnic Style among Third Generation Japanese Americans*. New York: AMS Press.

Kiefer, Christie. 1974. *Changing Cultures, Changing Lives: An Ethnographic Study of Three Generations of Japanese Americans*. San Francisco: Jossey-Bass.

Kikumura, Akemi, and Harry H. L. Kitano. 1973. Interracial marriage: A picture of the Japanese Americans. *Journal of Social Issues* 29:67–81.

Kimura, Yukiko. 1952. A comparative study of collective adjustment of the Issei. Thesis, Department of Sociology, University of Chicago.

King, Rebecca Chiyoko. 1997. Multiraciality reigns supreme? Mixed race Japanese Americans and the Cherry Blossom Queen Pageant. *Amerasia Journal: No Passing Zone* 23, no. 1:113–28.

———. 2000. Racialization, recognition and rights: Lumping and splitting multiracial Asian Americans and the 2000 Census. *Journal of Asian American Studies* 3, no. 2: 191–217.

———. 2001. Mirror, mirror on the wall: Mapping discussions of feminism, race and beauty on mixed race Japanese American women. In *The Sum of Our Parts: Mixed-Heritage Asian Americans*, edited by Teresa Williams-Leon and Cynthia Nakashima. Philadelphia: Temple University Press.

———. 2002. Eligible to be Japanese American: Counting on multiraciality in Japanese American basketball leagues and beauty pageants. In *Contemporary Asian American Communities: Intersections and Divergences*, edited by Linda Trinh Vo and Rick Bonus. Philadelphia: Temple University Press.

King, Rebecca C., and Kimberly McClain Da Costa. 1996. The changing face of America: The making and remaking of race in the African and Japanese American communities. In *The Multiracial Experience: Racial Borders as New Frontier*, edited by Maria P. P. Root. Newbury Park, Calif.: Sage.

Kitahara Kich, George. 1982. Eurasians: Ethnic/racial identity development of biracial Japanese/white adults. Thesis, Wright Institute Graduate School of Psychology, University of California, Berkeley.

———. 1996. In the margins of sex and race: Difference, marginality, and flexibility. Pp. 263–76 in *The Multiracial Experience: Racial Borders as the New Frontier*, edited by Maria P. P. Root. Newbury Park, Calif.: Sage.

Kitano, Harry H. L. 1993. *Generations and Identity: The Japanese American*. Needham Heights, Mass.: Ginn Press.

Kivisto, Peter, and Dag Blanck. 1990. *American Immigrants and Their Generations: Studies and Commentaries on the Hansen Thesis after Fifty Years*. Urbana: University of Illinois Press.

Kondo, Dorinne. 1997. *About Face: Performing Race in Fashion and Theater*. New York: Routledge.

Kurashige, Lon. 2002. *Japanese American Celebration and Conflict: A History of Ethnic Identity and Festival, 1934–1990*. Berkeley: University of California Press.

Lakoff, Robin Tolmach, and Raquel L. Scherr. 1984. *Face Value: The Politics of Beauty*. Boston: Routledge and Kegan Paul.

Lal, Barbara Ballis. 1986. The "Chicago school" of American sociology, symbolic interactionalism, and race relations theory. Pp. 280–98 in *Theories of Race and Ethnic Relations*, edited by John Rex and David Mason. Cambridge: Cambridge University Press.

Lan, Pei Chia. 2001. The body as a contested terrain for labor control: Cosmetic retailers in department stores and direct selling. In *Critical Studies of Work*, edited by R. Baldoz and C. Koeber. Philadelphia: Temple University Press.

Lazarre, Jane. 1996. *Beyond the Whiteness of Whiteness: Memoir of a White Mother of Black Sons*. Durham, N.C.: Duke University Press.

Le, C. N. 2004a. Interracial dating and marriage. *Asian-Nation: The Landscape of Asian America*. http://www.asian-nation.org/interracial.shtml.

————. 2004b. Multiracial/Hapa Asian Americans. *Asian-Nation: The Landscape of Asian America*. http://www.asian-nation.org/interracial.shtml.

Lee, Sharon M. 1993. Racial classifications in the U.S. Census: 1890–1990. *Ethnic and Racial Studies* 16:75–94.

Lee, Sharon M., and Keiko Yamanaka. 1990. Patterns of Asian American intermarriage and marital assimilation. *Journal of Comparative Family Studies* 21:287–305.

Leonard, Karen Isaksen. 1992. *Making Ethnic Choices: California's Punjabi Mexican Americans*. Philadelphia: Temple University Press.

Levine, Gene N., and Darrel M. Montero. 1973. Socio-economic mobility among three generations of Japanese Americans. *Journal of Social Forces* 29:33–44.

Levine, Gene N., and Colbert Rhodes. 1981. *The Japanese American Community: A Three-Generation Study*. New York: Praeger.

Lindsey, Karen. 1995. Race, sexuality and class in Soapland. In *Gender, Race, and Class in Media*, edited by Gail Dines and Jean M. Humez. Thousand Oaks, Calif.: Sage.

Loveman, Mara. 1999. Is "race" essential? *American Sociological Review* 64, no. 6:891–98.

Lyman, Stanford Morris. 1986. *Chinatown and Little Tokyo: Power, Conflict, and Community among Chinese and Japanese Immigrants in America*. Millwood, N.Y.: Associated Faculty Press.

Lyman, Stanford M., and William A. Douglass. 1973. Ethnicity: Strategy of collective and individual impression management. *Social Research* 40:344–65.

Lyon, M. 1972. Race and ethnicity in pluralistic societies. *New Communities* 1:256–62.

Magarifuji, Patti Shirakawa. 1982. A comparative study of ethnic identity in third-generation Japanese Americans in California and Hawaii. Thesis, Department of Psychology, California School of Professional Psychology.

Marchetti, Gina. 1993. *Romance and the "Yellow Peril": Race, Sex, and Discursive Strategies in Hollywood Fiction*. Berkeley: University of California Press.

Matsuo, Hisako. 1992. Identificational assimilation of Japanese Americans: A reassessment of primordialism and circumstanialism. *Sociological Perspectives* 35:505–23.

Mead, George Herbert. 1934. *Mind, Self and Society*. Chicago: University of Chicago Press.

Miles, Robert. 1982. *Racism and Migrant Labour*. London: Routledge and Kegan Paul.

Millard, H. 2002. Racial privacy act—Be careful what you ask for. http://www.newnation.org/Millard/Millard-Racial-Privacy-Act.html. Retrieved March 3, 2005.

Miller, Cindy. 1982. Letters to the Editor: More Re: Mixed-Ancestry Beauty Queens. *Rafu Shimpo*, Sept. 8, 2.

Mixed ancestry of Nisei Week Queens is a topic for concern. 1982. *Pacific Citizen*, 7–8.

Modell, John. 1977. *The Economics and Politics of the Japanese in Los Angeles, 1900–1942*. Urbana: University of Illinois Press.

Montagu, Ashley. 1964. *Concept of Race*. New York: Free Press of Glencoe.

Montero, Darrel. 1980. *Japanese Americans: Changing Patterns of Ethnic Affiliation over Three Generations*. Boulder, Colo.: Westview Press.

Moreno, Allys Mayumi. 1982. "Re: Mixed-Ancestry Nikkei Beauty Queens." *Rafu Shimpo*, Aug. 31, 4.

Morris, Aldon D., and Carol McClurg Mueller. 1992. *Frontiers in Social Movement Theory*. New Haven: Yale University Press.

Motoyoshi, Michelle M. The experience of mixed-race people: Some thoughts and theories. *Journal of Ethnic Studies* 18:77–94.

Munoz, Carlos, Jr. 1989. *Youth, Identity, and Power: The Chicano Movement*. London: Verso.

Mydans, Seth. 2002. Oh, blue-eyed Thais, flaunt your western genes! *New York Times, Bangkok Journal*. http://www.nytimes.com/2002/08/29/international/asia/29BANG.html.

Nagel, Joane. 1986. The political construction of ethnicity. Pp. 93–112 in *Competitive Ethnic Relations*, edited by Susan Olzak and J. Nagel. Orlando: Academic Press.

———. 1994. Constructing ethnicity. *Social Problems* 41:152–76.

———. 1995. American Indian ethnic renewal: Politics and the resurgence of identity. *American Sociological Review* 60:947–65.

Nagel, Joane, and C. Matthew Snipp. 1993. Ethnic reorganization: American Indian social, economic, political and cultural strategies for survival. *Ethnic and Racial Relations* 16:203–35.

Nakamura, Cayleen. 1996. Through the fire: Hapa or double: A question of identity. *Rafu Shimpo*, Sept. 17, 3.

Nakano, Mei. 1985. The other side of beauty contest. Pp. 6 in *Pacific Citizen*. Monterey Park, Calif.

———. 1988. Mirror, mirror, on the wall. Pp. 7 in *Pacific Citizen*. Monterey Park, Calif.

Nakashima, Cynthia. 1996. An invisible monster: The creation and denial of mixed race people in America. Pp. 162–78 in *Racially Mixed People in America*, edited by Maria P. P. Root. Newbury Park, Calif.: Sage.

Nishinaga, Linden. 1982. Letters to the editor: Mixed-ancestry beauty queens. *Rafu Shimpo*, Aug. 27, 3.

Nobles, Melissa. 2000. *Shades of Citizenship: Race and Census in Modern Politics*. Stanford, Calif.: Stanford University Press.

The numbers game. 1993. *Time* 142, no. 21 (November): 14–15.

Odo, Jonathan. 1994. Mixed race Japanese Americans and the future of the JACL. Unpublished essay, University of California, Berkeley.

Ogawa, Dennis. 1971. *From Japs to Japanese: An Evolution of Japanese American Stereotypes*. Berkeley, Calif.: McCutchan.

———. 1986. *Jan Ken Po: World of Hawaii's Japanese Americans*. Honolulu: University of Hawaii Press.

O'Hare, William P., and Judy C. Felt. 1991. *Asian Americans: America's Fastest Growing Minority Group*. Washington D.C.: Population Reference Bureau.

Okamura, Jonathan Y. 1981. Situational identity. *Ethnic and Racial Studies* 4:452–65.

Okamura, Raymond. 1982. Eurasian queens. *Pacific Citizen*, Sept. 24, 6.

———. 1984. 100 percent Japanese? *Hokubei Mainichi*, Jan. 13, 5.

———. 1985a. Letter to the Editor. *Hokubei Mainichi*, April 17, 5.

———. 1985b. Letters. *Pacific Citizen*, April 19, 6.

Okazaki, Suzie. 1985. *Nihonmachi: A Story of San Francisco's Japan Town*. San Francisco: SKO Studio.

Oliver, J. Eric, Fredric C. Gey, Jon Stiles, and Henry Brady. 1995. Pacific rim states Asian demographic data book. Pacific Rim Research Program, UC Office of the President, University of California, Berkeley.

Oliver, Melvin L., and Thomas M. Shapiro. 1995. *Black Wealth, White Wealth: A New Perspective on Racial Inequality*. New York: Routledge.

Olumide, Jill. 2002. *Raiding the Gene Pool: The Social Construction of Mixed Race*. London: Pluto Press.

Omi, Michael. 2000. Keynote address: Reorienting Asian Pacific America. Davies Forum Seminar Series. University of San Francisco.

Omi, Michael, and Howard Winant. 1994. *Racial Formation in the United States from 1960s to the 1980s*. New York: Routledge.

Osaki, Drew, David Omori, Jill Shiraki, and Rebecca Chiyoko King. 2000. Charting course and shifting direction for the Nikkei community. Japanese American Consortium of Community Related Organizations.

Penn, William. 1998. *As We Are Now: Mixedblood Essays on Race and Identity*. Berkeley: University of California Press.

Perlmann, Joel, and Mary Waters. 2002. *The New Race Question: How the Census Counts Mixed Race Individuals*. New York: Russell Sage Foundation.

Posey, Hedy. 1982. Letters to the Editor. *Rafu Shimpo*, Sept. 10, 2.

Racial Privacy Initiative. http://www.racialprivacy.org/content/index.php. Downloaded Feb. 12, 2004.

Reddy, Maureen. 1994. *Crossing the Color Line*. New Brunswick, N.J.: Rutgers University Press.

Reeves, Terrance J., and Claudette Bennett. 2004. *We the People: Asians in the United States*. Washington, D.C.: U.S. Bureau of the Census.

Riverol, A. R. 1992. *Live from Atlantic City: The History of the Miss America Pageant before, after, and in Spite of Television*. Bowling Green, Ohio: Bowling Green State University Popular Press.

Rockquemore, Kerry Ann, and David L. Brunsma. 2001. *Beyond Black*. Newbury Park, Calif.: Sage.

Roediger, David R. 1991. *The Wages of Whiteness: Race and the Making of the American Working Class*. London: Verso.

Rogers, Mark. 1998. Spectacular bodies: Folklorization and the politics of identity in Ecuadorian beauty pageants. *Journal of Latin American Anthropology* 3, no. 2 (Spring): 54-85.

Rooks, Noliwe. 1996. *Hair Raising: Beauty, Culture and African American Women*. New Brunswick, N.J.: Rutgers University Press.

Ropp, Steven Masami. 1997. Do multiracial subjects really challenge race? Mixed-race Asians in the United States and the Caribbean. *Amerasia Journal* 23, no.1:1–16.

Root, Maria P. P. 1992. *Racially Mixed People in America*. Newbury Park, Calif.: Sage.

———. 1996. *The Multiracial Experience: Racial Borders as the New Frontier*. Newbury Park, Calif.: Sage.

Sacks, Karen Brodkin. 1988. *Caring by the Hour: Women, Work, and Organizing at Duke Medical Center*. Urbana: University of Illinois Press.

———. 1994. How did Jews become white folks? Pp. 78–102 in *Race*, edited by Steven Gregory and Roger Sanjek. New Brunswick, N. J.: Rutgers University Press.

Saenz, Rogelio, Sean-Shong Hwang, Benigno E. Aguirre, and Robert N. Anderson. 1995. Persistence and change in Asian identity among children of intermarried couples. *Sociological Perspectives* 38:175–194.

Sandor, Gabrielle. 1994. The other Americans. *American Demographics* 16:36–42.

Sarasohn, Eileen Sunada. 1983. *The Issei: Portrait of a Pioneer, An Oral History*. Palo Alto, Calif.: Pacific Books.

Senzaki, Randy. 1994. Hapas and the future of the JACL. *Pacific Citizen* :3.

Shinagawa, Larry Hajime. 1994. Intermarriage and inequality: A theoretical and empirical analysis of the marriage patterns of Asian Americans. Ph.D. thesis, Department of Sociology, University of California, Berkeley.

Shinagawa, Larry Hajime, and Gin Yong Pang. 1988. Intraethnic, interethnic, and interracial marriages among Asian Americans in California, 1980. *Berkeley Journal of Sociology* 33:95–114.

Simpson, Caroline Chung. 2001. *An Absent Presence: Japanese Americans in Postwar American Culture, 1945–1960*. Durham, N.C.: Duke University Press.

Small, Stephen. 1989. Racial differentiation in the slave era: A comparative study of people of "mixed race" in Jamaica and Georgia. In *Sociology*. Berkeley: University of California.

———. 1994. *Racialized Barriers: The Black Experience in the United States and England in the 1980s*. London: Routledge.

Smedley, Audrey. 1995. "Race" and the construction of human identity. *American Anthropologist* 100, no. 3 (Sept.): 690–702.

Snipp, C. Matthew. 2003. Racial measurement in the American census: Past practices and implications for the future. *Annual Review of Sociology* 29:563–88.

Solomos, John, and Les Back. 1995. *Race, Politics and Social Change*. London: Routledge.

Song, Miri. 2001. Comparing minorities' ethnic options: Do Asian Americans possess "more" ethnic options than African Americans? *Ethnicities* 1, no. 1(April): 57–82.

———. 2003. *Choosing Ethnic Identity*. Oxford: Polity/Blackwell.

Spencer, Jon Michael. 1997. *The New Colored People: The Mixed Race Movement in America*. New York: New York University Press.

Spencer, Rainier. 1999. *Spurious Issues: Race and Multiracial Identity Politics in the United States*. Boulder, Colo.: Westview Press.

Spickard, Paul. 1989. *Mixed Blood: Intermarriage and Ethnic Identity in Twentieth-Century America*. Madison: University of Wisconsin Press.

———. 1996. *Japanese Americans: The Formation and Transformations of an Ethnic Group*. New York: Twayne.

Spickard, Paul, and G. Reginald Daniel. 2004. *Racial Thinking in the U.S.: Uncompleted Independence*. South Bend, Ind.: Notre Dame Press.

Streeter, Caroline A. 1996. Ambiguous bodies: Locating black/white women in cultural representations. In *The Multiracial Experience: Racial Borders as the New Frontier*, edited by Maria P. P. Root. Thousand Oaks, Calif.: Sage.

Taguma, Kenji. 2001. Emi Yoshioka crowned 2001 Cherry Blossom Queen. *Nichi Bei Times*, April 17, 1–4. Retrieved on May 9, 2005. http://www .nichibeitimes.com/news/queen-pagent.html

Takagi, Dana. 1993. *The Retreat from Race: Asian American Admissions and Racial Politics*. New Brunswick, N.J.: Rutgers University Press.

Takaki, Ronald. 1989. *Strangers from a Different Shore*. New York: Penguin Books.

Tamura, Eileen H. 1994. *Americanization, Acculturation, and Ethnic Identity: The Nisei Generation in Hawaii*. Urbana: University of Illinois Press.

Tanner, Mika. 1998. Pageants: Pride or puffery? *Asian Week* 19, no. 52(Aug. 20): 12.

Taylor, Charles. 1994. *Multiculturalism: Examining the Politics of Recognition*. Princeton, N.J.: Princeton University Press.

Thorne, Barrie. 1993. *Gender Play: Girls and Boys in School*. New Brunswick, N.J.: Rutgers University Press.

Thornton, Michael Charles. 1983. A social history of a multiethnic identity: The case of black Japanese Americans. In *Sociology*. Ann Arbor: University of Michigan.

———. 1996. Hidden agendas, identity theories, and multiracial people. Pp.

101–20 in *The Multiracial Experience: Racial Borders as the New Frontier*, edited by Maria P. P. Root. Newbury Park, Calif.: Sage.

Tighe, Lori. 1999. Queen says culture is a state of mind. *Honolulu Star-Bulletin*, March 22, A3.

Tinker, John N. 1973. Intermarriage and ethnic boundaries: The Japanese American case. *Journal of Social Issues* 29:49–65.

Tizard, Barbara, and Ann Phoenix. 1993. *Black, White or Mixed Race? Race and Racism in the Lives of Young People of Mixed Parentage*. London: Routledge.

Toth, Catherine E. 2001. Competing for more than a crown: Cherry Blossom queen discovers that success lies in personal journey. *Honolulu Advertiser*, April 8, E1.

Tuan, Mia. 1998. *Forever Foreigners or Honorary Whites? The Asian Ethnic Experience*. New Brunswick, N.J.: Rutgers University Press.

Uyeno, Steve. 1996. Committee cancels coronation: Organizers cite lack of participants, community interest. *Northwest Nikkei* (May): 1.

Valhouli, Christine. 2000. Asian eyes. *Salon.com*. http://archive.salon.com/health /feature/2000/02/16/asianeyes/print.html.

Van den Berghe, Pierre L. 1967. *Race and Racism*. New York: Wiley.

Wallace, Kendra R. 2001. *Relative/Outsider: The Art and Politics of Identity among Mixed Heritage Students*. Westport, Conn.: Albex Publishing.

Waters, Mary. 1990. *Ethnic Options*. Berkeley: University of California Press.

Webster, Yehudi O. 1992. *The Racialization of America*. New York: St. Martin's Press.

West, Candace, and Don Zimmerman. 1991. Doing gender. Pp. 13–37 in *The Social Construction of Gender*, edited by Judith Lorber and Susan Farrell. Newbury Park, Calif.: Sage.

West, Candace, and Sarah Fenstermaker. 1997. Doing difference. In *Women, Men and Gender: On Going Debates*, ed. Mary Roth Walsh. New Haven: Yale University Press.

Williams, Brackette F. 1989. A class act: Anthropology and the race to nation across ethnic terrain. *Annual Review of Anthropology* 18:401–44.

Williams, Teresa K. 1991. Marriage between Japanese women and U.S. servicemen since World War II. *Amerasia Journal* 17:135–54.

———. 1996. Beyond racial ambiguity and social displacement: The sociological reassessment of the "what are you?" encounters of biracial individuals. In *The Multiracial Experience: Racial Borders as New Frontier*, edited by Maria P. P. Root. Newbury Park, Calif.: Sage.

———. 1997. Race-ing and being raced: The critical interrogation of "passing." *Amerasia Journal* 23, no. 1:61–68.

Williams-Leon, Teresa. 2001. The convergence of passing zones: Multiracial gays, lesbians and bi-sexuals of Asian descent. Pp. 145–62 in *The Sum of Our Parts: Mixed Heritage Asian Americans*, edited by T. Williams-Leon and C. Nakashima. Philadelphia: Temple University Press.

Williams-Leon, T., and C. Nakashima, eds. 2001. *The Sum of Our Parts: Mixed Heritage Asian Americans.* Philadelphia: Temple University Press.

Williamson, Joel. 1980. *New People.* New York: Free Press.

Wilson, Anne. 1987. *Mixed Race Children: A Study of Identity.* London: Allen and Unwin.

Wilson, William Julius. 1978. *The Declining Significance of Race: Blacks and Changing American Institutions.* Chicago: University of Chicago Press.

Wilson, Robert A., and Bill Hosokawa. 1980. *East to America: A History of the Japanese in the U.S.* New York: William Morrow.

Wilson, Terry. 1992. Blood quantum: Native American mixed bloods. In *Racially Mixed People in America,* edited by Maria P. P. Root. Newbury Park, Calif.: Sage.

Wolf, Diane Lauren. 1994. *Factory Daughters: Gender, Household Dynamics and Rural Industrialization in Java.* Berkeley: University of California Press.

Wolf, Naomi. 1991. *The Beauty Myth: How Images of Beauty Are Used against Women.* New York: William Morrow.

Woodrum, Eric. 1981. An assessment of Japanese American assimilation, pluralism, and subordination. *American Journal of Sociology* 87:157–69.

Wright, Lawrence. 1994. One drop of blood. *New Yorker* (July 24): 46–55.

Wu, Judy Tsu-Chun. 1997. "Loveliest daughter of our ancient Cathay!" Representations of ethnic and gender identity in the Miss Chinatown USA Beauty Pageant. *Journal of Social History* 31:5–31.

Yancey, George. 2000. Introduction to interracial families and multiracial individuals. *Sociological Imagination.* 37, no. 4:205–8.

Yano, Christine. 2006. *Crowning the Nice Girl: Gender, Ethnicity, and Culture in Hawai'i's Cherry Blossom Festival.* Honolulu: University of Hawaii Press.

Zack, Naomi. 1993. *Race and Mixed Race.* Philadelphia: Temple University Press.

Index

access to social networks: race work for, 22

advertising for sponsors, 159, 160

African American/Japanese American mixed-race queen candidates, 38

agency of women in their beauty practices, 75–76

aggression: mixed race and cultural, 98, 99; stereotype of Japanese men as sexually aggressive, 47, 48

Aguirre, B. E., 54

Aihara, C., 178

Alba, R., 27

Ali, S., 3, 27, 28, 29

Alien Land Law of 1913, 62, 198

ambassadresses, queen and queen candidates as, 9, 119, 142–43, 150, 231; as community representatives, 152–58; at cultural events, 150–51; dealing with sponsors

and community politics, 158–66; financial relations with Japan and, 166–71; gendering Japanese Americanness and, 177–84; influence of Japan on Japanese Americanness and, 171–77

ancestry: eligibility based on. *See* racial eligibility rules

Anderson, B., 18

Anderson, R. N., 54

antimiscegenation laws, 46–47; repeal of (1967), 50, 202. *See also* intermarriage/interracial marriage

antirace, 24

anxiety about dilution of culture. *See* dilution of culture, anxiety about

appearance. *See* beauty; "looking Japanese"

archival research, 5, 6

Arima, C., 198

Armstrong, B., 168, 176

Arthur, Y. A., 102–3

Ashkenazi, M., 16

Asia: perpetuation of white or mixed image of beauty in, 108–9

Asian American communities: intermarriage and, 42, 43; Japanese American community shrinkage relative to, 38, 39; median ages of (1980), 41; multiracial Asians by racial/ethnic combinations, 44; population in U.S. during twentieth century, 41

Asian People's Friendship Society in Japan, 168

Asian Week (newspaper), 181

assimilation, 237n.2; collective anxiety about overassimilation, 4, 70; complexity of, 230; disintegrating community as cost of, 51; factors increasing Japanese American integration, 52; festivals' assimilationist tendencies, 11–12; interracial marriage as normal outcome of, 51–52; social control of pageant participants in name of, 61–62; structural, constraints of race on, 55–56; tension between exoticization of difference and, 141–42; after World War II, 49

Ato, Mr., 173–74

audience, 138–39; cultural and racial expectations in front of, 140–44; in Hawaii, 209; Japanese American community as primary, 8; from 1935 to 1950s, 62; role in talent competition, 113; variation from year to year, 164

authenticity: claims of Hawaii pageant to, 212–13; ethnic strategies for making racial claims, 35, 92–93, 102, 104–14; hierarchies of, 19, 79, 89, 103–4; of Japanese vs. Japanese American people, 167; knowledge of traditional cultural arts and, 126, 150; "markers" or "cues" of, 35; monoracial cultural impostors and, 9, 85–87, 89–90, 100, 114, 204; pureness of festival as mark of cultural, 174; race-ethnicity relationship and, 32, 69, 71, 91, 92, 192–93, 223

authenticity checks for mixed-race women, 191–92

Banet-Weiser, J., 7, 8, 75

Banner, L., 75

Banton, M., 7

Barbaree, E. T., 115

Barnes, J. S., 4, 202

Barrett, M., 36

Barringer, H., 40, 41

Barth, F., 104

basketball leagues, Japanese American, 2, 50, 96, 158, 178, 190, 195, 209, 231, 233

bathing-suit competition, 236n.2; elimination of, 183; feminist challenge to, 64–65, 67; in Miss Nikkei International pageant in São Paulo, 193–94

beauty: agency of women in their beauty practices, 75–76; alternative models of, 182, 198–99; Eurasian, 81, 108–9; influences on perceptions of, 199; as judging criteria, in Japanese American pageants, 8, 64, 65; popularity of blended features

in Hawaii, 214; racial/ethnic ideal type, 75–77; standards of, 12, 81–85, 180, 182–83, 198–99
beauty embodiment issues, 136–37
beauty pageant(s), 1–20, 59–73; antiquated cultural traditions enshrined in, 171; as arena for battle over feminism, 64–68, 72, 179, 183–84; as arena for conversations about Japanese Americanness, 178–79, 227–28; challenge of future, 232–33; claiming legitimacy for, 193–95; commodification of women in, 8, 60, 68, 159–61, 184; common issues, 11; community pageant as distinct from, 224; creating community through, 13–16; as cultural texts, 138; detractors, 17; evolution of Japanese American, 10–13; funding for, 164–71, 210–11 (*see also* sponsors); goal of, 16; judging interviews, 126–32; motivation for participation and community connections, 148–52, 156–57; from 1935 to 1950s, 60–64, 71–72; from 1970s to 1980s, 64–68, 72; in 1990s, 68–71, 72; as political act, 178–79; primary concerns of, since 1950, 72; public nature of, 102; as public reassertion of Japanese American masculinity and heterosexuality, 179; question-and-answer section of, 132–34; race work in Japanese American, 33–34; as racialized projects, 7–10, 16, 18–19, 33–34, 77, 186, 227, 232; rationalization for perpetuation of, 111; reasons for studying Japanese American, 16–19; resistance to, 178–84; as

response to being shut out of whiteness, 36; self-development through, 111; similarity in form, 10; social control after, 144–46; speech portion of, 109–11, 114; talent portion of, 112–13
beauty products, 109
beauty queen, 6–7; African American/Japanese American mixed-race candidates for, 38; career aspirations of, 66; changing racial ancestry of, debate over racial eligibility rules and, 69–71, 72–73, 202–7; characteristics of, debate about, 8–9; collective nature of candidates' campaigns to be, 110–11; collective self-definition in selecting, dynamic process of, 16–19; community created through participation, 13; outside connections made by, 15–16, 152; culture used as commodity to increase chances of becoming, 101–2; feminism of, 65–66, 68, 72; Japanese national businessmen's criteria for legitimate, 94, 175; as living symbol of collective identity, 9–10, 16, 17–18, 79, 101–2, 119, 142–43, 185; mixed-race (*see* mixed-race queen); motives for participating in pageant, 15–16, 148–52, 156–57; objectification of, 9–10, 64–65, 142; on racial eligibility rules, 70–71; as racial/ethnic ideal type, 75–77; as reflection of city reputation, 196; rules for producing, 117–20; selling, 164–66; as symbol/representative of local community, 3, 13, 14, 152–58, 224–25, 228–30; as touchstone for collective

Japanese American anxieties,
98–100; training and practicing
to be, 7, 120–32; travel to Japan,
168–71, 173
Beauty Queens on the Global Stage
(Cohen, Wilk, and Stoeltje), 16
Beech, H., 108, 109
behavior: gendered codes of,
130–31; social control of
candidates', 117–20; training
and practicing to be queen, 7,
120–32
Bennett, C., 4, 40, 41, 42
biases of judges, 82–83
bicultural association displayed
before World War II, 62
biological race: belief in, 21, 22, 23,
29–30, 191, 230, 232, 233
birth certificate: racial authenticity
proven by, 191, 237n.1
birth rates of mixed-race Japanese
Americans, 44
blood quantum: cultural style and,
99
blood-quantum rules: during
internment, 103, 203, 204, 205;
for pageants (*see* racial eligibility
rules)
Blumer, H., 35
Bobo, L., 97
bodily racialization, 7, 76–77; in
Japanese terms, kimono and,
122–26
body(ies): character and, 75–77;
as embodiment of cultural
practice, 162; linking sponsor's
name to queen's, 159; making
mixed-race, 27–31; mixed-race
people's heightened awareness
of, 25, 76–77; morality and, 87;
race/Japanese Americanness
problematized by multiracial, 7,

22, 70–71, 72, 174, 190; racial/
ethnic ideal type, 75–77
Bonilla-Silva, E., 22
Brazil: Miss Nikkei International
pageant in, 8, 167, 193–94
Brunsma, D. L., 24, 25
Bryman, A., 5
Burawoy, M., 229, 230, 231
Burbridge, C., 109
businesses sponsoring festival and
pageant, 158–66
Butler, J., 19, 76

California: antimiscegenation laws
in, 46, 47, 202
California Nikkei Leadership
Council, 167
Callahan, W., 8, 75, 138
"candidates," "contestants" vs., 68,
224
career aspirations of beauty queen,
66
censoring candidates' and queens'
politics, 145–46
census, U.S.: multiple racial choices
on, 24, 25–27, 28; using data to
understand ethnic identity of
mixed children, 54
Chang, D. Y., 66
chaperones: rules regarding, 118–19;
social control by, 145, 153, 154,
155
character: body and, 75–77
Chen, D. W., 178
Cherry Blossom Festival in Hawaii, 11–12; attendance of,
208; attention paid to queen
and, 208–9, 210; authenticity
checks for mixed-race women
in, 191–92; claims to authenticity, 212–13; close ties to Japan,
210–11; decision by merchandise

ballot, 207; decreasing participation in, 214; funding of, 163, 210–11; history of, 207–19; Japanese arts lessons required for participation in, 125–26, 150, 212–13; kimono section of, 121–22, 125, 212; lack of talent competition in, 112; motives of participants in, 16; outside connections made by queens in, 152; program booklets sales for, 165–66, 210; racial eligibility rules in, 71, 191, 195–96, 208, 210, 211–19, 225; racial eligibility rules in, changes in, 168, 215–19; residency rule for, 189; social context of, 197; sponsorship in, 162–63

Cherry Blossom Festival in San Francisco, x, 8, 12, 40, 115; appearance of queen and court during, 37, 139, 176; attempt to replace pageant with scholarship contest, 177–78, 180, 181; cochairmen of, 167; debates in 1988 about, 177–84; participants from Japan, 174; rules for visitation to Nisei Week Festival, 119; volunteers, 158–59. *See also* Northern California Cherry Blossom Queen Pageant

Cherry Blossom Festival Parade (San Francisco), 14; participants from Japan, 174

children: birth rates of mixed-race Japanese American, 44; racial/ethnic identification of mixed-race, 52, 53, 54–55; of Shin Issei, 57

China: status of women in, 46

Chinese: interracial marriage among, 46

citizenship: debates about U.S., 60–64; Japanese, importance of Japanese last name for, 106

civil rights movement, 12; outmarriage rate and, 50; resistance to beauty pageants based on civil rights, 181

class. *See* social class

Cohen, C. B., 16

collective consciousness: creation of, 13–14

collective nature of candidates' campaigns to be queen, 110–11

collective negotiations level of racework process, 35

collective racial and ethnic identity: beauty pageants as way to study, 17–19; power of, as social control, 145

Collins, P. H., 229

colorblind society: theories of, 28–29

colorism: racial meanings in Brazil based on, 194; standards, 84

committee members, 140–41, 142, 152; social control of queen, 145–46, 153–54, 155

commodification of women in pageants, 60; in community vs. mainstream pageants, 8, 68; of queen, 159–61; as "selling mechanisms," 184

community: of color, effect of mixed-race people on, 29; creating, 13–16; as extesion of family, 78, 119, 154; outmarriage/intermarriage as threat to, 9, 28, 45, 53–56; pageants as "of the community," 8; persistence of, 55–56; practical connections of queen to, 151–52; queen as representative of, 3, 13, 14,

152–58, 224–25, 228–30. *See also* Asian American communities; Japanese American community
community acceptance: race work for, 22
community membership: defining, 16–20, 56–58
community pageant: beauty pageant as distinct from, 224. *See also* beauty pageant(s)
community representation, social control through pressure of, 119, 152–58; after pageant, 144–46
community service, 8; claiming pageant participation as extension of, 127–28, 129, 131, 148–49, 150; focus in pageant judging criteria shifted to, 65
competition: learning to manage emotions in, 140–44
"contestants" vs. "candidates," 68, 224
Cornell, S., 23, 77
Craig, M. L., 77
Creef, E. T., 190
criticism of queens from community members, 155
cultural arts: classes required for Hawaii pageant, 125–26, 150, 212–13; knowledge of, 112; symbolic importance of, 212–13
cultural clash: at Miss Nikkei International pageant, 193–94; at Nikkei 2000 conference, 194–95
cultural events: queen's role as ambassadress at, 150–51
cultural impostors, 9, 85–87, 89–90, 100, 114, 204; learning cultural arts to avoid being, 126
culturalization of ethnicity, 31
cultural markers of Japanese Americanness, 78–79

cultural preservation: claiming participation for, 132, 149–50; growing anxiety in 1990s about Japanese American, 70, 90
cultural schools to teach heritage, 49, 236n.1
cultural values: defining Japanese Americanness and, 77–78; Japan Japanese and Japanese American, 172–73
culture: anxiety about dilution of, 53, 70, 90, 132, 149–50, 178, 184; claiming participation for learning, 149; as commodity to resurrect racial body, 101; conflicting notions about, 165; ethnicity as indivisible from, 28, 29, 30; Japanese vs. Japanese American, 168–71; pageant participants and "selling" of, 9–10; race and, 21, 22, 28, 95, 100, 114; race : culture nexus problematized by multiracial participants, 70–71, 72
Cuthbert, Elsa Akemi, 97, 202

DaCosta, K. A., 25
Dalmage, H. M., 25
Daniel, G. R., 31
Daniels, R., 48
dark skin: negative association with, 84
Daruma No Gakko (cultural school), 49, 236n.1
dekasegi (return migrants), 194
demographic shifts in Japanese American community, 2, 4–5, 37–58; elderly population, increase in, 39–40; factors causing changes in, 52, 53, 54; history of immigration to U.S. and, 39, 40, 45–48; immigration rates from Japan and, 39, 40; outmarriage

rates, 40–45; outmarriage rates, as threat to community, 53–56; outmarriage rates, explaining changes in, 48–53; racial eligibility rules and, 190–91, 195–96, 202

demographic size: of Japanese community in Hawaii, 208, 209, 213, 215; racial eligibility rules and, 190–91, 195–96, 222

deportment: learning Japanese, 124–26

deracialization: claims of loyalty to America through, 60–61

Dill, B. T., 92

dilution of culture, anxiety about, 53, 70, 90, 178, 184; cultural preservation as motivation for participation and, 132, 149–50

discrimination: against Japanese Americans, 198; against mixed Japanese Americans, ix, 30, 58, 184; multiple racial choices on census and difficulty in tracking, 27, 28

disrespect: motives for participation showing, 156–57

"doing gender," 184

"doing" race, 3–4, 34, 35, 229

Douglass, W. A., 35

Dower, J. W., 2, 176

DuBose, H. L., 26

Durkheim, E., 76

Duster, T., 35

Edgerton, R., 204

Edles, L. D., 33, 208

elderly Japanese American population, 39–40

eligibility rules. *See* racial eligibility rules

emotional labor, 9, 143–44

emotions of participants: learning to manage, 140–44

enclave neighborhoods: development of, 49

enryo (obligation): concept of, 119. *See also* obligation

entertainment industry: influence on Nisei Week Queen Pageant, 196, 199–200

ethnic identity of multiracial/ethnic people, 54–55; children, 52, 53, 54–55

ethnicity: culturalization of, 31; entry into, desire of mixed-race people for, 30; as equal way to determine community membership, 19; as indivisible from culture, 28, 29, 30; negotiating Japanese American race and, 100–103; persistence of, 55–56; race and, 8–9, 32, 69, 71, 91, 92, 192–93, 223; racialization of, 31–32; redefinition of, forced by mixed-race Japanese Americans, 16–20, 57–58

ethnic options of people of color, 32

ethnic strategies for making racial claims, 32, 92–93, 102, 104–14; language, 89, 106–8, 114; names, 104–6, 114; physical "racial" alterations vs., 108; speeches, 109–11, 114; talent, 112–13

ethnographic fieldwork, 5, 18

etiquette, pageant, 74, 76

Eurasians: debate over racial eligibility rules and, 202, 204–5; mixed beauty of, 81, 108–9; separation from other Japanese Americans, 96. *See also* mixed-race pageant candidates

evening gowns, 136
Exclusion League in San Francisco, 47
exoticization of difference: tension between assimilation and, 141–42
eyelid, physically altering, 236n.5
eyelid glue, 109

Face magazine, 206–7
familiarity and strangeness: travel to Japan and, 170–71
family: interview with, 191–92; thanks and recognition given to, 192
family photos, 192
farewell speech, 164
Feagin, C. B., 52
Feagin, J. R., 52
femininity: antiquated forms of Japanese, 124–25, 126; cultural clash in Miss Nikkei International pageant over, 194; hegemonic, 60–61
feminism: beauty pageants as arena for battle over, in 1970s–1980s, 64–68, 72, 179, 183–84; debate in San Francisco over, 12, 64, 65, 66–67, 223–24, 225; impact on judging, 12, 64, 65, 135–36; racialized by pageant candidates, 65, 68; resistance to pageant and, 181–83; visible challenge from, 17–18
Fenstermaker, S., 3, 229
festivals, 16. *See also* Cherry Blossom Festival in Hawaii; Cherry Blossom Festival in San Francisco; Nisei Week Festival (Los Angeles)
filial piety, 110

Filipinos: interracial marriage among, 46
films: American perception of war brides in, 48–49
financial relations with Japan, 166–71. *See also* funding for pageants
Fishburn, Monica Midori, 106
fitting in: importance in Japan of, 175
flirtatious movements in kimono: learning, 124
Forty-Fourth Cherry Blossom Festival Queen Contestants' handbook, 118
Foucault, M., 117
French, H. W., 168
Fugita, S. S., 55, 78, 111, 173
Fujiu, J., 195
Fukunaga, A., 11–12, 207
funding for pageants; 164–71; of Hawaii Cherry Blossom Queen pageant, 163, 165–66, 210–11; from Japan, 166–71. *See also* sponsors
furisode kimono, 173; donation of, 173–74

Gallagher, C. A., 25
gaman (perseverance), 77
Gardner, R. W., 40, 41
Garfinkel, H., 34
gender: imbalance in Japanese American community after World War II, 49; intertwining of gendering and racialization, 10, 19, 185; outmarriage rate and, 42–44; social control of race through. *See* social control of race through gender
gendering Japanese Americanness, 177–84

gender politics: linking of racial claims and, 228–29; as racialized object, 229

gender roles: racialized by pageant candidates, 65, 68

generational gap in racial understandings, 96

Gentlemen's Agreement, 47–48

gift exchange on visitations, 141

Gilroy, P., 3

Gimlin, D. L., 75

Glenn, E. N., 36, 45

Goffman, E., 18, 34–35

Goldberg, D. T., 23, 176

Gordon, M., 51–52, 55

Greater Seattle Japanese Community Queen, 8, 12–13

group orientation, 78

Guss, D. M., 8, 75

hair: traditional beauty in kimono and, 122

Hall, C. I., 55, 76–77

Hamamoto, D. Y., 51

Hamill, J. F., 188

Haney Lopez, I. F., 176

hapa girl, 89, 90, 114, 115, 236n.3. *See also* mixed-race pageant candidates

Hapa Issues Forum at UC Berkeley, ix–x

Harris, D., 24

Harrison, R. J., 42

Hartmann, D., 23, 77

Hawaii: economic and political power of Japanese community in, 210, 211; evolution of Japanese American beauty pageants in, 11–12; feminist critiques of pageants in, 66; interracial marriage in, 46; Japanese nationals in, 210–11; mainstreaming of Japanese in, 209–10; racial hierarchy in, 208; size of Japanese community in, 208, 209, 213, 215. *See also* Cherry Blossom Festival in Hawaii

hegemonic femininity, 60–61

height of queens, 182

Herman, M. R., 24

heterosexuality: pageants as public reassertion of Japanese American, 179

hierarchical negotiations level of race-work process, 35–36

hierarchies of authenticity, 19, 79, 89, 103–4

Hirabayashi, L., 4

Hiraoka, K. A., 164

Hochschild, A. R., 22

Hokubei Mainichi (newspaper), 6

Hollinger, D., 27

Hollywood, 225; influence on Nisei Week Queen Pageant, 11, 196, 199–200

Holmes, S. A., 42

Honda, H. K., 5

Honolulu: Japanese living in, 208. *See also* Cherry Blossom Festival in Hawaii

Honolulu Japanese Junior Chamber of Commerce (Jaycees), 3, 11, 12, 118, 162–63, 179, 207, 210, 213, 215

Honolulu Star-Bulletin, 66

hospitality committees, 11

Hutchings, V. L., 97

Hwang, S.-S., 54

hybridity in community beauty pageants, negotiating, 1–20; community beauty pageants as racialized projects, 7–10, 16, 18–19, 33–34; creating community and, 13–16; evolution of Japanese American beauty pageants, 10–13; shifting demographics in Japanese American community and, 2, 4–5. *See also* mixed-race pageant candidates; outmarriage rates in Japanese American community

Hyena, H., 109

icon, queen's body as cultural, 162

ideal type, queen as racial/ethnic, 75–77

Ideno, G., 143

identity, racial and ethnic: collective, 17–19, 145, 155–56; of multiracial/ethnic people, 52, 53, 54–55; process of race work toward, 34–36; social context and development of, x; on symbolic level, 55–56

Ignatiev, N., 22, 176

Immigration Act of 1924, 48

immigration to U.S. from Japan, 39, 40; Gentlemen's Agreement and, 47–48; of Japanese women, 45–48; middle stages of, 46

impostors, cultural, 9, 85–87, 89–90, 100, 114, 126, 204

individual negotiations level of race-work process, 34

Inouye, J., 4, 49, 53

Inouye, Y., 204

interest groups, 14; conflicts due to different agendas of, 14–15

intergenerational connections, 14

intergenerational nature of pageant, 151–52

intermarriage/interracial marriage: Asian American communities and, 42, 43; in Hawaii, 46; influences on, 48–51; making mixed-race bodies, 27–31; as

normal outcome of assimilation, 51–52; rates, 9, 46; as symptom of internalized racism, 49; as threat to community, 9, 28, 45, 53–56; total, in U.S., 41–42; before and after World War II, 48–49, 201–2. *See also* outmarriage rates in Japanese American community

internment, vii–viii, 134, 190; blood-quantum rules during, 103, 203, 204, 205; intermarriage rate of Japanese Americans and, 49; invoking history and impact of, 150; pageants during, 63

interpersonal negotiations level of race-work process, 34–35

interview(s): family, 191–92; judging the, 126–32; research through, 5, 6

Issei: antiquated Japanese language used by, 171–72; assimilation of children after World War II by, 49; as lost generation, 172; outmarriage rate for, 46–47

Iwasaki Mass, A., 55

Jan Ken Pon No Gakko (cultural school), 236n.1

Japan: beauty pageants in, 126; financial relations with, 166–71; Hawaii Cherry Blossom Festival ties to, 210–11; as homogeneous country, cultural modernization in, 172; immigration from, 39, 40, 45–48; importance of fitting in in, 175; influence on Japanese Americanness, 171–77; isolationist history of, 2; obsession with racial purity in, 2, 168; postwar idealization of Westerners, 2; queens' travel to, 168–71, 173;

reception of mixed-race queen in, 168; sister-city relationships with, 11, 169; status of women in, 46; U.S. occupation of, war brides as result of, 48–49

Japanese American: distinction between monoracial Japanese and, 98–99

Japanese American Citizens' League (JACL), 40, 67, 177; sponsorship by, 160–61, 162; targeted by Women's Concerns Committee, 179–80

Japanese American community: collective anxiety about over-assimilation, 4, 70; concern over future of, 195; demographic shifts in, 2, 4–5, 37–58; gender imbalance in, after World War II, 49; growth of, 48; queen as representative of local, 3, 13, 14, 152–58, 224–25, 228–30; racial hierarchies perpetuated by, 38; racial rules to ensure pageant participants' connections to, 188–89; range of participation of, 14; in Seattle, 220

Japanese American Consortium of Community Related Organizations (JACCRO), 235n.2

Japanese American Culture and Community Center in Los Angeles, 178

Japanese American feminist ideology: development of, 66, 68, 72

Japanese Americanness, 186–226; beauty pageant as important arena for conversations about, 8, 138, 227–28; beauty queen representing production of sense of, 16; collective production of, pageants as site of, 63–64;

defining, 2–3, 77–79, 195, 225–26; dynamic process of collective Japanese American self-definition, 16–20; gendering, 177–84; in Hawaii, less emphasis on, 211; hegemonic, West Coast understanding of, 194–95; influence of Japan on, 171–77; interest group conflicts over, 15; "looking Japanese" as unspoken nature of, 80–81; as passport to ethnicity and social network, 30; problematized by multiracial body, 7, 22, 70–71, 72, 174, 190; queen as ideal type of, 76; redefinition of, forced by mixed-race Japanese Americans, 16–20, 57–58

Japanese American Research Project (JARP), 51–53, 55

Japanese Americans, 176–77; in liminal position in terms of culture, 176; as minority in U.S., need for distinctive community/culture and, 172–73; women, racial rules to preserve pageant sphere for, 188

Japanese American Services of East Bay, 177

Japanese Culture and Community Center of Hawaii, 211

Japanese Junior Chamber of Commerce (Jaycees), Honolulu, 3, 11, 12, 118, 162–63, 179, 207, 210, 213, 215

Japanese nationals: criteria for legitimate queen, 94, 175; in Hawaii, 210–11; living abroad, rejected as true Japanese, 174–75; understandings of heritage and bloodline, 106

Japaneseness: Brazilian vs. North American understandings of, 194

Japanese New Year in San Francisco, 150–51
Japanese racial state, 176–77, 185
Japanese Tea Garden (San Francisco): as photo site, 160
Japantown (Nihonmachi), San Francisco, 12; renovation and redevelopment of (1968), 177–78
judges, 82–83; biases of, 82–83; choosing, 135; committee control over, 146; from Hollywood/ entertainment industry in Los Angeles, 199; preparation of, 137–38; social control and, 134–38
judging criteria, 8–9; feminism and alteration of, 12, 64, 65, 135–36; interpreting, 136–37; "looking Japanese," 80–85; removal of physical beauty as, in Hawaii, 216
judging the interview, 126–32

Kalish, S., 44
Kamisugi, K., 71, 215–16
Kawasaki, J., 203
Kikumura, A., 42, 53, 91
kimono, 114, 136; cost of, 120, 173; donation of, 173–74; learning how to wear, 123–24; rules of behavior while dressed in, 118–19; "selling" Japanese American culture through wearing of, 9, 10; speech section of pageant done in, 110, 114; as visual cues to Japanese American businesses/culture, 161–62
kimono section of pageant, 120–26; in Hawaii, 121–22, 125, 212; reason for, 165; symbolizing racialization of body in Japanese terms, 122–26

Kimura, A., 111
King, R. C., 34, 45, 69, 76, 131, 149, 178
Kintetsu building (San Francisco), 177
Kitahara Kich, G., 25
Kitano, H. H. L., 42, 45, 53, 91
Kobata, Y., vii
Kobata (Yoshimura), T., vii–viii
kokoro (inner feeling), 78
Kunitsugu, C., 161
Kurashige, L., 16, 62, 196, 236n.1

Lan, P. C., 159
language: changing role of, according to social context, 107; cultural clash at Miss Nikkei International pageant over, 193; Japanese of Issei vs. contemporary Japanese, 171–72; race and, 93; speaking Japanese as ethnic strategy for making racial claims, 89, 106–8, 114; speaking Japanese on trip to Japan, 169, 170, 171; using mastery of Japanese to compensate for race, 100–103, 114
Latin American model of racial stratification, 22
Le, C. N., 42, 43, 44–45
Lee, B., 238n.8
legitimacy: of mixed-race queen, challenges to, 94–98; for pageants, claiming, 193–95. *See also* racial eligibility rules
Leonard, K. I., 46
Levin, M. J., 40, 41
Levine, G. N., 51, 53
liberal Japanese American feminism: development of, 66, 68, 72
Little Tokyo (Los Angeles), 10, 60; geography of, 200–201; Nisei

Week to encourage business in, 196–98; renovation of, 200
Little Tokyo Service Center in Los Angeles, 178
"looking Japanese," 9, 35, 79, 92, 100–102, 103, 168, 169, 170, 188, 190, 236n.2; as judging criteria, 80–85; physical "racial" alterations for, 108, 109; racial rules and importance of, 196; speaking Japanese and, 106, 114
looks, racialization of, 79–85
Los Angeles: debate about mixed-race queens in, 82; dispersion of Japanese American communities in, 200–201; evolution of Japanese American beauty pageants in, 10–11; geographic arrangement of, influence of, 200–201; influence of Hollywood/entertainment industry in, 225; outside connections made by queens in, 152; relative anonymity of queen in, 209; reputation of queen in, 196. *See also* Nisei Week Festival (Los Angeles); Nisei Week Queen Pageant
Loveman, M., 77
Loving v. Virginia, 50, 202
loyalty to America: deracialization in pageant to claim, 60–61
Lyman, S. M., 35

Marchetti, G., 49
marketing of sponsors, 159, 160
masculinity: pageants as public reassertion of Japanese American, 179
Matsumoto, Vail, 216, 217
McKenney, N. R., 42
Mead, G. H., 34
media image of beauty, 82

membership in Japanese American organizations: demographic shift in Japanese American community and, 57–58; outreach efforts to mixed-race Japanese Americans, 56; recruiting Shin Issei, 56
methodology, research, 5–7
middle-class cultural capital, 137
Midwest: understanding of Japanese Americanness in, 195
Miles, R., 7
Millard, H., 69
Miller, C., 204
Miss America Pageant, 60, 61, 182, 198
Miss California Pageant, 198
Miss Congeniality, 166
Miss Nikkei International pageant in Brazil, 8, 167, 193–94
Miss Popularity: in Honolulu pageant, 166, 210
Mixed Blood (Spickard), 38
mixed-race bodies: as challenge to relations in racial production, 230–31; experience of, 25, 76–77; popularity of looks, 238n.8; repoliticization and problematization of race by, 7, 22, 70–71, 72, 174, 190
mixed-race identity choice: census data showing, 24
mixed-race Japanese Americans, viii–x; birth rates, 44; children, racial/ethnic identification of, 52, 53, 54–55; debate about impact on racial and ethnic meanings of, 4–5; discrimination against, ix, 30, 58, 184; ethnic strategies for making racial claims, 2–3, 104–14; increasing acceptance in Japanese American community, 38; negotiation between

two poles of standards of beauty, 85; organizational imperative to incorporate, 56; perceived advantage of, 81; redefinition of race, ethnicity, and community membership forced by, 16–20, 57–58

mixed-race pageant candidates: African American/Japanese American, 38; authenticity checks for, 191–92; in Brazil, acceptance of, 194; ethnic strategies for making racial claims, 32, 92–93, 102, 104–14; in Los Angeles' Nisei Week Queen Pageant, 201–7; motivation for participation, 149; negotiating Japanese American race and ethnicity, 100–103; in pageant interviews, 131, 132; proving their ethnic/racial identity to others, 91–92; "raced" as non-Japanese Americans, 30; in San Francisco, 222–23; using mastery of Japanese culture and language to compensate for race, 100–103, 114. See also mixed-race queen

mixed-race people: assumptions about, in theories of colorblind society, 28–29; as bridges between communities, 24; challenge to race by, 23–27; multiple racial choices on census for, 24, 25–27, 28; race work done by (see race work); racial frameworks constraining identity of, 34

mixed-race queen, 87–94; challenges to racial and cultural legitimacy of, 94–98; debate over, 192–93, 202–7; disruption of racial understandings by, 87; first in Nisei Week Pageant, 97;

in Hawaii, financial relations with Japan and, 168; pureness of festival problematized by, 174; race work intensified by, 228, 232

mixed-race research, 25–26

Modell, J., 47, 51

modesty, 128, 130

monoracial candidates: cultural impostors among, 9, 85–87, 89–90, 100, 114, 126, 204

monoracial Japanese: distinction between Japanese American and, 98–99

Montero, D., 46, 51, 53

morality: cultural clash in Miss Nikkei International pageant over, 194; link between body and, 87; moral link between gender and racial appearance, 117–18

Moreno, A. M., 203

mother: socialization into culture and values through, 92, 99

motivation for pageant participation, 15–16, 148–52; community service, 127–28, 129, 131, 148–49, 150; cultural preservation, 132, 149–50; learning culture, 149; screening participants for, 151; wanting to win, 156–57

multiculturalism, 5, 68; in San Francisco, 222, 223–24, 225

Multiracial Experience, The (Root), 55

multiraciality, 3; debate over racial eligibility rules due to increasing, 69–71; goals of multiracial movement, 32; multiracial Asians by racial/ethnic combinations, 44; race problematized and renegotiated by, 7, 22, 70–71, 72, 174, 190; race work done by multiracials, 22–23. *See also* mixed-race pageant candidates

Mydans, S., 109

NAACP, 26–27
Nakajo, S., 177–78, 181
Nakano, M., 17, 66, 178, 179–82
Nakashima, C., 26, 28
names: Japanese heritage claimed through, 104–6, 114
nape of neck: wearing kimono and exposing, 122
nasal inserts, 109
National Council de la Raza, 26
nationalism: debates about, 60–64
Native Sons, 47
Naturalization Law (1790), 62, 198
networks/networking. *See* social networks/networking
newspapers: archival research with, 6
Nichi Bei Times (newspaper), 6
Nihonmachi (Japantown), San Francisco, 12, 177–78
Niimi, V., 208
Nikkei 2000 conference, 194–95, 235n.2
Nisei, 150; outmarriage rate for, 46; volunteers, 159
Nisei Week Beautiful Baby Contest, vii
Nisei Week Festival (Los Angeles), 10–11, 16, 60, 69; feminist influences on, 64, 67; instruction packet given out before visitation to, 119; purpose of, 196, 198; queen contest added to, 196–98
Nisei Week Queen Committee, 162
Nisei Week Queen Pageant, 8, 11, 59, 103; decided by merchandise ballot, 198; decreasing partici-

pation in, 201; first mixed-race queen, 97; geographic arrangement of L.A. and, 200–201; history of, 196–207; Hollwood/entertainment industry influence on, 11, 196, 199–200; local pageants before finals of, 191; motives of participants in, 15; from 1935 to 1950s, 60–63; in 1954, 120; in 1981, 146; no-tanning rule in, 84; participant from Honolulu, 13; production scale of, 200; racial eligibility rules in, 69–71, 103–4, 188, 191, 196, 197, 201–7; rules and regulations, 153–54, 165, 189; speaking Japanese on stage not allowed in, 107–8; sponsorship, 162; theme of, 199
Nishikawa, M., 63
Nishinaga, L., 81, 202–4
Nobles, M., 25
Northern California Cherry Blossom Queen Pageant, 12; candidates, 88; conflicts over motives of participants, 15; debates in 1988 about, 177–84; emergence of, 12, 177–78; expansion of audience throughout pageant year, 139; Japanese-language translation ended in, 166; judging criteria, 136; judging interview in, 127–31; racial eligibility rules, 189, 222–23; residency rule, 189; sponsorship of candidates, 159–60; talent section, 112, 113. *See also* Cherry Blossom Festival in San Francisco
"nosei" generation, 129

obi (belt) of kimono, 122
objectification: feminism and

discouragement of, 64–65; of
queens, 9–10, 142
obligation: to the community, 151,
154; *enryo*, concept of, 119; to
others, recognizing, 110, 111; to
sponsors, 163–64
O'Brien, D. J., 55, 78, 111, 173
Odo, J., 40
Ogawa, D., 46, 51
Okamura, J. Y., 35
Okinaga, L., 216
Omi, M., 4, 7, 31, 45
omiage, 76, 78, 141
Omori, D., 149
"one-drop" analogy, 204
organizational imperative to incorporate mixed-race Japanese
Americans, 56
Osaki, D., 5, 149
outmarriage rates in Japanese
American community, 40–45;
current, 4; explaining changes
in, 48–53; as highly gendered,
42–44; before 1960, 2; as threat
to community, focus on, 53–56.
See also intermarriage/interracial
marriage
outreach efforts to mixed-race Japanese Americans, 56
outside connections, 15–16, 152
ownership of women by sponsors,
164–66

Pacific Citizen, 53
pageant. *See* beauty pageant(s)
Pang, G. Y., 42, 48, 50
participant observation, 6–7
participants involved in pageant:
diversity of, 151–52
participation: types of, 152
"passing" in mainstream society, 57
Penn, W., 26

performativity, 19
Perlmann, J., 25–26
photo-op appearances, 10
physical representation: racial eligibility rules to maintain, 189, 190.
See also "looking Japanese"
picture-bride system, vii, 46, 47–48
poise, 109, 137
politics: dealing with community
politics, 158–66; gender, 228–29;
pageant as political act, 178–79;
of racial eligibility rules, 190–93;
social control over queen's,
145–46
Posey, H., 204–5
postrace society, 3, 20; predictions
of deconstruction of race into,
27, 29
power: existence of racial groups in
hierarchy of differential, 36
pride: feelings of community, 14
privilege: perception of mixed-race
people in relation to, 29
professional service: pageant judging criteria focus shifted to, 65
program sales: raising funds
through, 165–66, 210
propriety: outside appearance of,
117–18
public events: studying collective
identity through, 18; performativity and, 19

queen. *See* beauty queen
question and answer, 132–34
questioning of mixed-race people,
37–38

race: believed biological basis
of, continuation of, 21, 22,
23, 29–30, 191, 230, 232, 233;
cultural challenge to biological

definition of, 2; cultural conceptual primacy of, 2, 4; culture and, 21, 22, 28, 95, 100, 114; "doing," 3–4, 34, 35, 229; ethnicity and, 8–9, 32, 69, 71, 91, 92, 192–93, 223; hyper embodiment in pageant setting, 77; as identity within individual, 34; as impermeable, assumption of, 203–4; kimono segment and the wearing of, 120–26; language and, 93; monoracial cultural impostors and, 9, 85–87, 89–90, 100, 114, 126, 204; negotiating Japanese American ethnicity and, 100–103; perceived racial commonalities producing social relations of, 231; persistence of role in defining Japanese Americanness, 16, 17; power of, as unchangeable idea in participants' minds, 109; race : culture nexus and multiracial participants, 22, 32–33, 70–71, 72; redefinition of, forced by mixed-race Japanese Americans, 16–20, 57–58; as relational and hierarchical, 35–36; social constructionist view of, 23–27, 232, 233; symbolic ethnic identity cultivated due to, 55–56

race thinking, 22

race work, 3, 4, 20, 21–36, 227; blurring of racial boundaries by mixed-race queens and, 228, 232; building racial social ties, 87; as collective social action, 147; ideal types of, 89; in Japanese American beauty pageants, 33–34; as labor of practice, 229; learning and performing racial culture, 87; levels of, 34–36, 231–32, 233; as link to ethnicity and culture,

30; to make claims about gender through race, 87–89; meaning of, 22; multiraciality and socially constructed nature of race, 23–27; process of, 34–36; purpose of, 22–23; reinforcing race : culture nexus, 32–33; through series of comparisons, 92–93; with white standards of beauty pageants in mind, 60–61, 62

racial and ethnic identity. *See* identity, racial and ethnic

racial boundaries: blurring of, 228, 232; controlling, 9, 20; made visible in pageant, 19

racial claims, ethnic strategies for making, 2–3, 104–14; language, 89, 106–8, 114; names, 104–6, 114; racial tactics and strategies vs., 108; speeches, 109–11, 114; talent, 112–13

racial eligibility rules, 2, 3, 7, 18–19, 20, 29, 30, 31–32, 50, 183, 227; compliance with, in making racial claims, 228, 232; cultural standards for, 103–4; debate in 1980s and 1990s over, 69–71, 72–73, 202–7; demographics and, 190–91, 195–96, 202; in Hawaii Cherry Blossom Queen pageant, 71, 168, 191, 195–96, 208, 210, 211–19, 225; in Los Angeles' Nisei Week Queen Pageant, 69–71, 103–4, 188, 191, 196, 197, 201–7; main purposes to, 188–89; politics of, 190–93; reflecting racial regimes, 231; in San Francisco, 188, 189, 191, 196, 197, 222–23; as screening device, 117–18; in Seattle, 13, 191, 221–22; social contexts of, 196, 197

racial/ethnic ideal type: queen as, 75–77

racial formation, 5, 231, 232; "doing" of race in specific social contexts, 229; studies, 26

racialization, 7, 29; bodily, 7, 76–77; of bodily movements, 124–25, 126; of body in Japanese terms, kimono and, 122–26; codified into concept of race, 231; of ethnicity, 31–32; intertwining of gendering and, 10, 19, 185; of looks, 79–85; process of, 7; of voice, 126–32

Racial Privacy Initiative in California, 26

racial production: relations of and in, 230–31, 232

racial project(s), 7, 17, 23, 229, 231, 233; community beauty pageants as, 7–10, 16, 18–19, 33–34, 77, 186, 227, 232; processual model for understanding microlevel, 34–36; production of queen as, 230

racial rules, 18, 19, 187–88; control through, 9; as demographically driven, 190–91, 195–96, 202; dependence on parts (percentages or fractions) for meaning, 188; financial relations with Japan and, 168–71. See also racial eligibility rules

racial states, 176–77, 185

racial stratification: Latin American model of, 22

racism, 97; internalized, interracial marriage as symptom of, 49; within Japanese American community, 97; Women's Concerns Committee's criticism of pageants based on, 184

raffle tickets and tickets to the pageant: pressure to sell, 110, 139, 160, 165–66

Rafu Shimpo (newspaper), 6, 69, 81, 195, 202–3

Reeves, T. J., 40, 41

regimes, race work, 231, 232

research methods, 5–7

residency rules, 189, 219–20

responsibility to community, sense of, 153–54; of collective voice, 154–55; community representation and, 152–58; after term as queen ended, 157–58

return migrants (*dekasegi*), 194

Rhodes, C., 51, 53

Rockquemore, K. A., 24

Roosevelt, T., 47

Root, M. P. P., 24, 55

Ropp, S. M., 24, 29

Saenz, R., 54

San Francisco, 12, 175; debate between general committee and queen pageant subcommittee in, 175–76; debate over feminism in, 12, 64, 65, 66–67, 223–24, 225; Exclusion League in, 47; fieldwork in, 6–7; history of pageant in, 12, 222–24; interviews in, 131–32; Japanese New Year in, 150–51; progressive and multicultural nature of, 222, 223–24, 225; racial eligibility rule in, 188, 189, 191, 196, 197, 222–23; relative anonymity of queen in, 209; reputation of queen in, 196. See also Cherry Blossom Festival in San Francisco; Northern California Cherry Blossom Queen Pageant

San Francisco Chronicle, 47

San Francisco Pageant Committee, 119

Sansei: outmarriage among, 46, 50, 52–53; renovation and redevelopment of Japantown (San Francisco) and, 177; volunteers, 159

Sanwa Bank in San Francisco: closing of, 166–67

Sawa, N., 12, 219

Sayonara (film), 48

scholarship pageant, 13; attempt in San Francisco to replace queen pageant with, 177–78, 180, 181; in Seattle, 189, 219–22

screening of candidates, 162–63; eligibility rules as screening device, 117–18; for motivation, 151. *See also* racial eligibility rules

Seafair Festival (Seattle), 8, 221

Seattle: community membership defined in terms of geography and social networks, 225; International District in, 220; Japanese American community in, 220; progressive political context of, 221; Seafair Festival, 8, 221

Seattle Japanese Community Queen Pageant, 12–13, 219–22; cancellation in 1996–97 of, 219–20; history of, 12–13, 219–22; interview in, 128–29; racial eligibility rules in, 13, 191, 221–22; residency rule, 189, 219–20; as scholarship pageant, 189, 219–22; social context of, 197; talent section, 112–13

self: Goffman's theory of, 34–35; Mead's theory of, 34; transformed into reflection of collective community, 158

self-definition: dynamic process of collective Japanese American, 16–20

self development: pageant participation and, 111

self-preservation: Japanese Americanness maintained as form of, 229–30

sexism: Women's Concerns Committee formed to combat, 179–81

sex ratio among Japanese in America, 47–48

sexuality: formal and informal rules around, 10; stereotype of Japanese men as sexually aggressive, 47, 48

shame: of losing pageant, fear of, 129; social control through use of potential to, 118

shashin kekkon (picture-bride system), vii, 46, 47–48

Shikataganai (It can't be helped), 77

shikoku kyujo (children of Japanese nationals living abroad), 174–75

Shinagawa, L. H., 9, 42, 48, 50, 97, 235n.1

Shin Issei, 56; children of, 57

Shiraki, J., 149

Shiroma, T.-A., 66

Shiseido cosmetics, 159

Simpson, C. C., 2

sister-city relationships, 11, 169

skin color, 84; mixed-race skin against kimono, look of, 121; no-tanning rule, 84, 120, 150

skin-whitening cream, 109

Small, S., 7

Smedley, A., 32

Snipp, C. M., 26

social capital, 30, 78

social class, 137, 166; ability to afford travel and appearances, 167–68; class mobility, 117; upward mobility after World War II, 50, 52

social constructionist view of race, 23–27, 232, 233

social control of race through gender, 9, 116–47, 179; audience and, 138–39; chaperones and, 145, 153, 154, 155; committee members and, 145–46, 153–54, 155; community representation and, 119, 152–58; examples of failed, 120; judging and the judges, 134–38; learning to manage emotions in pageant, 140–44; in name of assimilation, 61–62; after the pageant, 144–46; question-and-answer section of pageant, 132–34; rules for producing queen, 117–20; training and practicing to be queen, 7, 120–32

socialization: mother's role in, 92, 99

social networks/networking: developing, 143; outside connections, 152; pageants as opportunity for, 65–66, 68; pageants' claim to racial/ethnic authenticity through, 193; practical connections to community, 151–52; race work for access to, 22

Song, M., 32, 93

Spam *musubi*, 126

speech: controlled by larger social collective identity, 155–56; as ethnic strategy for making racial claims, 109–11, 114; farewell, 164; themes of, 110–11. *See also* language

Spencer, R., 25

Spickard, P., 31, 38, 49, 91, 111

sponsors, 1, 12, 14, 67, 102, 110, 120, 138, 139, 141, 149, 152, 184; dealing with, 158–66; emotional relationship with, in abstract sense, 163–64; financial relations with Japan, 166–71; funding from, 164–66; in Honolulu, 162–63; linking body of woman and her mastery to, 159; in Los Angeles, 162; marketing of, 159, 160

standards of beauty, 12, 81–85, 198–99; Japanese, pageant as place affirming, 83–85; white, 180, 182–83

state regimes: racial ideologies embedded in, 176–77

stereotype(s): of Asian men, outmarriage rate of Japanese American women and, 50; of Japanese men as sexually aggressive, 47, 48; of Japanese women, outmarriage rate and, 51; of mixed-race children as products of illicit unions during World War II, 48

stigma of maintaining queen image after reign, 157–58

Stoeltje, B., 16

Streeter, C. A., 29

structural assimilation: constraints of race on, 55–56

Super Japanese American, 90

surveys for mixed-race identity studies, 24–25

symbol, kimono wearing as, 124–25

symbol, queen as: both body/symbol and racial/symbol, 101–2; living symbol of collective identity, 9–10, 16, 17–18, 79, 101–2, 119, 142–43, 185; of local community, 13, 14, 224–25, 228–30; racialized, 79

symbolic capital, 142–43

symbolic ethnic identity, cultivation of, 55–56

Taguma, K., 103
Tajima, L., 237n.4
Takagi, D., 68
Takaki, R., 45, 46, 47, 61
talent portion of pageant, 112–13
Tamura, E. H., 46
Tanner, M., 17
tanning: rule against, 84, 120, 150
tattoos, 141
Tea House of the August Moon (film), 48
textual analysis of pageants, 138
thankfulness of queen, 164
Thirty-Fifth Anniversary Seattle Japanese Community Queen Scholarship Program Booklet, 164
Thornton, M. C., 55
threat of cultural dilution. *See* dilution of culture, anxiety about
Ties That Bind conference, 235n.2
Tighe, L., 219
Toth, C., 216, 218
training and practicing to be queen, 7, 120–32; control over outcome through cultural coaching, 146; kimono segment and wearing of race, 120–26; racializing voice, 126–32
travel expenses, 167
triangulation, 5
Tuan, M., 56

U.S. Census. *See* census, U.S.
U.S. racial state, 176, 185
unity between Japanese Americans, pageants and, 13–16. *See also* community
upward mobility after World War II: increasing outmarriage rate and, 50, 52
Uyeno, S., 219, 221

Valhouli, C., 109
Van den Berghe, P., 75
vetting of candidates, 159, 162–63
visitations, 141, 142–43, 216
voice: racializing, 126–32; responsibility of collective, 154–55
volunteerism: rhetoric of, 149

walking Japanese, 124; walking American vs., 63
walk-through visits, 142–43
Wallace, K. R., 25
war brides, 48–49
Watanabe, A., 198
Watanabe, B., 178
Waters, M., 25–26, 27, 93, 105
WCC. *See* Women's Concerns Committee (WCC)
West, C., 3, 34, 87, 229
West Coast understanding of Japanese Americanness, hegemony of, 194–95
white America: Japanese American pageants as response to being shut out of, 36; Japanese American ties to, 41; outmarriage to whites, 42–44
whiteness: as advantage vs. liability, 101–2; increased interest in mixed Eurasian beauty and, 81, 108–9; white standards of beauty, 180, 182–83
whitening cream, 109
white womanhood: supposed sexual threat of Japanese men to, 47, 48
Wilk, R., 16
Williams, T. K., 25, 38, 55
Williams-Leon, T., 25, 26
Wilson, T., 188
Wilson, W. J., 68, 97
Winant, H., 7, 31
Winters, L. I., 26

women: blamed for changing community demographics, 53–54; immigration to U.S., 45–48; as important procreators of race, 28; as maintainers of family and group culture, 28, 45, 92, 99; outmarriage rates of Japanese American, 28, 42–44; status in Japan, 46

Women's Concerns Committee (WCC), 66–67, 160, 178, 179–84, 232

Woodrum, E., 47, 50, 51

World War II: blood quantum rules during internment in, 103, 203, 204, 205; internment during, vii–viii, 49, 63, 103, 134, 150, 190, 203, 204, 205; interracial marriages rate after, 48–49, 201–2; postwar stigma and isolation of community, 63

Wu, J. T.-C., 129

Yancey, G., 25

Yano, C., 71, 117, 163, 179, 189, 192, 216, 237n.6

Yoshimura, T., vii

Yoshinari, K., 168

youth involvement: importance of, 130, 131, 134, 150

Zack, N., 24

Zimmerman, D., 34, 87

Rebecca Chiyoko King-O'Riain
is a lecturer in the Department of Sociology
at the National University of Ireland, Maynooth.